SPEAKING WITH THE DEAD

IMMIGRANT COMMUNITIES & ETHNIC MINORITIES IN THE UNITED STATES & CANADA: NO. 75

Series Editor: Robert J. Theodoratus
Department of Anthropology, Colorado State University

Continued at back of book

SPEAKING WITH THE DEAD

Development of Afro-Latin Religion
Among Puerto Ricans in the United States

A Study Into the Interpenetration of Civilizations in the New World

by

Andrés Isidoro Pérez y Mena

AMS Press, Inc.
New York

Library of Congress Cataloging-in-Publication Data

Pérez y Mena, Andrés Isidoro.
    Speaking with the dead : development of Afro-Latin religion
among Puerto Ricans in the United States : a study into the
interpenetration of civilizations in the New World / by Andrés
Isidoro Pérez y Mena.
    (Immigrant communities & ethnic minorities in the
United States & Canada ; 75)
    Includes bibliographical references.
    ISBN 0-404-19485-0
    1. Spiritualism—New York (N.Y.)   2. Santeria (Cult)—New York
(N.Y.)   3. Puerto Ricans—New York (N.Y.)—Religious life.
4. Bronx (New York, N.Y.)—Religious life and customs.
5. Emigration and immigration—Religious aspects.   I. Title.
II. Series.
BL2490.P39   1991
299'.67—dc20   91-8469
                                                             CIP

All AMS books are printed on acid-free paper that meets the
guidelines for performance and durability of the Committee on
Production Guidelines for Book Longevity of the Council on
Library Resources.

AMS PRESS
56 East 13th Street
New York, N.Y. 10003, U.S.A.

MANUFACTURED IN THE UNITED STATES OF AMERICA

Para Mis Hijas
Micaela y Julia Li y
Nuestros Antespasados
Emma y Justa

ACKNOWLEDGMENTS

I received encouragement for this book from my mentor and friend Dr. Gwendolyn Midlo Hall, Professor of History and Chairperson of Puerto Rican and Hispanic Caribbean Studies at Rutgers - The State University of New Jersey, at New Brunswick. She worked with me from the publisher's first inquiry many years ago, to completion. A "thank you" can never suffice as an expression of my gratitude. The editor of this series, Professor Theodoratus provided much needed guidance, Professor J.J. Chambliss of the Rutgers School of Education made many valuable contributions to the completion of this text. Many enthusiastic class discussions on Puerto Rican Spiritualism are reflected in my book. I thank my students at Rutgers, at Bank Street College of Education (GEPFE), at City College - CUNY, and Brooklyn College - CUNY. A heartfelt thank you to the Rev. Camacho. Without him there would be no book. Dr. Antonio Stevens-Arroyo of Brooklyn College - CUNY spent many hours going over the manuscript and made a significant and much needed contribution to its re-structuring. I received much needed support and encouragement from my friends at Papyrus Books, NRS-Antiquarian Bookstore, and from Raul "K.O." Caban. Ms. Rosa Maria Masdeu, my compañera, encouraged me, and was always helpful - I am fortunate. I owe a special appreciation to my mother who taught me survival did not mean subservience; blood of my blood is most important; demand reciprocity; and say what you feel. Lastly, I should thank the many innovative educators and administrators with whom I worked in Community School District 4 in East Harlem who encouraged and supported my efforts and Ms. Miriam Castillo for her patience in typing this manuscript. For the appearance of the text I am indebted to Mr. Ronald S. Freeman at LightSpeed Communications & Computer Services who typeset this book. Ms. Vilma Perez, my secretary at Rutgers was also helpful. Without these individuals this book would not have been possible--I thank you all! Nevertheless, I alone take responsibility for what is said.

A.I.P. y M.

TABLE OF CONTENTS

An explanation of research methodology and a description of the *centro espiritista.* Each stage on the path to becoming a Spiritual-ist is described and an idiosyncratic dictionary of terms used at this *centro espiritista* is provided.

Part I. A review of the roots of ancestor worship among the Puerto Rican people, also reviewed is the emergence in the United States of an ancestor worship which is neither French Spiritism nor Cuban *Santería.* This new development is a combination of these beliefs for the Puerto Rican national formation especially for those residing in the United States. Part II. Review of the literature, on Puerto Rican Spiritualism.

A discussion of the roles filled by the congregation at the *centro.* Services at the *centro espiritista* are described and spiritually derived ailments are reviewed.

A review of the transition between the congregation and becoming a Godchild (*ahijado*). To be a Godchild requires a baptism. This then entitles one to become a member of the ritual kinship system to which all the godchildren belong. The ritual clothes worn are explained.

LIST OF TABLES

LIST OF PHOTOGRAPHS

LIST OF FIGURES

INTRODUCTION

S pir-itualism was born in the United States in 1848, the year three young sisters from Hydesville, New York, claimed they were able to communicate with the dead by means of wall rapping. The girls, Leah, Kate, and Margaret Fox, who lived with their parents in a small cottage, had been hearing the strange knocking for some time. One night they decided to start a conversation with their invisible visitor. The code was one knock for yes and two for no. Through the rapping they were able to learn that the spirit with whom they were speaking was that of a murdered peddler whose body had been buried underneath their cellar. The news of their ghostly conversations spread like wildfire and were the foundation upon which the practice of Spiritualism was first started. It was not until 56 years later that the remains of a human body were found underneath the Fox's cellar next to the implements of a peddler's trade.

From the United States Spiritualism spread to Europe, specially to England and France, where it soon enjoyed the patronage of many exalted personages, such as Queen Victoria, Napoleon III, Marconi, and Conan Doyle.

The practices of Spiritualism involved mostly demonstrations by different mediums of their much heralded abilities to speak with the dead. They also demonstrated other powers, such as table rapping, levitations, automatic writings and sometimes the emission of ecto-plasm, a gaseous, luminous, substance that allegedly emanated from some mediums during a trance. Naturally there was much fraud con-nected with Spiritualism, although there seemed to have been several authenticated cases of true mediumship, such as that of the famous medium Douglas D. Home.

The differences between Spiritualism and Spiritism are quite marked. Spiritualism is mostly concerned with a medium's psychic pow-ers and her ability to communicate with the dead for the benefit of her clients, for a price. Spiritism is an actual movement, where a group of people get together in a temple-like setting for the purpose of communal healing, counseling and communication with higher spirits to obtain guidance and illumination. Another aim of Spiritism is the enlightenment of "intranquil" or dark spirits who are in need of light and help.

Spiritism is the result of a mixture of Spiritualism and the beliefs and philosophy of a Frenchman called Hippolyte Leon Denizard Rivail, better known under the pseudonym of Allan Kardec. He believed that spiritual progress must be physically achieved through a series of progressive incarnations and that each person has a group of guardian angles and protecting spirits who guide him or her through the "tests" of life (*pruebas*). Kardec stressed the importance of communicating with these spirits, which were compiled in several books. Two of the most famous are The Book of The Spirits and The Gospel According to Spiritism, better known as El Evangelio.

Kardec's books were swiftly translated into several languages, including Spanish and Portuguese. They soon made their way to Latin America through contraband, and in spite of the vociferous prohibitions of the Catholic Church against its practices, Spiritism soon became a way of life among Latin Americans, especially in Brazil, Argentina, Cuba, and Puerto Rico.

In Puerto Rico, Spiritism grew so swiftly that virtually every Puerto Rican today either practices Spiritism or has knowledge of someone who does.

A typical Spiritist seance (*sesión espiritista*) is conducted with several mediums, all dressed in white, sitting around a table, always covered by a white table cloth. At the head of the table sits the person who directs the seance, invariably a man, known as the *presidente de mesa*. On the table there are usually flowers, several water bowls, a bottle of Florida Water mixed with curative plants and one or two of Kardec's books. Behind the table sit those who are not mediums and who come to be healed or helped in some way by the spirits and the mediums.

When Puerto Ricans began to migrate to the United States, they brought with them their very special Spiritist beliefs. Many Spiritist temples, known as *centros*, began to make their appearance in Puerto Rican neighborhoods, and very soon each had its own group of followers. But then a very curious phenomenon began to take place in the form of a definite syncretism between the practices and beliefs of Spiritism and those of an Afro-Cuban religion known as *Santería*. The *presidente de mesa* was suddenly known as the *padrino* or godfather, a *Santería* term used to denominate the person who confers initiations into the religion. Among the spirits who are invoked or consulted by the mediums can now be found some of the *orishas* or deities worshipped in *Santería*. The religious paraphernalia used by *santeros*, including the bead necklaces, is also part of the *centro*, as well as some of the cleansing and healing rituals of *Santería*. This syncretic phenomenon, as well as the actual practices of the *centro*, are the subject of this scholarly work by Dr. Andrés I. Pérez y Mena, SPEAKING WITH THE DEAD: Development of Afro-Latin Religion among Puerto Ricans in the United States.

In order to write the book, Professor Pérez y Mena did exhaustive research in a *centro* in the South Bronx, attending seances, interviewing the members, filming and recording the seances and carefully studying their methodology and modes of expression. The result of this meticulous work is SPEAKING WITH THE DEAD, the first book to describe the syncretic fusion that is taking place between Puerto Rican Spiritism and *Santería* in the United States, particularly New York City. It is important that this distinction be made as this syncretism does not seem to have taken place in Puerto Rico or anywhere else in Latin America.

The importance of this pioneering work cannot be overemphasized as it provides a much needed in-depth study of a fascinating phenomenon. The book is social research; it is a participatory collective happening, where the reader is guided with a firm but inspired hand through the tantalizing but often incomprehensible world of the spiritist. Research for this book began in the spring of 1978 and lasted three years. During this period, Professor Pérez y Mena became an accepted member of the *centro*, working with various mediums, being present and taking part in seances and conducting several enlightening interviews with the *padrino* and *madrina* (the *padrino's* wife).

The book takes good care to underline the distinctive roles of men and women in the *centro*, and carefully delineates the various problems brought to *padrino* for solution. The different spiritual entities who are used to provide help with all these problems are assessed and their characteristics painstakingly analyzed. Among these entities are the saints/*orishas* worshipped in *Santería*. Examples of the benefits received from these entities through the work in the *centro* is one of the most interesting parts of the book.

Professor Pérez y Mena does not see the work at the *centro* as fodder for Western psychology, but rather as an indigenous form of therapy which is intrinsically Puerto Rican and distinct from any other. His book should be a welcome addition to the literature on the magico-religious practices of the Carribbean and could easily become a classic in its genre.

Migene Gonzalez-Wippler
New York City
May, 1990

CHAPTER I

From The Outside Looking In

This first chapter contains an explanation of the methodology used and a description of the *centro espiritista*. Each role at the *centro* is broken down into the stage of development which that role represents on the path to becoming either one of the mediums or the spiritual leader of a *centro*. Moreover, these individuals maintain their own idiosyncratic vocabulary, and a dictionary is provided. These terms are unlike the traditional terms used in either Spiritism or Cuban *Santería*. A glossary of traditionally held definitions has been appended at the end of this book.

This study was conducted at a *centro espiritista* in the South Bronx of New York City. The *centro espiritista* -- or Spiritist Center - is a Puerto Rican storefront church where spirits of the dead communicate with members of the congregation through the intercession of trained mediums. The majority of those who come to pray at this *centro* are Hispanic Puerto Ricans who have migrated to the United States. The non-Hispanics are, for the most part, African Americans from the former British West Indies.

Although this kind of spirit communication is actually a form of ancestor worship that combines ancient African Yoruba beliefs, Spanish and Puerto Rican forms of Catholic worship and French Spiritism, neither the congregation nor the mediums have any real knowledge of the historical background of their Spiritist Center. The congregation as a whole views itself as strict followers of Spiritism (*Espiritismo*), as founded by a Frenchman named Allan Kardec a century ago. In actuality, they are far from followers of Kardec's Spiritism. What is practiced at the *centro espiritista* is a combination of *Cuban Santería* (syncretism of Roman Catholicism and Yorubaland practices as practiced in Cuba) and aspects of Kardec's Spiritism. Consequently, while more of the language used is from the Spiritist tradition, the iconography and the clothing are from *Santería*.[1] The services begin as a sedate French Kardecian Spiritist session and end as a *Santería* service with its music, dancing, and trance-like spirit possession.

What members of the *centro* say they are practicing and what they are actually doing are in contradistinction. In order to develop a system to understand the language of the *centro* and ferret out the idiosyncratic usage, it became necessary to distinguish the participants' perspective from definitions traditionally used in historical research. This distinguishing of viewpoints facilitated an understanding of the language-behavior contradistinction occurring at the *centro*.

With these priorities in mind, the study was designed as a field exploration using George Herbert Mead's ideas on symbolic interaction and socialization into roles. And it was designed with several prime objectives: to present for the first time an in-depth historical review of the creation, growth and development of a Puerto Rican *centro espiritista* in the United States. Such a *centro*, which synthesizes Afro-Puerto Rican ancestor worship, Cuban *Santería*, and French Kardecian spiritism do not exist in Puerto Rico, but exist only in the United States. Thus, we see the emergence of a magico-religious belief system which transcends the parochialism of narrow national boundaries in the Caribbean, creating a more universalist consciousness among peoples of Caribbean origin and descent in the United States. It is therefore very important to develop an understanding of this new belief system emerging within the Puerto Rican community in the United States. This study sets out to understand and delineate the process of socialization into the particular roles available to members of the congregation at different stages of their involvement in the *centro*.

In order to obtain the necessary data, affairs at the *centro* were both filmed and recorded while the researcher participated directly in its activities.[2] In addition to this participant observation, members were interviewed and life histories were taken at different stages of their involvement. The interviews were informal, often taking place concurrently with other scheduled activities.

George H. Mead's theoretical approach served as a means of looking at certain types of human behavior within social settings.[3] These interviews gave the participants an opportunity to explain their own perspectives of reality. The use of life histories as a research tool made it possible to understand the process by which individuals move from one role in a given stage of development to the next. Mead's concept of symbolic interaction explains role taking as the means by which individuals fall into a pattern of behavior which others expect of them.[4] By focusing on the evolving role played by various individuals from the most elementary to the most complex, one begins to understand their particular perspectives of reality.

All individuals who were interviewed were asked how and why they became involved in the activities of the *centro* and why they continued to attend the services. Effort was also made to determine whether or not the socialization process operating at the *centro* differed for men and women. There was also a need to differentiate their various perspectives on the belief system and to develop a way of describing the apparent rationales for either success or failure to move from one role in a given stage to the next role at another stage.

The *centro* is located in a predominantly Puerto Rican neighborhood and although the windows of this storefront church are boarded up to prevent anyone from looking in during services, there is a large sign painted in white letters on a red background across the top proclaiming, this is a *centro espiritista*.

About 200 individuals attend the services each week. They take place on Monday and Thursday nights -- never on Sunday so that they will not conflict with the Masses held at local Catholic Churches. Interesting enough, while the congregation at the *centro* are encouraged to worship in their neighborhood Roman Catholic Churches the Roman Catholic Church in the area where the *centro* is located discourages participation of parishioners in the activities of the *centro*. The Spanish priest who conducts the Mass for the Hispanic - Caribbean community has cautioned the members of the congregation about becoming involved in "things condemned by the Pope in Rome as outside the Church's teachings".

Pentecostal groups will sometimes make their appearance in the hope of dissuading individuals from going into the *centro* to engage in "Satanic-Saint worshiping." They arrive early in the afternoon and remain across the street playing religious revivalist music until 6:30 pm.

Photo 1. Pentecostal Group Urging People Away From "Satanic Saint Worshiping"

Photo 2. Godchild Guarding The Centro Prior to Services

A small crowd gathers to listen while the chorus of five women and three young girls with tambourines, accompanied by a male guitarist, play and sing. The Pentecostal leader remains inside a van parked near the curb while the singing goes on. Some Pentecostal males mingle in the small crowd.

Once the Godfather and godchildren arrive, arrangements are made for one of the godchildren to stand outside and watch the Pentecostal crowd. The spiritualists feel harassed by this unwanted attention. However, as the dinner hour approaches the Pentecostal group packs up and leaves. This is usually about an hour before services begin at the *centro.*

The preparations at the *centro* take on the ritualized structure of most religious preparations and services. The Godfather arrives at about 6:00 pm, opens the steel gates on the *centro's* door, and then unlocks the red doors. He usually arrives with his wife, the Godmother. They enter the *centro* and begin lighting candles or replacing flowers that are drying out.

Slowly the godchildren and the mediums arrive from home or work. They sit around and chat about the day's activities on the job or at home. The *centro* begins to fill up with individuals from the public hoping to speak to the Godfather before the services. When someone requests a consultation with the Spiritualist, he asks them to enter the consultation room. The Godfather also will see the godchildren, the mediums, and the associates of the *centro* who need to speak to him or seek advice on some problem. These consultations occur with a limited number of individuals prior to the services.

Individuals will come into the *centro* requesting that the Godfather spiritually bless the figurines they keep in their homes. They bring rosaries, statues of saints, statues of Indians, chains, and pendants bearing figures of saints. The Godfather takes each of these and says a prayer over it.

Services begin once the godchildren and the mediums have been seated at about 7:30 pm. Those that arrive at the *centro* for the first time are called the public (*público*) and tend to remain in the rear. Many of those who regularly attend arrive early to avoid sitting on folding chairs once the pews are filled. The folding chairs have to be placed in the middle of the aisle, and are moved every time someone moves to the front of the *centro*, especially when someone wants a *causa* worked.

The number of people who attend the *centro* depends on the weather and the season. If it rains, snows, or is very cold, fewer people attend the services. Consequently, in late spring, summer, and fall, there are more people attending services than in winter.

The *centro* itself is a rectangular room 60 feet long and 30 feet wide. At the far end of the room is a bathroom, the consultation room (*cuarto de consulta*) and a sink which stands between the two. The altar is set up against the consultation room and a seven - foot statue of the Virgin Mary stands against the bathroom wall. Next to the front entrance is a refrigerator which is used for storing fresh herbs and plants. On either side are about 10 pews constructed of plywood and painted with brown shellac. The aisle in the middle leads to the table in front of the altar where the mediums communicate with the spirits. Above the pews are shelves with candles, statues of saints, and offerings of flowers, iron, gold, and copper to the spirits. The candles are housed in different colored glasses, and the walls are painted red from the bottom to the middle and dark blue from the middle to the ceiling (see Figure 1).

There is a centrally placed white table for spirit communication. On the wall running from the altar to the first pew there are about six chairs; on the other wall directly across are about eight chairs. There are nine chairs around the table used for spirit communication, which brings to 23 the number of chairs tightly placed in the front of the *centro*. Only the godchildren, the mediums, and the Godfather sit at the table, with the head reserved for the Godfather who is nearest to the altar. There are two Head Mediums to either side of the Godfather. Next to each Head Medium are two apprentice mediums or godchildren, making four apprentices at the table. At the far end is one auxiliary medium on each side nearest the congregation. In case of absences, the auxiliary medium can substitute for the Head Medium and the best of the apprentice mediums becomes an auxiliary medium. A medium, nevertheless, is never demoted from one category to another for the purposes of spirit communication.

The godchildren sit in the first pew and on the chairs against the walls at the altar. The associates who sit nearest the front hope to be asked to become godchildren, while those associates further back are not inter-

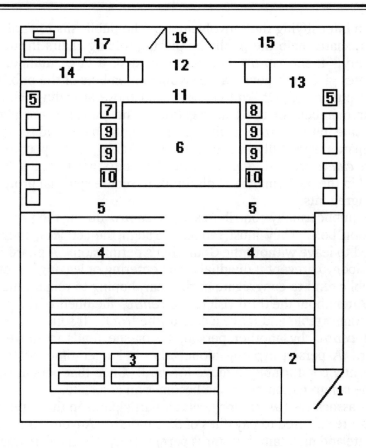

1. Entrance
2. Male Godchild Guard
3. Folding chairs
4. Pews
5. Seating for Godchildren
6. Table for Spirit Communication
7. Principal Head Medium--right
8. Head Medium--left
9. Apprentice Mediums
10. Auxiliary Mediums
11. Godfather
12. Male Godchild--for Godfather
13. Male Godchild--for Mediums
14. Altar
15. Bathroom
16. Sink
17. Consultation Room

Figure# 1. Layout of the *Centro*

ested in intensifying their involvement. The public sits toward the rear. The associates help the public by placing folding chairs in the aisles if necessary. If the *centro* becomes crowded, a large number of male associates give their pew seats to women members of the public.

The public (*el público*) consist of all those attending who are not regular members of the congregation. The public is not allowed to participate in the *centros* activities on a regular basis, and is expected to participate respectfully in the services. Usually, these people come to have a *causa* treated, and evaluate the Godfather to see if he can be trusted in the performance of his duties to secure spiritual protection for his congregants.

The public usually contributes to the *centro* during the passing of the collection box. They must remain through the services; they are not allowed to leave without the Godfather's permission. A guard is placed at the door to prevent individuals from entering or leaving. Members of the public tend to congregate at the rear, hoping to remain inconspicuous. After about the third visit to the *centro,* members of the public feel more comfortable and move closer to the front. If someone is brought to the *centro* by another person, he or she tends to move forward sooner. A person arriving alone takes a longer time before feeling sufficiently comfortable to move forward. Once that person decides to join the congregation he or she becomes an associate.

The associates (*asociados*), as full participants in the services of the *centro,* are required to pay dues of $5 a month. Anyone can become an associate and maintain that status permanently, but they are encouraged to become godchildren, and later, mediums. Since all godchildren and mediums are associates they too are required to pay dues. This means that at least half of those attending the services are dues paying members whose fees help defray the cost of maintaining the *centro.*

Sometimes associates fall behind in their dues, especially when they are unemployed. An associate who is a bus driver from Connecticut says that he has not paid dues for five months. Driving a school bus is not a full - time job. Nevertheless, he arrives at the *centro* twice a week for the services. He understands the financial needs of the Godfather, but he does not feel he can make up past dues until he can upgrade his license enabling him to drive out-of-state buses. His major concern now is to keep his spiritual side protected while getting his high school equivalency diploma.

Some associates are middle-class individuals who are better off than the majority of the congregation. They live in suburban areas of Northern Westchester and arrive at the *centro* in large cars. They are interested in insuring that the material (worldly) benefits they have received are not taken away for a lack of spiritual protection.

There is one suburban couple who have been involved with the *centro* for years. They arrive with teenage daughters for the services. They are associates who pay their dues promptly. They do not attend both weekly sessions because of the distance they travel.

Another suburban man arrives at the *centro* one day a week, sometimes with his wife, from Northern Westchester near the Connecticut border. He makes large personal contributions to the Godfather and offers to send him on vacations to Puerto Rico to see his (the Godfather's) mother. The associates also contribute during the passing of the collection box.

The Godfather (*Padrino*), who is the leader of the congregation, insures the daily functioning of the *centro*. Often called a Spiritist (*Espiritista*), he is responsible for the spiritual development and training of those associates ready to become godchildren (*ahijados*) and mediums. His wife is called the Godmother (*Madrina*) and is never referred to as a Spiritist, although as the wife of the Godfather she is a person of great status.

In time some of the godchildren learn to communicate with the spirits in public and begin the process of becoming full-time mediums. As mediums they are ranked in order of their ability to communicate with the spirit world.

The Principal Head Medium is the closest in experience to the Godfather and sits next to him on his right when working the spirits of the dead at the table. During services on Monday and Thursday nights there are between 10 and 18 godchildren present. Only the eight most developed godchildren participate as mediums, sitting at the table which is centrally located in front of the congregation. The Godfather sits at the head and, in the French Kardecian Spiritist tradition, is regarded as the President of the table (*Presidente de la Mesa*).

All the mediums are Puerto Rican, whether born on the Island or in the United States. Both the Godfather and the Godmother were born in

Puerto Rico and, as has been said earlier, most of the congregation is Puerto Rican as well.

Research at the spiritualist center (*centro espiritista*) began in the spring of 1978, and continued over a three year period, with major portions of the research being done during the summers of 1978 and 1980. Since the focus was on participant observation and the gathering of informal life histories of individuals at the *centro,* the researcher was accepted as a member of the congregation after establishing sincerity of purpose to the Godfather and the group. The Godfather made several efforts to recruit the researcher, attempts which provided the researcher with many opportunities to participate in activities restricted to members of the congregation (*público and asociados*), godchildren (*ahijados*), and mediums (*mediaunidades*).

The Principal Head Medium (*Mediaunidad de Mano Derecha*) was helpful in providing insight into the different roles available for socialization into each stage of the belief system. Both Head Mediums were extremely helpful in insuring that members of the congregation, the godchildren, and the mediums would be comfortable while talking to the researcher. The Principal Head Medium was the most articulate informant. She explained many aspects of what the researcher saw or heard.

Observation focused on all members of the congregation and all but one of the life history interviews were conducted at the *centro,* either before or after the services or while individuals waited for consultations (*consultas*). The Principal Head Medium continued to be the major source of information throughout the investigation.

Data were collected during different activities in the following manner:

1. Monday and Thursday nights when the congregation as a whole participated in the services.

2. The Godfather or Spiritualist and his wife, the Godmother, were interviewed.

3. Two women godchildren were interviewed: an auxiliary and an apprentice.

4. Three women members of the congregation who were preparing to become godchildren and were awaiting the saints' permission to be ritually baptized

into the godchildren were interviewed.

5. One male was interviewed who wished to remain as part of the public because he did not want to increase his commitment to the belief system.

6. The Principal Head Medium and the Head Medium were interviewed.

The informal life history interviews were originally typed from notes and tapes and then translated from Spanish into English. Not all of the interviews were conducted completely in Spanish or English. Names of persons interviewed or mentioned in this study were changed to safeguard their privacy. These interviews required extensive editing to assure readability. Since different concerns tended to appear throughout the interview a content analysis was undertaken. It also became necessary to sort the content of each interview into distinct categories. The topic categories were different for each individual and at each stage of socialization. As a result, it was assumed that the amount of time an individual spent on a given topic was a measure of its importance. Later the interviews were typed into a logical sequence of events. Consequently, the interviews do not appear in verbatim form, although the content of the interviews has been kept intact.

There are five stages of socialization operating at the *centro* and the research centered on these five naturally occurring stages. Stage I focuses on the congregation at large: the public and the associates in the periphery. The congregation's greatest number of individuals are represented by the roles of the public (*público*) or associates (*asociados*). The associates, although recruited from the public, are unlike the public because they are regular dues-paying members. Both groups, however, have limited roles. Their involvement is peripheral because they remain mostly in the congregation. They are nevertheless essential since they are the *centro's raison d'etre* and are also a major source of financial contributions. In this stage one finds a generalized but nebulous belief in spirits. The family imparts a generalized belief in spirits among Puerto Ricans. This belief operates on the individual prior to arrival at the *centro*. What brings an individual to the *centro* as a member of the public is initially within the larger cultural realm or the family, and is independent of what occurs at the *centro*.

For the other four stages and their significant roles, socialization occurs within the *centro*. Stage II of socialization is a transitory stage. It represents an individual's desire to leave the boundaries of the public or associates of Stage I and begin preparation for development into a godchild. Stage III, represented by the godchildren, is a group which has gone through a rite of passage, the baptism. This semi-peripheral group is not a part of the public or associates. They are apprentice mediums. They are not highly developed in their ability to communicate with the dead. It is, nonetheless, from among the godchildren that the spiritual leader of the *centro* picks those individuals who have proven themselves sufficiently prepared to participate publicly in communicating with the dead.

The mediums in Stage IV are a group representing the core of the *centro's* activities. These mediums are hierarchically arranged by experience and ability. There are head mediums, auxiliary mediums, and apprentice mediums. The mediums enter spirit possession during services while sitting at a table near the altar with the leader of the congregation, the Godfather. It is through the mediums during services that spirit communication occurs for members of the congregation.

The final stage, Stage V, is that of the Godfather. He is the high priest of the *centro* and an authority on the Spiritualist belief system. He represents the highest stage of development. As Godfather to the congregation he is the only male who regularly sits with the mediums at the table used for spirit communication. He also provides private consultations to congregation members who wish to communicate with the spirits.

From Stage I to Stage V the participants' perspective is always reflected by their definition of the social phenomena they experience. This is why it became necessary to re-examine the importance of language to socialization in the process of translating and finding equivalent English terms. Language is not only an important symbol, but also vital in understanding the perspectives which make up the roles defined by the individuals at the *centro* in each of the five stages. Language mediates the relationship of the individual with the role he or she is going to assume. Defining the terms used by the participants not only helps clarify what is being said and done, it is emblematic of the status of a given stage and role in the religious service.

Insights on Language Use and Research

The use of language and its variations is a means for a people to build their own sense of who and what they are, especially in an urban metropolis such as New York. Misinterpretations of the issues which are under investigation can occur if the researcher fails to notice that what is being communicated on one level may not be what is intended. What is communicated, no matter what the intent of the articulation, may not be what is later translated. It is through language that mankind can truly describe his level of consciousness and, in the final analysis, distinguishes himself from the rest of those with whom he coexists and interacts.

The Puerto Rican Community in the United states is an in vivo research laboratory of the varieties of non-traditional usages of the Spanish language. The reasons for this situation can be partly explained by the impact of the United States occupation of Puerto Rico in 1898 and the Americanization effort of the United States in Puerto Rico. This Americanization effort was facilitated by the cooperation of some of the ruling sectors of the Puerto Rican national formation through their acceptance of the imposition of the English language in the public schools. The overwhelming number of those Puerto Rican migrants arriving in the United States were from the marginalized sectors of the society. Puerto Rican government agencies contributed to the displacement of large numbers of undereducated rural and urban proletarians and displaced peasants and subsistence farmers into the menial labor market of the United States. There are large numbers of Puerto Ricans in North America who represent a marginal sector of the working class. Educationally they represent a group which speaks neither standard English nor standard Spanish. Within the island, there are marked variations in the language from one small community to the other. These conditions have not been previously acknowledged as having created problems for the interviewer. Caution should be the prime concern of the researcher whenever the interviewer is not a native speaker of the language used by those under study and is not familiar with variants of the Spanish language spoken by Puerto Ricans in the island as well as in the United States. The anthropologist must avoid misusing his "veil of objectivity" by accepting the communication on one level and possibly negating the impact of the social phenomena observed and as represented by the language on other levels.

The late Margaret Mead's lectures on anthropological methods introduced the writer to the prominence of language, explaining the impact of the variations of language use from one island of the South Pacific to another upon her own research. Her emphasis on language use has served this researcher well. The existing research on Puerto Ricans in the area of Afro-Latin Caribbean religions has proven to be highly inaccurate with respect to defining the manner in which Puerto Ricans distinguish their belief systems within the Continental United States. This situation is compounded by a lack of historical understanding which falsely views the Puerto Rican national formation outside the context of the rest of Latin America. This is especially true in the case where Puerto Ricans distance themselves from other Hispanics, especially Cubans, who practice forms of Afro-Latin religions in the United States.

A constant problem in this research is the contradistinctive and often seemingly contradictory manner in which Puerto Ricans describe their belief in the spirits of the dead. They describe themselves as believers in Spiritism, distinguishing themselves from believers in the Afro-Cuban system of *Santería*. And yet, both Spiritism and *Santería* are present in the rituals of Puerto Rican Spiritualist congregations in the United States. A combination of French Spiritism and forms of *Santería* exist in both Cuba and Brazil. This research makes a special effort to distinguish between French Spiritism, Cuban *Santería*, and the combined belief system of Spiritualism practiced by this *centro's* congregation. The idiosyncratic definitions that operate in the Spanish spoken at this *centro* has given a new perspective to the meaning of Puerto Rican Spiritualism. This research perspective is crucial in studying the distinct belief systems and their sources in the history of Afro-Latin peoples in the Americas. The writer has therefore created a dictionary which provides some insight into the differences between the traditional use of language in its historical context and its idiosyncratic use by Puerto Ricans at this *centro*.

Dictionary of Idiosyncratic Terms

The following dictionary of idiosyncratic terms illustrates the importance of language, at this *centro*, as a medium of communication. Still, these definitions are unlike those used by social scientists and represent the code words which members of this *centro* use in their efforts to establish their *comunidad* or, community, of historically based idiosyncratic individuals. In other words, they have defined the language to represent them as they want to be understood.

Light (*Darle Luz*). Once a medium communicates with a spirit, the spirit begins its development out of darkness and into the light. An enlightened spirit is a more knowledgeable and worldly spirit who is gaining experience in helping to solve people's problems. Saints are the most enlightened spirits at this *centro*, and present themselves with the greatest light.

Godfather (*Padrino*). The leader of a Spiritist *centro* is also called the President of the table (*Presidente de la mesa*). As the Godfather to the congregation, he is responsible for the activities and services at the centro. As President of the table in the Spiritist tradition, he refers to his role as the person who asks questions of the spirits while the mediums are possessed. He also provides consultations to individuals in the privacy of his office, confirms the mediums' divining, and as a result trains mediums.

Godmother (*Madrina*). The Godfather's wife. She is not ritually important at the *centro*, and remains with the godchildren during services. She never works the table during spirit communication.

Godchildren (*Ahijados*). These are the individuals who make up a semiperipheral group within the *centro*. To become a godchild, a person must go through a baptism which is a rite of passage at the *centro*. The godchildren are primarily responsible for praying during the services, passing incense through the congregation, cleaning up, and passing the collection box. The most experienced godchildren become apprentice mediums when they are called to the front table for spirit communication.

Medium (*Mediaunidad*). The terms apprentice medium, auxiliary medium, Head Medium, and Principal Head Medium appear only as a means for the participant observer to distinguish the mediums' roles. These terms are not in use at the *centro*.

Principal Head Medium (*Mediaunidad de Mano Derecha*). The highest level of mediumship that an individual can attain has always been held by a woman. Consequently, her next level of development within the belief system is that of establishing her own *centro*. The Godfather confides most in the Principal Head Medium who sits at his right side. There is a second Head Medium to the left side of the Godfather, and she is not allowed to work the table on the right side.

Santería or *Santerismo* (no English language equivalent). The use of sorcerers, mostly Cubans, who use their powers to intervene and destroy others' happiness. They work for large amounts of money, and specialize in conjuring up evil forces. They are considered second to those who work *Vodum*, who specialize in the conjuring up of high-level evil spirits.

Sorcery (*Brujería*). This sorcery is practiced mostly by Puerto Ricans, although it is understood that a Cuban *Santero* can also be a sorcerer. A Puerto Rican sorcerer works for low wages and specializes in working for the simpleminded who seek satisfaction of their envy by destroying the happiness of others. The *Cuban Santero* can work spirits that are either low or high level in the spirit hierarchy. In contrast to the *Santero*, the sorcerer is seen as capable only of influencing low-level spirits. These low-level spirits, who are looking for light, are often set loose by the sorcerer to do harm indiscriminately. Most problems brought to the *centro* are caused by sorcerers using low-level spirits.

Spiritism (*Espiritismo*). The belief in the spirit world as developed by Allan Kardec. This belief system requires mediums (*mediaunidades*), godchildren (*ahijados*), and a Spiritist whose role is to be Godfather to a congregation. This Spiritism serves to remove the evil that plagues the Puerto Rican community. The saints are the most enlightened spirits which can intervene in an individual's behalf. The saints require animal sacrifices, an altar, and beads. They must be invoked by using both their Roman Catholic and Yorubaland *Orisha* name.

Facilitating an Understanding of the Belief System

This classification of definitions held by participants and those traditionally held by researchers facilitated an understanding of the complex nature of the socialization process when language use is considered at the *centro*. The confusion of Spiritism and *Santería* has its reasons in the historical development of each belief system. Books on Spiritism, however, have been circulating in Latin America since the 1860s and are presently available in inexpensive editions. In contrast, *Santería* is an orally transmitted belief system with a limited number of recent expensive publications. As a consequence, at the *centro* there is a predominance of terms from Spiritism, with a slow movement toward using some terms from *Santería*.

By analyzing the definition of terms at the *centro*, one can understand that the socialization process also has language variables which complicated the research process. An individual who first arrives at the *centro* is accustomed to the language that operates out of Spiritism. As that person progresses into more significant roles at the *centro*, the oral tradition aspects of *Santería* are incorporated into his or her total belief system. In the end, this combination of Spiritist language and growing use of terms out of *Santería* represents an initial language orientation out of Spiritism and a behavioral - ritual orientation into *Santería*. As a result, when a participant describes a belief in Spiritism, while actually meaning Spiritualism, it will appear thusly in the text, "Spiritism (Spiritualism)."

Spanish is the dominant language even though non - Spanish speakers from other areas of the Caribbean also come to the *centro*. Parts of the services are conducted in a bilingual format using English and Spanish. But the spirits always communicate in a Spanish characterized by a wide range of intonation similar to the speech patterns noted by Lydia Cabrera in her pioneering work, <u>El Monte</u>. Miami: Ediciones Universal, 1975.

ENDNOTES

[1] This study differentiates between Spiritism, which is taken to mean French Kardecian Spiritism, and Spiritualism, which is used to denote the merging of French Kardecian Spiritism and *Cuban Santería.*

[2] Services at the *Centro Espiritista* were filmed with a 16mm camera. This film project emerged from a student excercise in team fieldwork for the late Dr. Margret Mead's Research Methods in Anthropology course at Columbia University. The film begins with a discussion of syncretism (merging) of the Yoruba Pantheon and the Catholic Saints. The film includes scenes from a *botánica* (an herbal magico-religious store), the congregtion at the *centro,* spirit possession at the *centro,* and healing of a *causa* by the mediums. The film was shot without sound and utilized voice-over and commercially recorded music used at the *centro.* The film was produced by the researcher as "Puerto Rican Espiritismo in the South Bronx," runs eighteen minutes, is black and white (1978) and was shown for the first time at the September 1978 Margaret Mead Film Festival at the American Museum of Natural History.

[3] George H. Mead, <u>Mind, Self and Society</u>, (C. W. Morris, Ed.), (Chicago: University of Chicago Press, 1962), 76.

[4] For a classic example of a socialization study using George H. Mead's approach, see H.S. Becker, B. Greer, E.C. Hughes and A.L. Strauss, <u>Boys in White</u>, (Chicago: University of Chicago Press, 1961).

CHAPTER II

Historical Development of Puerto Rican Spiritualism

Part I. A review of the roots of ancestor worship within the Puerto Rican national formation. A form of ancestor worship has been exhibited among the inhabitants of Puerto Rico since before the discovery of the Island by the Spanish. These forms of ancestor worship were later reinforced by the ideologically liberal French Spiritist belief system founded as a reaction against Roman Catholicism. A new development occurred in the United States, previously unknown among the Puerto Rican people, but identified among researchers in the United States as Puerto Rican Spiritualism.   This new development is a combination of those beliefs among the Puerto Rican people reinforced by the paraphernalia of *Cuban Santería*. The end result is that Puerto Rican Spiritualism can be viewed as an incorporatin of *Cuban Santería*. Part II. A review of the Psychological Research literature on Puerto Rican Spiritualism in the United States.

PART I

I ndividuals who attend the *centro* are generally unaware of the historical background and development of their belief system and ritual practices.   There is actually a definitive historical component reflected in their services and it is only by identifying the ideological content that one can begin to understand the practices.

There are three distinct ideological configurations which compete for survival within the Puerto Rican national formation. The first is that of the *Taíno* people, who were the indigenous inhabitants of Puerto Rico. The second group were the Spanish who conquered the *Taíno*. The third group were brought over by the Spanish as slaves from Africa.

Each group maintained a distinct ideological content inherent to its people which is represented, primarily, by the group's religious beliefs.

The *Taíno* of Puerto Rico used *buhuitihu*, men who conversed with ancestor spirits (Pane, 1969, pp. 19-22). It can therefore be said that some form of belief in spirits had existed in Puerto Rico prior to its discovery and conquest by the Spaniards. Nevertheless, by the 1600s the *Taíno* population of Puerto Rico had been decimated by the Spaniards,[1] who arrived in the Americas with the "indissoluble union" of the Roman Catholic Church and the Spanish Crown (Haring, 1963, p. 166). The manpower represented by the *Taíno* was replaced with Africans who were reported within the Spanish Empire by the 15th century (Herring, 1968, p. 104).

The Yoruba people who came to Cuba from West Africa as slaves, brought with them a powerful religious belief system which became a counter-consciousness to the ideological hegemony imposed by the Roman Catholic Church and the Spanish State. The belief system is most prevalent in Cuba, where it is known as *Lucumí* and in Brazil, where it is known as *Candomblé*. Significantly, the Yoruba belief system, like the Taínos', is organized around the worship of ancestor spirits. Similarly, African and Spanish religious ideology represents the major contributions to the development of a Puerto Rican national culture. Importantly, social classes in Puerto Rico were not only distinguished by their relationships to production, but also by allegiances to belief systems.

African ancestor worship took root on the plantations and among the peasantry where slavery was most prominent. In contrast, the Roman Catholic Church was wielding its ideological hegemony in the urban centers, facilitated by the use of the Spanish State's repressive apparatus. The countryside worshipping at home became "nominally Roman Catholic"; at the same time, the urban areas were more closely monitored by the Church and State.

As political activity mounted against the Spanish State, so did political activity mount against the Spanish Church. It was left to a group in the late 1870s, after the failure of the 1868 Lares rebellion for Puerto Rican independence, to initiate a process of generating an ideological content to be used in countering the dominant ideology of Spain. This counter-hegemonic force (Boggs, 1976, p. 78) had to unite the aspirations of the rustic settler (*jíbaro*) in the countryside, and the urban classes within the cultural context of the emerging Puerto Rican national formation.   In other words, a political ideology was called for which would transcend class bounds and facilitate the building of a national consciousness.

The factor combining these two distinct classes in opposition to Spain was not a lay political philosophy but the absorption of French Kardecian Spiritism.   This Spiritism created the opportunity for an unconscious co-participation between those in the countryside and those in the urban centers.   Spiritism nonetheless was not the direct result of immigration, but was the result of an intellectually derived belief system from France. What developed in Puerto Rico was the continuation of ancestor worship, which was initially *Taíno*, and was later reinforced by African forms in the countryside.

As privileged classes evolved in Puerto Rico the historical trajectory brought them to believe in some form of ancestor worship as well. Nevertheless, their justification was projected as European, not African in ideological content. Ultimately, what occurred was the development of a counter-hegemonic unity of consciousness between the rural ancestor worship which was African in content and the Puerto Rican upper class forms of ancestor worship which were formally French but represented a repressed African behavior pattern.   Both of these forms of ancestor worship were in opposition to the Roman Catholic Church and Spanish State which represented the hegemonic power of the society and opposed all other forms of religious expression.   This counter-hegemonic unity of consciousness between the privileged and under-privileged, both rural and urban, reached national proportions in Puerto Rico just prior to the Cuban - Spanish - American War (1898) and the United States occupation of Puerto Rico.

An Inherent Belief in Spirits

According to Rudé (1980, p. 33), an inherent ideology can be defined as the culture of a population at large.   In the case of Puerto Rico, spirit communication can be said to have been inherent.   Further, an inherent ideology can be supplemented by a derived element which, in the case of Puerto Rico, was Allan Kardec's Spiritism.   The derived element can provide political content to the inherent ideology, setting the stage for the development of a popular ideology that is forward looking and not backward looking, aiming towards reform rather than restoration.

In Puerto Rico, spiritism became a popular ideology that was forward looking and which clandestinely attacked the Spanish State and the Roman Catholic Church. The Spiritists rejected the Roman Catholic Church and, in the process, rejected the state, which in the Spanish Empire were very closely linked.

The Roman Catholic Church contributed to the development of Spiritism as a popular ideology by focusing its attention on the populated urban sectors in Puerto Rico, ultimately creating a church which few Puerto Ricans identified as their own. The church and state in Puerto Rico were so intertwined that after the Cuban-Spanish-American War, with the collapse of the Spanish colony, what was left of the Roman Catholic Church also collapsed.

> Although the source is obscure, Father Sherman - son of the famous Civil War general and Roman Catholic chaplain with the American forces which occupied the island in the Spanish-American War - is widely quoted at the time as having written, "Porto Rico is a Catholic country without religion whatsoever....The Church has been so united with the State and so identified with it in the eyes of the people that it must charge the odium with which Spanish rule is commonly regarded. Religion is dead on the island." (Fenton, 1969, Sec. 1.1)

African Ancestor Worship and Spiritism

Among the rural settlers (*jíbaros*) an "unorthodox Creole Catholicism" developed. Consequently, the development of Spiritist beliefs was reinforced by the Roman Catholic Church's "preaching loyalty to Spain, even under the tyranny of military rule" (Wagenheim, 1970, p. 162). At the same time, Afro-Puerto Ricans and Jíbaros were engaging in ancestor worship and folk medical practices. In the Development of the Puerto Rican Jíbaro (originally published in 1935), Rosario (1975) acknowledges that the rustic settlers (*jíbaros*) called on spirits and also revered and worshipped saints of the Roman Catholic Church.

Paradoxically, the upper classes turned to the French Spiritist beliefs, not wanting to identify themselves with the African and *Jíbaro* elements within their society. Yet the upper classes, by practicing Spiritism, provided legitimization of the ancestor worship already flourishing in Puerto Rico.

Historical Development of Spiritism in Puerto Rico

The roots of Puerto Rican Spiritism lie deep in its colonial history. During Spanish absolutism and the domination of Puerto Rico, products destined for the colony had to be exported from Spain. Any other products entered the Empire by special license or were brought in by pirates as contraband (Fernandez Mendez, 1970, pp. 154-155; Haring, 1963, pp. 308-313). Puerto Rico became a pirate haven because it was the furthest point into the Atlantic and the least populated island of the Major Antilles. It developed into a major outpost for clandestine trade, especially with the non-Hispanic Caribbean, e.g., Dutch, English, and French (Morales Carrion, 1972; 1974). In the late 19th century, The Book of Mediums by Allan Kardec (1970) arrived in Puerto Rico among a shipment of unsanctioned and contraband books. It promoted the belief that people should communicate with God through his intermediaries, the spirits.

Speaking to spirits of the dead was a common phenomenon wherever the African people settled. Consequently, the French Kardecian Spiritist phenomenon of the 1860's had fertile ground in the Afro-Latin Caribbean. The greatest impact of Spiritism was on the literate incipient bourgeois sectors of the population in Puerto Rico. Other classes within Puerto Rico began practicing French Spiritism because the culture was prepared to absorb a doctrine from France that reinforced, in a Eurocentric manner, the spirit belief already present on the Island.

A Spiritist Political Leadership

The Spiritist beliefs were reinforced by such well-known figures as Rosendo Matienzo Cintron and Luisa Capetillo, who were in the process of crystallizing a popular ideology when the United States' military occupation of Puerto Rico took place. It was, however, the renowned lawyer and nationalist Rosendo Matienzo Cintron (1855-1913) who made Spiritism a popular ideology. This process came to the fore during the military occupation of Puerto Rico by the United States at the end of the Cuban-Spanish-American War.

Joseph Bram (1972) documents an extensive list of publications in Puerto Rico dealing with Spiritualism or Spiritism. The 21 periodicals listed cover a period of 75 years, and all but 4 were published after the United States' occupation. It was unlike the Spanish occupation of Puerto Rico, when Spiritists functioned clandestinely because of the mandatory persecution involved in veering from the fundamental ideas of the Spanish Church and State. Subsequently, the newspaper La Conciencia Libre, December 11, 1910 (Diaz Soler, 1960, Vol. 1, p. 604, and note) published with the help of Matienzo Cintron, was openly attacking the Roman Catholic clergy, calling them "fanatics who make the soul dumb and pervert the heart." Ideal Católico, the newspaper of the Catholic Church, remembering its political hegemony in religious affairs, asked the United States military governor to suspend publication of La Conciencia Libre because of its anti-Roman Catholic pronouncements.

The rejection of the church and state in Puerto Rico reached higher levels with Journalist Luisa Capetillo (1880-82 to 1922), who is recalled by many as the first woman arrested for wearing pants intended "only for men to wear" (Valle, 1975). She was a well-known labor organizer for the Free Workers' Federation of Puerto Rico (Federación Libre de Los Trabajadores) and traveled extensively throughout the Island as an organizer lecturing to farm workers on the importance of unionization. She was constantly attacked by the Roman Catholic clergy for her scandalous remarks about the church. Later, reflecting on her life, she said:

> I stoutly attacked Catholic fanaticism. I think they do well to defend themselves,as long as it is on reasonable and scientific grounds. For example, since belief in the usefulness of baptism is widespread, they might answer me as to why in all justice they don't baptize people who having nothing to eat can't bring the dollar fee. (Capetillo, 1976, p. 48)

Her anti-Roman Catholicism was combined with Spiritism and a desire for socialism.[2]

All the elements of a forward-looking Puerto Rican popular ideology are found in her thinking: a break with Roman Catholicism[3], advocacy of free love, Spiritism, Socialism, and Materialism. She said, "I am a socialist because I want all the advances, discoveries and inventions to belong to everyone, and that socialization be established without privileges." (Capetillo, 1976, p. 49)

Spiritism's practice was simple, facilitating its diffusion. A believer needed only a white table cloth, a glass of water, and a centrally located table at which to recite prayers. This ritual combined with the study of mediumship from Kardec's texts, would secure spirit communication. In Puerto Rico's hinterland, Spiritism spread unopposed and encouraged by the absence of institutional Roman Catholicism. Consequently, the literate classes represented by the incipient bourgeois, in their political protest against the Spanish Church and State, invested energy and time in the diffusion of the Spiritist belief system and with the Africans' ancestor worship present in Puerto Rico, its diffusion was not difficult.

The United States Occupation of Puerto Rico

The United States' occupation of Puerto Rico undercut the possibility that the inherent ideology of a belief in spirits among Puerto Ricans would combine with the derived ideology of French Kardecian Spiritism and evolve into an anti-absolutist, anti-Roman Catholic popular ideology. The influence of the United States in Puerto Rico implanted progressive elements unknown during Spanish domination. The separation of the church and state, unionization of labor, freedom of the press and religion made their appearance, eliminating the causes fought for by a generation of Puerto Rican pro-independence Spiritist activists.

The appearance of the liberal juridical state brings political parties into direct support of the United States' colonization of Puerto Rico. This support can best be noted in the platform of the Republican Party of Puerto Rico (1898) and the platform of the Federal Party of Puerto Rico (1898). Both platforms advocated annexation by the United States, viewing the U.S. as liberal and forward looking. The Republican Party said in its 1899 platform that the U.S. represented the "highest culture in human destinies."

Considering the status of African-American people residing in the

United States at the time, the Puerto Rican Republican's pronouncements of 1889-1899 assume an ironic tinge because they represented the views of the Afro-Latin people in Puerto Rico.

> Although an obscured theme in the sociological literature of Puerto Rico, there is some evidence suggesting that blacks were a fundamental component of the annexationist movement. As U.S. rule increasingly undermined the political hegemony of the white creole classes (among which racist attitudes were widespread), the Puerto Rican black population saw in the new situation the opening of avenues for social and political mobility. The fact that Barbosa[4] was black may explain in part black support for the Partido Republicano. (Gamaliel Ramos, 1980, p. 261)

In opposing the Spanish Empire and siding with the United States' occupation, Puerto Rico was thrown into political convulsions. The possibility of a popular Spiritist ideology and its incipient leadership died. The situation was complicated further when the North American Protestant and Catholic Churches developed vigorous programs to win Puerto Rican converts. The result was a political and religious breakdown within Puerto Rico.

The United States Roman Catholic and Protestant Churches

Protestantism openly entered Puerto Rico in 1900 as a new religious institution. There had been a period of tolerance under the Spanish Republic (1868-1885) and Anglican church services were allowed for the English-speaking community of Ponce, which held its first service in 1873. When the Spanish crown was restored, the gothic-style Anglican church was allowed to continue functioning

> on appeal by Queen Victoria, to continue holding services provided it did so unobtrusively - spoke only English, possessed no books in Spanish, used a side door as the main entrance, and did not ring its bell. (Fenton, 1969, Sec. 1.2)

United States Catholicism & Protestantism

North American Protestantism could proselytize openly after the

United States' occupation. Fenton (1969) commented that,

> the agreement remains a landmark in comity arrangements; unfortunately, today the wording and circumstances of the agreement are lost and it is not known when it was signed (though 1902 is the traditional date), who participated in the discussion, or how sectors were assigned. (Sec. 1.2)

The Island was divided among Protestant religious organizations. However, Pentecostal groups who were not included in these agreements soon began a vigorous campaign of evangelization throughout Puerto Rico, disregarding the territorial divisions agreed upon among other protestant sects. (Fitzpatrick, 1971, p. 121).

Spiritist centers and publications continued to flourish while the Roman Catholic Church went from a Spanish-dominated church prior to 1900, to an Americanized Roman Catholicism after 1900. Therefore, "the church revealed itself as the new defendant of compulsory Anglicanization," as the personnel and structure went from Spanish to North American (Lewis, 1963, p. 221). The renowned dramatist and short story writer, René Marques (1976), notes that "if the impartial observer did not have his sense of humor somewhat dulled, he might perhaps think that the practitioners of the New Catholicism in Puerto Rico cherish the mystic hope of a moving scene: Saint Peter opening the gates of Heaven to the chords of the Star Spangled Banner" (p. 51). In the long run, the Church never attracted large numbers of Puerto Ricans to either the hierarchy or the congregation.

Undermining Ideological Cohesiveness

Roman Catholicism, with its clear relationship to the Spanish State and its alienation from the Puerto Rican people, had contributed to the development of a noninstitutional framework for religious affairs. Further, with the United States' occupation, Protestant religious organizations divided the Island in an effort to gain converts, while the Catholic Church was taken over by North Americans. Undermining the formal religious institutions, Spiritism had become widespread while developing into a popular ideology.

While Garcia (1974) views Protestantism as the initial ideological vanguard of the Americanization effort in Puerto Rico, Gordon Lewis (1963, p. 221) points out that only 4 out of 40 Protestant schools taught in English while 40 out of 92 Roman Catholic schools taught in English, making the Roman Catholic Church the true vanguard of the Americanization effort.

> [That] Catholicism is the Puerto Rican religion par excellence is more than proved. The Roman Church on the island clearly enough is less and less the church of the people. That fact, perhaps, may explain the recent phenomenon of conversion to the faith of a number of University intellectuals; for as the church becomes less popular its appeal might be increased for the spiritual snob. (Lewis, 1963, p. 221)

Such a shifting religious atmosphere contributed to what Lewis (1963) called the failure of Puerto Rican society "to build up a cohesive community consciousness" (p. 219). The end result of the clash in religious beliefs in Puerto Rico is that an Afro-Latin syncretic belief system such as Haitian *Vodum* [5] or Cuban *Santería* cannot be identified today among the inhabitants of the Island. According to Nieves Falcón (1980), "What can be said is that there was a cultural erosion of the black heritage." (personal communication). Although many African religious practices still exist in Puerto Rico, the tendency is to deny that they are in fact African.

Brameld (1959), in The Remaking of a Culture, found a belief in Spiritists, fortune-tellers, and *Santiguadores* (spiritual faith healers who use oils and herbs) in Puerto Rico. He found "one respondent who insisted 'witchcraft' is common in his municipality and sick persons are often considered ` bedeviled' " (p. 124). He reported what he felt was a "rather ironic practice: local drugstores do a thriving business in native herbs and oils which are sold for higher prices then scientifically tested prescriptions" (p. 124).

Spiritism: An Anomic Trait?

Seda Bonilla (1969) more recently studied Spiritism and sorcery (*Hechicería*) in *Tipán*, Puerto Rico. His view is that Spiritism's rise is the end result of collective insecurity and can be seen at this point as an anomic cultural trait. To Seda Bonilla, Spiritism is dysfunctional for the individual as well as harmful for the entire social structure.

> The resurgence of Spiritism in the last ten years is a sign of
> collective insecurity provoked by confused and suspicious
> situations in the structure of community life. In our judg-
> ment, it is evident that there has been a massive disruption
> of the traditional norms of community life, and the cultural
> amorphism bewilders the possibilities of systematic predic-
> tion as to who is who, and as to how one should behave ac-
> cording to who he or she is. (p. 152)

Seda Bonilla adds that the alleged inferiority complex of Puerto
Ricans is manifested in their devaluation of what is theirs. In this
manner they escape envy, but enter a state of nothingness (*nadismo*).
This ambiguity of self-esteem created by the massive disruption of
traditional community norms became the basis for the revival of Spiritism in Puerto Rico today. Spiritism provides people there with an
integrative atmosphere in which accumulated frustrations can be expressed.

I am in complete disagreement with the position which Seda Bonilla
has on the issue of what Spiritism means within the social context of
Puerto Rico. He sees Spiritism as a "disruption of traditional norms"
instead of viewing it as part of the history of the Puerto Rican people. It
is obvious to me that he has engaged, perhaps unknowingly, in negating
that which is his own and the impact of ancestor worship in the history
of Puerto Rico.

In the end, it can be said that what Seda Bonilla studied is not clear
since sorcery (*Hechicería*) is not a part of Spiritism but is clearly part of
some form of African ancestor worship as expressed mainly in the
Caribbean.

Kardecian Spiritism: A Means of Negating Blackness

The Spiritist belief system has been described as a means of arousing
and manipulating fear among people. Seda Bonilla also (1969) points
to a collective projection of fear among the members of *Tipán* Spiritists
toward the black population of Puerto Rico. This hostility toward the
black Puerto Rican Spiritists, who live in the predominantly black areas

of Puerto Rico, occurs "without an understanding about the African origin of these practices" (pp. 112-113, note). Bastide (1978) adds that the Spiritist belief system in and of itself becomes one means of negating the African cultural heritage which can be encountered in societies where large numbers of descendants of former slaves reside. He states:

> Spiritism (Kardec's) represents a means of ascent to the man whose hopes and aspirations are blocked by the dual barrier of color and social class. It is the only means through which children of darkness, imprisoned in their skin, can dream of transforming themselves, in their future existence, into children of light. (p. 338)

In Puerto Rico, among blacks as well as whites, there was an erosion of understanding of the origins of black religious practices, making it possible for the population to engage in forms of ancestor worship without considering these practices black in origin. The U.S. occupation, furthermore, had the effect of reinforcing a denial of the African aspect of the Puerto Rican cultural heritage, making a society where few Puerto Ricans identify themselves as Afro-Puerto Rican.

Two events far removed from the shores of Puerto Rico provide an opportunity for the privileged classes to join with the *jíbaro* and the Afro-Puerto Rican in developing a popular culture. The first event was the American Spiritualist phenomenon which occurred in New York State, while the second was a reaction against this North American Spiritualism by the founder of Spiritism, the Frenchman Allan Kardec.

It was Kardec's Spiritist movement and its pronouncements which had an impact on the Puerto Rican national formation. The French Kardecian Spiritist belief system viewed itself as progressive and "scientific." Consequently, for the privileged classes of Puerto Rico, Spiritism from France became a means of whitewashing their African ancestor worship with a European belief system.

The class forces represented by the *jíbaro* and the Afro-Puerto Rican on the one hand, and the privileged classes on the other hand, united their incompatible beliefs represented for the former by an African ancestor worship and for the latter by Kardec's "scientific" Spiritism. It was this syncretism which brought the two classes together to undermine the ideological hegemony of the Roman Catholic Church.[6]

Toward an Understanding of Syncretism

The concept of syncretism is neither new nor used exclusively in reference to religion in Latin America. The earliest mention of syncretism appears in Plutarch as "the act or system of blending, combining or reconciling inharmonious elements...to forget dissensions and to unite in the face of common danger" (Showerman, 1910-1911, pp. 292-293). George Calixtus (1586-1656), a Lutheran Professor at the University of Helmstedt in Germany, popularized the term in his effort to forge religious unity and develop a conciliatory attitude toward Christian syncretism (The Compact Oxford English Dictionary, 1971). The term regained prevalence when the Brazilian anthropologist Ramos (1935, 1940, 1943, 1944) used it to describe the process of combining or mixing different religious systems that seem incompatible. His focus was on Afro-Brazilian cults and the process of syncretism between Yorubaland religious beliefs and Roman Catholicism.

Herskovits (1937), a North American anthropologist writing about African cultural "retentions" in the New World, popularized the term among English speakers. His pioneering article on Haiti, Cuba, and Brazil, entitled "African Gods and Catholic Saints in New World Negro Belief," developed the thesis that syncretism between African belief systems and Roman Catholicism was not an isolated incident. Herskovits focused on the survival of Yorubaland deities in the images of Roman Catholic saints. Herskovits applied the concept of syncretism interchangeably with the word "synthesis" when discussing the Africans' "nominal Catholicism while at the same time they belong to 'fetish cults' " (1937).

The least complicated form of syncretism resorts to either plaster images or chromolithographs of Roman Catholic saints addressed by either their Roman Catholic name or their Yorubaland name. (For example, Santa Barbara, a Roman Catholic Saint, becomes *Chango*, an ancestor deity of the Yoruba people.) These figures become a means of worshipping either the saints or the *orishas*.

This process of syncretism has not been uniform, and Herskovits (1937) suggests this process of merging and combining the images of the saints with the *orishas* is idiosyncratic. He details the inconsistencies which syncretism displays from one geographic area to another. In an area of Brazil around Bahia, Herskovits links *Changó* with the female Santa Barbara, while in another area of Bahia, Herskovits identifies him with Saint Jerome. In Rio, he is again syncretized with Saint Jerome. At the same time, there is no *Changó* or Santa Barbara associated with *Vodum* cults in Haiti.

Gonzalez-Wippler (1975) has a Herskovits oriented interpretation of syncretism:

> In their confused imagery, they [Africans] identified their gods and goddesses with the saints of the Catholic faith. This was the beginning of *Santería,* which is a term derived from the Spanish word "santo" (saint), and literally means the worship of saints. *Santería* is a typical case of syncretism, that is, the spontaneous, popular combination or reconciliation of different religious beliefs. This syncretism can be appreciated in the fact that most of the Yoruba gods have been identified with the images of Catholic saints. (p.3)

In contrast to Gonzalez-Wippler and Herskovits, Bastide (1978) does not view the believers' inconsistencies in detailing the syncretization process as either idiosyncratic or due to "confused imagery" but as the researchers' failure to recognize the different ethnic and geographic contributions to the process. Most significantly, researchers have failed to understand that the *orishas* are protean or variable in form. Consequently, a Yorubaland deity or *orisha*, unlike saints, assumes various forms.

> It is therefore likely that each form (or at least the principal ones) will have its Catholic equivalent. Hence it comes as no surprise to find one orixa (Portuguese spelling) corresponding in our table to several saints or virgins. What at first seemed capricious now appears as a more harmonious arrangement. Nina Rodriguez identified *Yemanja* (Portuguese spelling) with our Lady of the Rosary, whereas today she is identified with the Virgin of the Immaculate Conception. The explanation is that we are dealing with the two different *Yemanjas.* (p. 270)

Research by Cabrera (1975) details the protean nature of the *orishas.*

In short, "*Obatalá* is one, call him or her by whatever names one may wish, *Obatalá* female, *Iyala*, and *Obatalá* male, all are one," without excluding the daring and warlike *Allagguna*. "...the first generation of saints in *Oyo*....were the *Obatalas* who formed the family of *Ocha*, as the placing of the soup bowl offering in the highest part of the altar shows, and that *Obatalá* is always placed above all of the other saints, because they (the *Obatalas*) are the Fathers-Mothers, young, old men--lords of the world." (p. 313)

In discussing the *orishas*, it must be remembered that the different saints are chosen on the basis of given characteristics. For example, *Obatalá* is generally identified with Our Lady of Mercy but, as Cabrera's informant explains above, *Obatalá* is a family and there are male and female *Obatalá* which contain different characteristics. This combination of animus (male characteristics) and anima (female characteristics) is common in the *orishas*. Similarly, Carl G. Jung (1954, pp. 68-69) views anima and animus as representing the contrasexual components of the integration of the personality. Consequently, the use of the different characteristics identified in both the saints and *orishas* contains many forces, one of which is the combining male and female aspects of the personality.

The *orishas* are further represented by stones invested with divine power. It is thought that these stones were swallowed by enslaved Africans prior to the Middle Passage to the Americas and concealed in their stomachs. These stones today are prepared and empowered, ritually fed, maintained, and are considered to be alive, with the ability to reproduce.

> The real power of the Santos resides in the stones, hidden behind a curtain in the lower part of the altar, without which no *Santería* shrine could exist. The stones of the Saints are believed to have life. Some stones can walk and grow, and some can even have children. (Bascom, 1971, p. 523)

The process of the preparation of stones is detailed by an informant of Cabrera (1975) thusly:

> but we fix it (the stone) like this: We wrap it in a white handkerchief and we bury it for seven or twenty-one days in a cemetery. At the end of seven or twenty-one days I go to get it and I bring it home. I kill an all white rooster for it, and

I bathe the rock in the blood so that it drinks it. The bones of the rooster are wrapped in the same handkerchief that was used for the stone, and I return them to the cemetery. The wrapped bones are then buried in the same spot as the rock was. Later, I wash the stone with holy water and I give it sweet wine or dry wine with cinnamon. I then place it in a small clay casserole or in a cup and cover it with metal filings. I give it small pieces of gold, silver, and copper, nails from a horseshoe, needles or pins, a magnet: a horse-shoe made of magnet, and mercury. Moreover, we the "*mayomberos*"[7] also place a piece of Jamaica rosewood and another of "verraco" wood and two pieces of "sabedor" wood, cinnamon sticks, cloves and pepper. (pp. 140-141)

The magnetic stones' power or the "*Piedra Imán*" (the all-powerful stone) is determined by their proximity to the altar, with the Roman Catholic saints representing the *orishas*. It is the stones which empower the Catholic saints. Consequently, many a worshipper sees the altar with its Roman Catholic saints as a historical residue from the time when "whites had to be given the impression that members of the 'nations' were good Catholics" (Bastide, 1978, p. 272).

This use of the Catholic saints is made possible by the Yoruba belief system which does not focus on the world as "good" or "bad." The saints are there to be used as the *orishas* are to be used, that is, to combat malevolent or benevolent powers. Therefore:

Unlike the European, the Yoruba does not conceive the world as a conflict between good and evil, light and darkness, God and Devil. He is realistic and recognizes that all forces--even divine forces--have destructive as well as constructive possibilities. The secret of life, then, and the purpose of the *Orisha* worship is to establish a constructive relationship with these powers. (Jahn, 1961, p. 64)

This relationship building is further intensified because, within these powers, each *orisha* is assigned colors which must be worn as a string of beads and as clothing. The *orisha* called *Obatalá* is represented by white beads only, while *Yemayá* is represented by "seven white beads alternating with seven blue beads, then one white and one blue until seven of each have been threaded; the cycle is repeated until the necklace is of suitable length" (Gonzalez-Wippler, 1975, p. 32).

Similarly, the *orishas*, with each attribute, identified by a *santero / santería* (priest or priestess) or *babalao* (High Priest), must be consulted through process of divination using cowrie shells. This initiates individuals into ancestor worship, since spirits of the *orishas* or saints are called upon for advice. The *santero* builds up protection for the individual by communicating with spirits (ancestors) and providing the neophyte with necklaces (*collares*). These necklaces are provided as the *babalao* attains complete understanding of the powers represented by the neophyte's *orishas* or saints, which the neophyte spiritually manifests (*montar*) within him.

> The necklaces are believed to protect their wearer against all evil as long as they are being worn. While he is wearing the necklaces, the neophyte may carry on his normal everyday routine, but he is not to bathe or to undertake any form of sexual activity. If he wants to take a bath or have sexual intercourse, he must remove the necklaces and put them back on when he is finished. (Gonzalez-Wippler, 1975, pp. 31-32)

Witchcraft (*brujería*) or sorcery is a part of *Santería*. Gonzalez-Wippler (1975) describes one form as "Natural Magic" which finds its power in the use of

> herbs and trees that are found in the steaming, tropical forests of the Antilles. In these dark, brooding woods live the spiritual entities of the *Yorubas* and the Bantus. Everything comes from the forest, from the fertile womb of the earth, say the *Santeros*. Magic cannot be practiced without the help of the woods. (p. 85)

The other types of magic involve spells to entice lovers, invite good luck, dispel bad influences, and exorcise spirits that often involve the ritual sacrifice of animals.

> Before the *Santero* offers an animal to an *orisha*, he must find out by the means of the sea shells whether the god accepts the animal, and what is to be done with it. If the animal is to be sacrificed it is also necessary to learn what parts of its body are to be offered to the god. It is forbidden to divide an animal among several saints. (Gonzalez-Wippler, 1975, p. 51)

Garrison (1977a) explains:

> *Santería* is an alternative religion which involves a life-long commitment and a large financial investment on the part of the initiate. It is organized in a system of fictive kinship[8] in which each initiate is the *ahijado* (godchild) of the *Santera* (*madrina*, godmother) and the *babalawo* (*padrino*, godfather) that initiate him or her. The initiate is correspondingly related to all others initiated. (p. 91)

Consequently, all initiates or neophytes become part of a given house of worship (*casa*) which they enter as godchildren of the high priest. But most importantly, and contrary to what is found in the South Bronx, "There are no public meeting places in traditional *Santería*, except out-of-doors in the mountains (*el Monte*)" (Garrison,1977a, p. 91). *Santería* is a complex religious system that has a syncretic facet with Roman Catholicism. It involves attempting to establish relationships with the *orishas* or saints, relationships that are reinforced by the ritual kinship system.

Anglo-American Spiritualism

Spiritualism began in the State of New York during the religious revival of the 1840s. In the late 1840s, the Fox family of Hydesville, Wayne County, New York reported spirit communication with the dead. After celebrated investigations the family moved to Rochester, New York, where they gained popularity as Spiritualists. They became known as the Fox Sisters, the Rochester Knockers, the Fox Girls, and the Rappers. Daughters Katie, Leah, and Margaret became well-known mediums who would listen for spiritual communication through knocks, raps and other noises. One famous seance took place at the New York Academy of Music, where lights, sounds, and knocks were caused by manifesting spirits (Cadwallader, 1917; Asociación Escuela Científica Basilio, 1976, pp. 60-61; Sidgwick, 1910-1911, pp. 705-708).

French Scientific Spiritism.

Frederick Engels (1908), reflecting on his times, noted it was necessary for a man of free thought to consider himself a materialist because it was one of the "necessary qualifications of a cultivated man" (p.34). As spirit communication became more popular in Europe, Engels (1940) denounced the movement as one that was exalting mere experience at the expense of thought, criticizing those who had "fallen a hopeless victim to the spirit rapping and spirit-seeing imported from America" (pp. 297-298).

Kardecian Spiritism developed in France during the 1850s. The American spirit manifestations were rejected in France as unscientific, pseudo-Spiritism. Attuned to the times, Allan Kardec proceeded to develop a form of "scientific" and materialist spirit communication intended for the cultivated, but which rejected the American experiences of the Fox sisters (*Asociación Escuela Científica Basilio*, 1975, pp. 65-69).

Allan Kardec (1808-1869) (pseudonym for Denizarth Hippolyte Rivail) published several treatises on scientific communication with spirits. Among the better known titles presently available are *El Evangelio Segun El Espiritismo* (Kardec, 1969), *El Libro de Los Espíritus* (1975), and *The Book of Mediums* (Kardec, 1970), all originally written in French.

Kardec saw Spiritism as a religious innovation which attempted to incorporate aspects of the Scientific Revolution. Vivian Garrison (1977a) wrote that Kardec:

> was a mesmerist and engineer who attempted to explain and rationalize the beliefs in spirits then popular in Europe with the science of his day. [Consequently,] Kardec later distinguished between "spiritualism" and "spiritism," defining the first as any belief in a non - material aspect of life - the opposite of materialism, and the latter as "the science" or "doctrine" of "the interrelationship between the material world and the espiritus (spirits) or seres (beings) of the "invisible world." (p. 80)

Parenthetically, it should be remembered that the period had its effects on August Comte (1798-1857), a major figure in sociology, who in his later years proclaimed himself the "High Priest" of the Religion of Humanity (Aron, 1965, pp. 100-109; Coser, 1977, pp. 38-41). This effort to bridge the gap between science and religion which Kardec, like Comte and Saint-Simon were attempting, is a familiar 19th century concern. The concept that spirits are seeking "light" (Enlightenment) becomes the cornerstone of the Kardecian Spiritist tradition. The spirits are seen as progressively seeking light from the moment they cease being material (tangible living beings) and become spiritual. *Dar La Luz al Espíritu* (giving a spirit light) and underdeveloped spirits provide the first and second conditions for calling upon mediums. Once invoked and enlightened the spirit can ascend to the next spiritual level, where it can become a more potent instrument for providing advice to the living. The spirits exist in a hierarchy, as Kardec (1970) states:

> Now, the superior spirits are the upper circles of the spirit world: their very elevation places them so much above us that we are frightened at the distance that separates us. Spirits more bourgeois (may they excuse the expression) make the circumstances of their new existence more palpable to us. (p. 363)

Several definitive spirit types manifest themselves through mediums. These types represent different levels of the hierarchy, and in *El Libro de Los Espíritus*, Kardec (1975) sets forth three categories with nine levels through which a spirit must pass to become pure and enlightened. Kardec's three categories encompass all aspects of the spiritual world.

The first category contains the most enlightened spirits. Intellectually superior and pure in feeling, these spirits are not influenced by material things. Closest to God, they act as His Messengers, assist God in His quest for universal harmony, and assist inferior spirits to secure perfection (Kardec, 1975, pp. 78-86; Ruiz, 1979, p. 30).

Kardec's second category includes benevolent spirits who understand God and possess spiritual power greater than their material power. This category subsumes four levels:

1. Spirits (superiors) who, through mediums, transmit morality, wisdom, and scientific knowledge, and only manifest themselves on missions that facilitate progress toward these ends.
2. Spirits (prudents) which manifest themselves with morality but only limited wisdom.
3. Spirits (sapients) which become manifest with limited scientific knowledge.
4. Spirits (benevolents) who manifest themselves with limited

wisdom but with higher levels of morality and ethics (Kardec, 1975; Ruiz, 1979).

The third category of spirits has the last five of Kardec's nine levels. These are imperfect spirits who enjoy behaving in a malevolent fashion, overcome by material forces, they manifest themselves as egoistic and ignorant.

1. Spirits (perturbers) who marshal themselves through air, water, or matter.
2. Spirits (neutrals) who are inspired to manifest themselves by material objects but are neither benevolent nor malevolent.
3. Spirits (false instructors) who manifest themselves as all-knowing.
4. Spirits (ghosts) who manifest themselves as superficial, ignorant, and mocking.
5. Spirits (impures) who manifest themselves as preferring-malevolence (Kardec, 1975; Ruiz, 1979).

Kardec's three categories with its nine levels of spirit manifestation define the characteristics inherent in his spiritual hierarchy. These spirit types manifest themselves through mediums, with the more skilled mediums able to communicate at higher levels. Mediums also must have the "faculty" to receive spiritual communication and distinguish mocking spirits from "bantering spirits, who amuse themselves at their expense" (Kardec, 1970, p. 394). The important spirits are those that "while advising us, leave us to our own energy, as a skillful teacher does for his pupils" (Kardec, 1970, p. 394).

The process through which mediums' abilities develop hinges on each medium securing his or her own protectors (*protecciones*); only some mediums can do this. Protectors are mediums' spirits which represent the mediums' spiritual being (*propio ser*), a nonmaterial aspect. The mediums' spirits attached themselves to the medium at birth, and attempt to help the future medium ultimately make contact with higher level spirits.

The development of these disincarnate spirits along the hierarchy is promoted by carnate spirits already in the medium. But spirits within the medium begin to lose their protective features and even become subversive if the medium does not seriously establish contact with spirits outside him or herself. In the end, the medium's carnate spiritual development reflects his or her ability to enlighten disincarnate spirits (Garrison, 1977a, pp. 80-89).

The process of developing spiritual protectors (*protecciones*) or guides (*guías*) becomes all-important for the relationship of the mediums with the spirits. This development of protectors cannot occur without the help of the medium's Guardian Angel.

> The primary point consists in putting one's self, with sincere faith, under the protection of God, and imploring the assistance of one's guardian angel, who is always good, while the familiar spirit, sympathizing with the good or bad qualities of the medium, may be trifling, or even bad if these indications are suspicious, a fervent appeal must be made to the guardian angel, and the bad spirit repulsed with the whole strength, proving to him that you are not his dupe, in order to discourage him. (Kardec, 1970, p. 254)

Through the magnetic fluids (*fluidos*), a mysterious source of energy, the mediums are able to detect the type of spirit present at the seance. The mediums become aware of the fluids through the physical feelings generated by spirit communication. Various cues help the medium identify different types of spirits. Feelings of freshness and coolness in the medium denote enlightened spirits. In contrast, feelings of pain and warmth imply less enlightened spirits (Ruiz, 1979, p. 31). Initially, developing mediums communicate with base, earthly bound spirits looking for light.

As the mediums become practiced, they eventually start communicating with developed spirits, which increases their ability to communicate at even higher levels until they achieve communication with deceased enlightened heroes and leaders. In the 1970s, in the Puerto Rican area of New York City, Harwood (1977c, p. 41) found Spiritists consulting Los Tres Difuntos (The Deceased Three), John F. Kennedy, Robert Kennedy, and Martin Luther King, Jr.; whereas more than 10 years earlier, Rogler and Hollingshead (1972, p. 49) had reported that Franklin D. Roosevelt and Mahatma Gandhi were being communicated with spiritually in Puerto Rico. The medium's ability determines the type of spirit contacted; the more enlightened the spirit the higher the quality of the communication.

Puerto Rican Spiritualism in the United States

By the 1980s there were over 2 million Puerto Ricans residing the United States, mostly migrants in search of better and higher-paying jobs. Presently, Puerto Ricans make up less than 1% of the population of the United States. Still, there are 860,552 Puerto Ricans in New York City, which is 12.2% of the total population. (The Puerto Rican New Yorkers, The New York City Department of City Planning, December, 1982.)

Puerto Rican migration to the United States resulted in a process of religious syncretism similar to that described by Bastide in Brazil (1971). Besides the chanting and paraphernalia of the Yoruba cults, he identified the cult of the dead through Allan Kardec's Spiritism, saying, "...it is clear that what we have here is a reinterpretation of the African ancestor cult." (p. 168).

Puerto Rican Spiritualism in the United States today connotes the contribution of the religious objects (paraphernalia) and ideology of Cuban *Santería* with aspects of french Kardecian Spiritism. This merger is facilitated by Kardec's (1970) statement that spirits "identify themselves with the habits of those to whom they speak, and take the names calculated to make the strongest impression on the man by reason of his belief" (p. 345). Therefore, spirits can identify themselves as saints, especially if believers in *Santería* are involved in seances. Spiritism is not viewed as an antagonistic philosophy by *Santeros* in New York today, since they too use spirit communication. Gonzalez-Wippler (1980) emphasized that "all Santeros are Spiritists [sic] but not all Spiritists are *Santeros*" (personal communication). The rites of passage, the complicated nature of empowering orishas to be used as a weapon, the animal sacrifices to satisfy the blood demands of the *orishas*, and the process of divination in *Santería*, all contribute to making Kardecian Spiritism a much less complex system of ancestor worship when compared with Santería.

Toward the Reaffirmation of Blackness

Inadvertently, Steiner (1974), Garrison (1977a), and Harwood (1977c) have found in New York City what no researcher has reported in Puerto Rico: the development of a syncretized system of Puerto Rican Spiritualism, combining spiritism and aspects of Cuban *Santería*, especially the Yorubaland orishas. Nieves Falcón (1980) believes this is possible because *Santería* was latently present in Puerto Rico, but that Puerto Ricans in the United States were capable of making it manifest because of

> the search for identity and the positive approach to the African heritage (in the United States). In the acceptance of herbs, *orishas*, and *botánicas* (herbal magico - religious stores) the white ethnic background was substituted by a black background. (personal communication)

Ultimately, what has developed in the United States is a "collective positive approval for an element in Puerto Rico that is negative" (personal communication).

In Brazil, the Yorubaland religion syncretized with Roman Catholicism and *Candomblé* developed. Later, in a similar manner to the Puerto Rican case, through a syncretism with French Kardecian Spiritism, *Umbanda* developed. What makes this notable is that *Umbanda* maintains seven major syncretized orishas in Brazil, while Puerto Ricans in the United States, with a completely different history, are also using seven major syncretized orishas. In Brazil the orishas remained in the historical trajectory toward the incorporation of Spiritism, while among Puerto Ricans the main historical trajectory was a dormant ancestor worship, combined with the use of Catholic home altars, which later became manifest with a pronounced use of French Spiritism and Cuban *Santería's* orishas in North America.

Consequently, without the extensive migration of Puerto Ricans to the United States this manifest development of a religious syncretism might not have occurred. Bastide (1978) wrote:

> Religious syncretism results from the development of trade and the rise of cities where seafarers and travelers gather. It simply transposes to the level of superstructures the economic ties that link country to country, making them interdependent. But each "syncretism" has its own character and each one struggles against the others. (p. 12)

Notwithstanding, it should be noted that the Seven African Powers do not appear in the traditional sources on *Santería* such as Cabrera (1975) and Ortiz (1973). Researchers in Puerto Rican and Cuban communities of the United States (Garrison, 1977a, 1977b; Halifax & Weidman, 1973; Sandoval, 1977, 1978) have never identified the Seven African Powers.

Gonzalez-Wippler (1975), working in New York City, nevertheless identified the Seven African Powers, or Yoruba Pantheon, when describing the syncretic *orisha* -saint combination of *Santería*. The Seven Powers have been identified in field studies by different researchers. Confusion often occurs when different spellings are encountered, and because some researchers who have acknowledged the existence of the Seven Powers have failed to identify all of them. Both Gonzalez-Wippler (1975) and Pérez y Mena (1977) found the Seven African Powers and their syncretized equivalents among Puerto Ricans in New York City. Hence:

> The septet of African Powers controls every aspect of life with *Changó* (Santa Barbara) representing sensual pleasure; *Eleggua* (Holy Guardian Angel), opportunity; *Obatalá* (Our Lady of Mercy - Las Mercedes), peace and harmony among people; *Oshun* (Our Lady of La Caridad del Cobre), marriage; *Oggun* (Saint Peter), war and work for the unemployed; *Orunla* (Saint Francis of Assisi), gives power by opening the doors to the past and the future; and lastly, *Yemaya* (Our Lady of Regla) fertility and maternity. (Pérez y Mena, 1977, p. 133)

Other identifications have occurred in New York City. Saint Anthony of Padua has been identified by Borrello and Mathias (1977) and Harwood (1977c) as syncretized with *Eleggua*. Saint Martin of Porres was identified without a syncretized orisha equivalent by Borrello and Mathias (1977). St. Francis of Assisi, who is usually syncretized with *Orunla*, is now, among Puerto Ricans in New York City, being syncretized with *San Juan Bautista*, the patron saint of Puerto Rico. There is a significant correlation between the work of researchers identifying the existence of the Seven African Powers in New York City. The *orishas Eleggua, Oshun, Yemaya,* and *Changó* have been identified by Borrello and Mathias, Pérez y Mena, and Steiner, and most importantly, by Harwood. Furthermore, Borrello and Mathias (1977) did not ac-

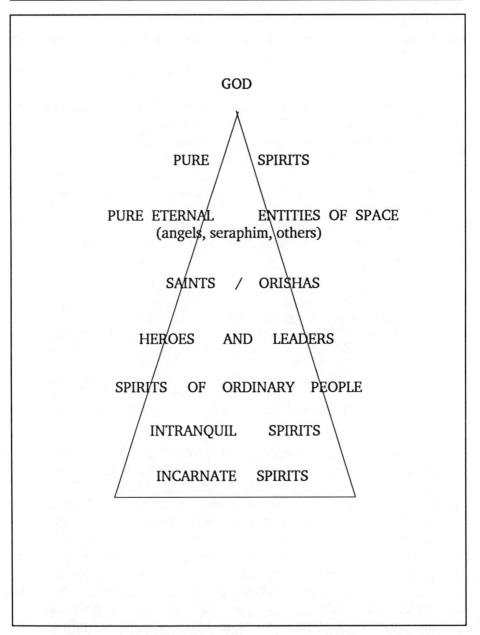

Figure# 2. The Spirit Hierarchy (Harwood, 1977c, p. 40)

knowledge all seven of the syncretized forms, limiting themselves to four out of the Seven African Powers. Harwood (1977c) identified the Seven African Powers and included some not found by other researchers.

Figure 1 represents Harwood's (1977c, p. 40) findings of a syncretized system of Spiritism and *Santería*, among Puerto Ricans which in Brazil goes under the name *Umbanda*. One can see that this belief system, which combines the worship of the *orishas*, the Catholic saints, and Kardecian Spiritism, is not unique to Puerto Ricans. What makes this situation unique is its manifest appearance in New York City.

Researchers need to differentiate between those who maintain a belief system which is primarily influenced by French Spiritism and one which is influenced by *Santería*. The degree of syncretism becomes a better barometer of the complexity of the belief system. It is not sufficient, consequently, to say that someone believes in spirits, since Spiritualism or *Espiritualismo* is used to refer to any occult practice (Garrison, 1977a, p. 80).

Wakefield (1960) participated in a Spiritist session in the late 1950's and gave a pioneering description of French Spiritism among Puerto Ricans in New York City. He made no mention of Yoruba orisha worship. Just as importantly, he criticized Mills' finding that 2% of Puerto Ricans in the United States claim membership in Spiritist churches. Wakefield (1960) contended it was meaningless to write of formal membership, pointing out that spirits can be worshipped just as easily in a home.

> The consistently small percentage...is often a misleading figure to outside observers who assume that the Puerto Ricans conduct their religious life by the same rules and rituals as, say, Irish Catholics or Midwestern Protestants.... There is actually little difference, though, between the beliefs and practices of the work with the spirits in the home or in the Puerto Rican Spiritualist church. (p. 65).

Glazer and Moynihan (1963) acknowledged the strength of Spiritualism among Puerto Ricans, but mistakenly characterized it as "more akin to an occult science like astrology" (p. 106). In this sense they failed to appreciate the complexities of Spiritualism as a belief system. Oscar Lewis (1965) also failed to appreciate the significance of the belief system by never focusing on Spiritualistic beliefs among his informants, even though some told him of their belief in spirits. Steiner (1974, p. 481) encountered a form of Spiritualism among Puerto Ricans in New York City which contained chants to the "Seven African Powers," one facet of Yorubaland *orisha* worship within *santería*. He erroneously stated that "Spiritism was ecumenical." Nonetheless, he correctly but inadvertently identified the dynamic process of syncretism between Puerto Rican Kardecian Spiritism and the already syncretized Cuban *Santería*. Moreover, by Steiner recording this form of Spiritism with attributes of *Santería*, he goes beyond the findings of Fitzpatrick (1971), Glazer and Moynihan (1963), Lewis (1965), Padilla (1958), Rogler and Hollingshead (1972), Wakefield (1960), and Wagenheim (1970).

Wakefield (1960) provides, through the omission of any mention of Cuban *Santería* in Puerto Rican Spiritism, an indication that its syncretism did not occur in the 1950's. It began its appearance in the late 1960's and was recognized as apparent by Steiner in the early 1970's.

There were two underlying factors contributing to activating syncretism. The first was that during the 1950's major Cuban and Puerto Rican bands performing in the United States and Latin America played music which was predominantly influenced by chants, instruments, and lyrics used in *Santería* to praise the deities of the Yorubas. My informant says that Cuban bands such as the popular Sonora Matancera, and those led by *Benny Moré* and singer *Celia Cruz*, often played on the same bill at the Palladium in the Hotel Taft in New York City with Puerto Rican singers Rafael Hernandez and Daniel Santo. Also the *Sonora Matancera* was a backup band for both the Puerto Rican singer Daniel Santo and for the Cuban singer Celia Cruz in Cuba, in the United States, and in South America during the late 1940's and 50's. Significantly, *Celia Cruz* has produced an immense repertory of music to the Yoruba Pantheon, the most memorable piece was to the Yorubaland deity *Changó*, syncretized with Santa Barbara. This situation leads one to assume that at the cultural level there was considerable exchange of Afro-Cuban musical expressions between Cuban and Puerto Rican performers. Another contributor to the cultural dissemination of the Yoruba Pantheon in North America was the Cuban band leader and actor *Dezi Arnez* who regularly sang to the Yorubaland deity *Babalú-Ayé* on television during the situation comedy "I Love Lucy". His signature so became the chants and music to *Babalú-Ayé* (syncretized with Saint Lazarus the Leper) that almost twenty years after the "I Love Lucy" show was last filmed, he performed it on National Broadcasting Company's (NBC) "Saturday Night Live". Today the popular Afro-Latin Music *Salsa* is the musical expression mostly of Puerto Ricans residing in the United States, with the Cuban Celia Cruz as a major performer, and is similarly influenced by *Santería*, and Afro-Cuban rhythms.

Secondly, and probably the most important factor contributing to this renewed syncretism, was the arrival of nearly one million Cubans as refugees, fleeing the Cuban Revolution and settling in the United States. Further, contributing to this syncretism was their re-settlement on the east coast of the United States in predominantly Hispanic areas.

The fuse which ignites all these forces into a syncretism within the Puerto Rican community is the turmoil of the 1960's. The psychological repercussions on the Puerto Rican Community's battles for equal rights, equal accesses to education, anti-racist struggles, Puerto Rican independence, and the loss of loved ones in Vietnam. This then forms the social bases for syncretism. This syncretism occurred because of an on-again and off-again conscious effort by the Puerto Rican community to distance itself from the policies of the Euro-American superstructures of the society as was occurring in the English Speaking African American communities residing in the United States. The positive re-appraisal of blackness among Africans residing in the United States similarly influenced the Puerto Rican community. They found in their ancestor worship a renewed sense of positive meaning in the orishas as represented in the popular music of the 1940's and 50's.

Once in the United States the "nominal Catholicism" among Puerto Ricans became more pronounced, as Puerto Ricans distanced themselves from the traditional forums of religious expression, and it manifested itself as a form of ancestor worship in search of its African form. Consequently, in the United States, the Yorubaland *orishas* of Cuban *Santería* gained prominence within Puerto Rican Spiritism. Herein orishas became a vehicle of expressing frustrations, while at the same time alleviating those frustrations, all this from within what was thought to have been French Spiritism, which can now be defined as Puerto Rican Spiritualism.

PART II

Psychology and Puerto Rican Spiritualism in the United States

Puerto Rican Spiritualism has become the catch-all category to describe Puerto Rican forms of ancestor worship. In the migration to the United States the belief system was transplanted, took root, and entered into a syncretic process with Cuban *Santería*. This rapid and ongoing syncretism created difficulties for the psychologically oriented researcher, especially when a significant number of Puerto Ricans in the northeast of the United States reported consultations with "spiritualists." These practices went un-differentiated as to whether what was being practiced was either French Spiritism, Spiritualism, or *Santería*.

What psychotherapists in general felt they had identified in their practice with Puerto Ricans in the United States was an indigenous form of therapy. This indigenous therapy often competed with Western trained therapists, and was at the same time identified as a belief operating alongside Western therapies.

The difficulty of securing information about Puerto Rican adherence to forms of African ancestor worship has been one of the major problems in psychological research efforts. Abad and Boyce (1979, p.35) found as a rule that Puerto Rican patients in the United States do not volunteer information about their beliefs when visiting a psychiatrist. Mumford (1972, p. 772) cautioned clinicians that if a Puerto Rican said he did not adhere to a belief in spirits, they had not gained his confidence. Despite efforts of concealment, findings in the Hispanic communities of New York City have shown a dramatic use of Spiritualists which researchers have mistakenly identified as a belief in Spiritism.

Research has shown that 73% of all Puerto Rican outpatients in a mental health clinic in New York City reported concurrent visits to Spiritualists (Mumford, 1972). In another study, out of 79 households, 53% had one resident who admitted consulting a Spiritist (Harwood, 1977c, p.28). In a sampling of 80 Puerto Ricans in the South Bronx, 30% consulted Spiritists (Garrison, 1973). Lastly, in a Washington Heights study of 52 Puerto Ricans, 31% consulted Spiritualists (Lubchansky, Egri, & Stokes, 1970). Undoubtedly, ancestor worship is wide spread in the Puerto Rican community.

In an important study, supernatural causation among Puerto Ricans became the focus of Lubchansky et al.'s (1970) research. The subjects were Spiritualist and community leaders. A third category, which contained a probability sample, provided a cross-section of male Puerto Rican household heads and their wives. Each group was given fictitious cases for evaluation and referral. One of the salient findings was that Puerto Ricans have both a natural and supernatural belief system about the etiology of illness. Those with mental illness requiring professional treatment are often taken to Spiritualists. Out of 20 interviews, 16 were done at Spiritist centers where seances were conducted. Public meetings and private consultations were held regularly at the temples (*centros*). Part of the healing technique included the use of herbs, baths, and ointments. Distinction of Spiritualist or Spiritist and use of paraphernalia is absent. Therefore, simpler Spiritist beliefs are not distinguished from the more complicated Spiritualist beliefs which contain aspects of *Santería*.

Because the belief systems are not differentiated, the amount of syncretism involved in amelioration of ailments are undefined. Lubchansky et al. maintain that the Spiritualist's conceptions of mental illness is idiosyncratic, and unlike professional psychiatric interpretations (1970).

A study of Puerto Rican community in Connecticut was conducted by Gaviria and Wintrob (1976). They found that psychiatric outpatients and the community maintained similar views on natural and supernatural causes of mental illness. The principal natural causes identified for nervousness were alcohol, drug abuse, heredity, and malnutrition. A positive relationship was said to exist between mental illness and Spiritism by 80% of the community subjects and 90% of the patients interviewed. The researchers' short coming is that they did not question the component parts of the belief system although half the psychiatric outpatients were convinced a positive relationship existed between mental illness and witchcraft. French Kardecian Spiritism does not contain the use of witchcraft (sorcery), which Puerto Rican Spiritualism inherited from *Santería*, and ancestor worship from Afro-Puerto Ricans.

Gaviria and Wintrob (1979) found that in 80% of the families they interviewed in two Connecticut towns, at least one spouse believed in Spiritism; in 48% of the families, both spouses did. They identified a tendency among Puerto Ricans toward a belief in the supernatural which can produce benevolent and malevolent spirits. This was unlike the black and white ethnic sample of their study.

Still, some researchers have taken syncretism into account in analyzing the Spiritualist belief system. Harwood (1977a) identified Spiritists, Spiritualists, *Santeros*, and sorcerers *brujos* (witches), and focused on the role of Spiritualism in family relations in a Hispanic neighborhood in New York City. Salgado (1974) found a significant number of Puerto Rican families employing Spiritists in family related problems. Leutz (1976) also found that Spiritualists most actively responded to requests for help in family-related problems. Leutz experimented by providing human services information in the Puerto Rican community to merchants, Spiritualists, social club owners, and the clergy. He found that the Spiritualists and the clergy used the information the most. Ruiz and Langrod (1976) maintain that Spiritualists and clergy have similar roles, although the authors complain that psychiatrists, especially Anglo-North Americans, tend to reject this possibility, precipitating poor doctor-patient relations.

In contrast to Leutz (1976) and Salgado (1974), Harwood (1977a) recognized the differences between Spiritist and *Santero*, and acknowledged the process of syncretism between the two belief systems. Nevertheless, Harwood (1977c) incorrectly identifies *Santería* as a Spiritist tradition, saying "in New York today syncretism of the two spiritist [sic] traditions is rapidly taking place" (p. 49). He found *centros* which practiced a mixture of both Spiritism and *Santería*. Furthermore, Harwood (1977c, p.47) recognized the Seven African Powers with their syncretic saint equivalents, which is a salient attribute of *Santería*. He postulated that syncretism occurred in the United States because of the "socioeconomic heterogeneity" of Puerto Ricans in New York, unlike in Puerto Rico, where the different belief systems are practiced by "socio-economically distinct" groups (p.52). As has already been suggested, there is no evidence of cultural retention in Puerto Rico of manifest syncretism between Yoruba beliefs and Roman Catholicism, that would bring about the development of ancestor worship with the *Orishas*. Harwood's contention that Spiritists perform the rites of *Santería* is questionable, even if he is referring to Spiritualists who practice a syncretic system.

The complicated services a *Santero* works require large investments by clients, and Spiritists traditionally do not have the background for the rituals. It is easier to postulate that it is the language homogeneity among Hispanics in New York, the Cuban Revolution and the monetary investments required by *Santería* as the contributing factors helping to ignite syncretism. The *asiento*, a rite of initiation into a house of worship in *Santería*, which contains a ritual kinship system, cost $3,000 in 1975 in New York, and $5,000 in Miami (Garrison, 1977a, p.98). Garrison further states:

> "The mixed practices of *Espiritismo* and *Santería* in which records of drum rhythms of the *Orisha* are played or the African powers are "mounted" in mediums during essentially *Espiritista* (spiritist) reunions are considered deviant exploitative practices by the *Santero* (*a*)s and most of the *Espiritistas* that I have studied. "Fully made" *Santero* (*a*)s are distressed to see the practices of many *Botánicas* in which *collares* or factory-made hollow images of *Eleggúa* and other ritual items of the cult can be purchased without the elaborate "preparation" and ceremonies with which these are bestowed in the traditional cult practices. (p.95).

As with Garrison (1977b) and Harwood (1977a, 1977b), 1977c), the focus has been on the folk-therapeutic components of Spiritualism. Harwood (1976, p.139) views the metaphysics of psychiatry as based on Anglo-Protestantism and those of Spiritism as based on Folk-Catholicism. Garrison (1977b) follows the treatment of her informant, Maria, by a psychiatrist and a Spiritualist. Maria's treatment by the Spiritualist is filled with the combined traditions of Spiritism and *Santería*. To cleanse Maria of her evil spirits, saints (*orishas*), cigar smoke, and the calling of African (Congo) protector spirits were employed. The diagnosis held that low-grade spirits had been hired to make Maria crazy. Although there is no concept of low-grade spirits in *Santería*, there is the concept of spirit intrusion, which sends a malevolent spirit into an individual to spread disease.

Sandoval (1977) considers spirit intrusion the most dreaded cause of disease. In the French Kardecian Spiritist system spirits cannot be manipulated, whereas in *Santería* spirits are manipulated for malevolent and benevolent purposes. Garrison identified the syncretic treatment of disease even though the Spiritist tradition was manifestly exhibited by the standard prayers read at the *centro, Colección de Oraciones Escogidas de Allen Kardec y Otros Autores.*

In 1978, Garrison focused on how Spiritualism can act as a support system for schizophrenic Puerto Rican women in the South Bronx of New York. Out of four adaptive categories for migrant women, she named Spiritualism in the "cultic pattern" category which provided a natural support system. This "cultic pattern," is a general category that does not differentiate between Spiritism or *Santería* and does not distinguish levels of syncretism within belief systems.

All too often women patients who complain of being hexed are diagnosed as psychotic and institutionalized (Griffith & Ruiz, 1977) and natural support systems go unconsidered. This occurs because clinicians are unable to distinguish culturally prescribed behavior that differs from their Western therapeutic models. The alternative to institutionalization of those labeled psychotic is not utilized. The cure therefore becomes reinforcement of alienation from the culturally prescribed natural support system. The inability of the Western diagnostician to differentiate between what is culturally defined behavior and what are Western clinical models acts of psychotic behavior tends to reinforce patient resistance to psychiatry. This resistance has been recorded by Abad and Boyce (1979), Garrison (1977a), Mumford (1972), and Ruiz and Langrod (1976).

Koss' (1977b) study of a female-centered family is a clear-cut case study of the use of French Spiritism to reinforce male authority in the home through the spirit of a deceased grandfather. Here there is no involvement of either aspects of *Santería* or Roman Catholicism.

Koss (1975) does not focus on syncretism and its role in the belief system, concerning herself only with the therapeutic aspects. In her pioneering work on "Therapeutic Aspects of Puerto Rican Cult Practices," she does not address herself to the structure of the belief system. She identified a maneuver used by Spiritualists which psychiatrists employ. The maneuver, conceptualized by Erickson (1959), is called the "Utilization Technique," and is used to shift patient behavior in the direction of cooperative activity while in therapy.

Ruiz and Langrod (1976) feel that Puerto Rican folk healers such as Spiritualists communicate in the same terminology as, and understand the non-verbal communication of, their Puerto Rican clients, unlike Western therapists. Lastly, the client can act out wishes in the presence of Spiritualists that would not be accepted by the mainstream of society. More importantly, Ruiz and Langrod (1976, p.394) criticize psychiatrists for rejecting the possibility of concurrently believing in two religions, such as Roman Catholicism and Spiritualism. Their feeling is that Western-trained therapists view having two religions as a psychotic behavior rather than part of Hispanic culture. The Western clinician with this in mind rejects the possibility of nominal Roman Catholicism which makes use of "spiritualism, witchcraft, and Black magic" (p. 393).

Ruiz and Langrod's (1976) finding that folk healers can be viewed as more likely to provide correct diagnosis and treatment was later recognized by Harwood (1977a), who saw therapeutic effects "through dramatic enactments and suggestion within the framework of spiritualist concepts" (p. 91). Griffith and Ruiz (1977, p. 36) point out that providing information to a psychiatrist about his patients' cultural background is not the solution, although transcultural therapeutic training is viewed as an improvement.

Griffith and Ruiz (1977) focused their attention on a nebulous conception of "folk healers" and do not discuss the role of syncretism in the treatment of patients. These researchers do not discuss the differing practices of Spiritism, *Santería*, and Spiritualism encountered in the Hispanic community nor do they distinguish differences in treatment based on the belief system of their clients. Consequently, Ruiz and Langrod's (1976) finding that the Puerto Rican Spiritualist as a folk healer uses the patient's "symptomatology" corresponds to the finding of Lubchansky et al. (1970) that the Spiritualist's conception of mental illness is idiosyncratic and unlike professional psychiatric interpretations. Koss (1977) also echoes Lubchansky et al (1970) when she says that "curing techniques vary with personal ideologies and styles of cult leaders" (p. 462).

Harwood indicates that the Puerto Rican Spiritualist's skill is in his ability to " 'facilitate the clients' alienation from certain patterns of behavior" by having the individual focus on the spiritual (1977a, p. 91). The patient is therefore attributing his or her problems to the spiritually reifiable. Consequently, Occidental therapeutic benefits from Spiritualism are not consciously derived models, but ritual enactments that "approximate" therapeutic techniques (Pérez y Mena, 1978). Although approximations in this therapeutic enactment between Spiritualism and Western therapy may occur, the underlying premise of Spiritualism which attributes one's problems to the spiritually reified works against Western therapeutic conceptions about the benefits of therapy, where it is the individual who becomes responsible for his acts. Ultimately, the contradiction between reifying spirits who are responsible and the Western ideal of making the individual responsible can not be resolved.

ENDNOTES

1 See Stevens Arroyo (1988) for an extensive discussion of the Taínos and their form of ancestor worship.

2 Luisa Capetillo's combining of Spiritism and Socialism was not unusal in her day. The British utopian socialist, Robert Owen (1771-1858), was a Spiritist. See Heilbroner (1972, p. 112).

3 In Spain followers of Karl Krause (1781-1832) were influenced by his "mystical belief". Krause's influence is found in Jose Marti and Eugenio Maria de Hostos. As in Spiritism they viewed Roman Catholicism as inferior, see Raymond Carr, 1966.

4 José Celso Barbosa, Afro-Latin leader of the Peurto Rican Republican Party, was educated in the United States. Lewis (1963) states that Barbosa's "well-known stand on the race question in the island could be seen as little more than a battle conducted in the interest of the colored professional middleclass group to which he belonged" (p. 61). In contrast to Barbosa's position, Spiritist Matienzo Cintron, by the 1900's, was leader of the Unionist Party and rejected participation in the United States-appointed local government. See Sariola (1979, pp. 78-81).

5 Herring (1968, p. 113) says that the term *Voodoo* is a popular pronunciation of the Dahamean word *Vodum*, meaning either "spirit" or "God." Tallant (1971) sees the correct usage as *Vodu*, while both regard the usage of the term *Voodoo* as incorrect.

6 This situation in Puerto Rico is unlike the Bolivian example of parallel religious belief reported by June Nash (1979) in which instead of a syncretism the indigenous and Spanish Colonial beliefs are separated by assigning them a different place, time, and context for worship.

7 Palomayombe a Bantu religion is the source of much of the sorcery in *Santería*, for a more extensive description see glossary.

8 Fictive kinship system is the same as ritual kinship system. In both cases it is a kinship system that does not have a common ancestor.

CHAPTER III

STAGE I: The Public (*El Público*) and Associates
(*Los Asociados*) in the *Centro*

The Periphery

A discussion of the role filled by the congregation that
attends services at the *Centro*. These individuals
make up the public and are the least active members
of the *Centro*; here one also finds the associates who
have a greater level of involvement than do those who
are members of the public. The services are described
and the *causas* (spiritually derived problems) are
worked by the mediums with the help of the spiritual
leader - the Godfather. The different types of causas
brought to the *Centro* are detailed. This Chapter is
introduced by an interview with Calibán who is a
member of the public and has thought of becoming an
associate.

C alibán, who is interviewed in Stage I, remains a member of the
public, although there have been attempts to recruit him into the associates. Calibán has been coming to the services at the *centro* for over a
year.

Calibán was born in Puerto Rico and reared in the United States. He
is 27 years old, and full time graduate student in educational psychology
at an Ivy League University.   He is viewed by the congregation as a
member of the public. The interview with Calibán follows:

Yes, I view this as a religion. I feel that it is a religion because it is a belief in God. God is God even if you worship as
the Jew or the Moslem: God is God. Everyone has their own
way of praying to Him. I say that to people and they don't

understand.

About eight months ago I started coming to this *centro* because my mother told me to. She said, "Listen, it's in our family. We should all be together at the *centro*. Your grandmother used to do it as well as everyone else in the family." It was sort of a tradition, and in the back of my head I understood it had something to do with me. So, as far as what I was told, I was interested. Then I let the Godfather do the rituals of the spiritual cleansing of the hair. I did not expect to get anything else done for me.

But the spiritual cleansing of the hair, as far as I understood, gave me a little more ease. It helps in letting one see problems a little clearer. Also it takes away influences that disturb, in the sense that they don't allow you to concentrate on those things you need to concentrate on. When I had to take an exam, it alleviated the tension; it was like an outlet, something I could focus on to let the tension out.

When I sit at the *centro*, I check out the people from a social science point of view. In my mind, I check out the people and I record what I see for my own knowledge, such as what is Spiritism (Spiritualism) and what do the saints represent. Just what do certain things represent?

My first role at the *centro* was that of being curious. I was not sure if I was interested enough to spend time there. I saw that being involved in the *centro* would take time away from other things I wanted to do. I felt there were other things that were more important for me to do and I did not see the *centro* as an important part of my life. But, as I started going to the *centro*, I felt more comfortable in the place, and I started making time to attend the services at the *centro*. But, even after attending in the beginning, I did not see it as one of my roles.

I understand what is going on, but in the back of my head I have always had a little question mark: Is that real? Is what's going on there real or not? How much value can I place on that....you know the Godfather, he's a man and I am a man. He could do anything up there, fake or real, and it is left for me to judge whether it is real or not. While I am sitting here, I am still in that kind of limbo. And I don't know whether to put my whole belief in some of the things that are going on. I think it has to do with my background. In school one is taught that certain things follow certain events. Sometimes I see things up there at the altar that don't follow the right pattern. Let me give you an example. Once he (the Godfather) was saying that he was going to spiritually operate because a person had a bullet in his back which the doctors were finding difficult to operate on. And so he took two magnets to help him move the bullet, and he spoke to the spirits about moving the bullet. He said, "We are going to move it to make it safer for the doctors to operate."

Afterwards he took the two magnets, and as he placed them so that the magnetic fields opposed each other, he said, "This is the force that's keeping them apart." He was saying that the spiritual powers were involved in keeping the two magnets apart. But in my head, I know that when you have opposing forces, they don't meet. So right there I had it in my head that something wasn't clicking right. What my eyes and my intelligence were telling me had nothing to do with what was going on out there at the altar. Some things like that happened and that kept me uncertain.

I also saw a vaginal operation where coconuts were used to absorb the evil. The coconuts were to be gotten rid of along with the knives that were used and the sheet from the operation. The sheet is put over the person; they get rid of the water used in cleansing. They used the two coconuts in this spiritual operation. They always use two coconuts.

I have other problems in getting involved. Problems on the side that are trying to pull me away from the *centro*. Like my girl friend on one side; she doesn't dig the scene. You know how it is, she's negative about it. And sometimes she puts me into a predicament that comes down to the *centro* or her. I have to be very cool about what I do and how I approach her and the *centro*. On the other side I have my mother telling me, "Well, don't miss the *centro*." Then I have a friend telling me not to get involved in the *centro*. So I am in the middle, bouncing back and forth, it's terrible! You can get into a bind when you're trying to please opposing sides.

There are those who come to the *centro* because they are looking for something. Most likely they are like me; they are looking for something they feel might be there for them. Then there are those who are very active possibly due to respect and maybe it's the only role they play. One of these system things that they do in their lives; they participate in the services in the same way that they marry or go home to their wife. If you have a *centro*, you go to the *centro*. Then there are those that go because they are needed to help the Godfather.

Then there are those who also go to be involved in rumors (*bochinches*); those that just go to the *centro* to talk. That's all they do. They don't involve themselves in the praying of the "Our Father's," and they don't even mumble a word of prayer.

The services are supposed to be something of unity, like the praying during the session. Everybody is supposed to be united in prayer. Sometimes the Godfather or one of the male godchildren has to tell everyone "Come on, let's get going and say the 'Our Father.' " Everyone seems so quiet and asleep sometimes. That happens a lot and all one gets to see is talking on the side. I haven't heard what it is they are talking about. But I do know it has nothing to do with what is going on. It has to do more with what someone did somewhere else--rumors (*bochinches*).

A lot of them show up regularly; they are used to it; they have no place else to go, so they show up where they know their friends are going to be. I am telling you, I sit there sometimes and I don't believe it; some people are there to just bullshit.

There are a lot of things that people will do for money and I am not sure that they all call themselves sorcerers (*brujos*). Anybody can say "I am a sorcerer (*brujo*)," and then ask you, "What is it that you need done to this person?" It is a mind set, a mentality which depends on the individual. I have never seen a sorcerer and I don't know how popular they are. I do know that some of these people exist.

Because of sorcerers, photography has always been a problem within this religion. People must get themselves together as far as what pictures mean and determine what can happen if a sorcerer gets his hands on a picture. In this *centro*, it was the first time that I came across people who didn't shy away from having their picture taken. Maybe I noticed this because I haven't been involved in the *centro* that much.

I got involved in Spiritism (Spiritualism) through my mother. I've known about it from as far back as I can remember. She used to take me to the *centros*. It was boring at first because when you're young you don't really understand what is going on. All you sense is that you're frightened. So I always ended up going, although I didn't want to. I sensed all that moving around, it kind of scared me. I really was not that interested. After a while as I got older, I just stopped going. I had the choice of going or not going, and I stopped going.

Attending *centros* in Puerto Rico, I don't remember too much. But according to my mother my grandmother was very involved in Spiritism. My grandmother left it for a while, my mother said. And it was for my mother to carry it on.

When we arrived here in the United States, it was for my mother to find *centros* right here in the Bronx. Most of my life I lived in the Bronx. When we first arrived, I was living with my aunt in Manhattan. I don't recall going to any *centros* while in Manhattan, but in the Bronx I do. We used to go to a couple of *centros* in the Bronx. I wasn't afraid of it, except when I was young, and that was because I didn't know what was going on. But, I know better now; I am a little older and I understand what is going on.

As to growing up, the realization that my mother could communicate with spirits seemed like something that she was doing that was quite common, because I had to accept it for what it was. I could not say that she wasn't communicating with spirits or that she was. I haven't experienced it myself. But you have to take that as faith and you've got to take it at face value, for what you see. From what I have seen, I would tend to agree that she does communicate with spirits.

As a child it was not that important to me that I was afraid. It wasn't like something I felt or was going to believe in some day. Whether my mother communicated with a spirit or not was not important to me and I wasn't interested.

Once I left, I was away from it since 1968, maybe 10 years. I was brought back by wanting to see if this was something that was right for me or wrong for me. I wanted to know if it was part of me. I was interested in it because I had always been interested in Spiritualism.

The *centros* she took me to when I was small didn't have saints. They had the tables with the white tablecloth. They had the water bowls and sometimes a crucifix and white candles. Usually there were 8 to 10 people sitting at a table; it was dark and there were no saints.

But those *centros* always had problems when the Spiritist turned out not to be what he was saying he was. The *centros* frequently closed down. The Spiritist just wanted money. And that's what they wanted from the people. They wanted the women also, to do with them what they wanted. After that experience I didn't go back to Spiritism (Spiritualism) until recently, and the same with my mother.

I saw a baptism at the *centro*. I hadn't seen the male godchild before up at the altar in the *centro*. He was baptized by having some water put on him, on his forehead and on his palms. Some white powder was also put on him. After that session, he was in the *centro* dressed in white, but before the baptism he was never up there. It was about a half-hour thing. The Godfather put beads on him, and some handkerchiefs with different colors. When the Godfather gives you one type of bead you're ready to become baptized. The Godfather takes your old beads off and gives you new ones once you're baptized.

The baptism of a man was unusual since the men at this *cento* are given inactive roles. Men are not given those important roles of sitting at the table as a medium. Men as mediums, I've seen it before when I used to go to other *centros* with my mother. As far as I remember the men were good mediums, but the men did similar things to what the women do here.

In this *centro* I don't see the men playing an equal role to the women. But on one occasion the Godfather explained to those present why it was that there were few men, but it was not clear to me. He said something about the men not being advanced enough. There are ony three men left in the godchildren. The Godfather checks everyone out before you can advance and you go through the baptism and all that. But he's the one!

The Godfather 's going to get new godchildren, maybe one or two. He's going to baptize some soon. As you noticed there are less godchildren now. When I first arrived at the *centro* there were a lot more people there. The front was almost full. Now there are a couple of chairs that are empty, so a couple of people haven't come back. Maybe he's going to initiate some more. Somebody told me that of the 12 that were initiated last year there are only 6 left among the godchildren. The Godfather says that they often leave due to material problems because they begin to confuse their material and spiritual problems.

I just know two of the mediums by name. The Head Medium is very good. And the other medium that sits to the Godfather's left is very good. I've focused on the two and they are on the ball. I've seen them act out, especially when they take the spirit. I am interested in the things they say. When the Godfather asks them questions while they have the spirit, they know the problem because they are in that person with the *causa*. Some of the things that they say are right on the dot.

The Godfather tells me about those things such as the material and the spiritual. But he doesn't explain what it is they mean. Maybe he has explained, but I haven't picked it up. If he sees that there is something wrong with you he'll tell you to read something. He will tell you to do this or that. He'll tell you to say the "Our Father" or any other prayer of that type.

He does not put me in a trance. When he does the cleansing by fire (*despojo*) I get a little feeling, but I don't get the feeling that I am losing consciousness. I do feel at times like there is something next to me. My mother can go into a trance and so can my sister, but they are way ahead. My mother has already been a medium. My sister can feel the spirits and actually go through some type of change, but I haven't experienced that yet. I would like to experience it and see if that's what I want or not. But I haven't. Yesterday at the services I felt something. I didn't feel dizzy or anything like that, but I felt this strange feeling in me. Like I felt cushioned from two sides and it was inside of me or coming into me.

I don't know if I could become a medium. I go there to participate because it is something that I feel I should do. But I don't think that I will become a medium because I am not too sure about what my role will be nor do I know how much I will be willing to put into it. I am going to be at the *centro* a while and then I am not going to be there any longer.

There are many ways to pray but many people feel that

there is only one way to pray to God and that is through being a Catholic. I went to Catholic school and I was indoctrinated. I know a lot about the Bible. I can interpret the Bible because I know it from Catholic school; they just fed it to me every day.

Every day I had to go to school and read the literature they had on the Catholic Church. I spent elementary school and junior high in Catholic school. My first and second grade education was in public school in Puerto Rico and I started going to Catholic school upon my arrival in the United States. From the third until the eighth grade I was in Catholic school. At first I was going to school in Manhattan and later in the Bronx. Then I went to public high school in the Bronx.

I am confronted now and again by people who have a little knowledge of Spiritism (Spiritualism). They will always talk about the negative experiences and say that it's no good. I have had to study Spiritism (spiritualism) while at the same time studying Christianity because I was brought up a Catholic. I have tried to bridge the gap between the two. In this fashion I feel I can better explain things to people. I show them the similarities between Spiritism (Spiritualism) and the rest of Christianity. In other words, I show them that the roles played here in the *centro* are similar to the roles they see institutionalized elsewhere. A lot of times people don't understand because they don't know about the institution of Christianity or about their rights or the powers of the Church. Among Puerto Ricans, they don't know what the priest is supposed to represent. And a lot of Puerto Ricans who are supposed to be 100% Catholic have no understanding of what it is to be Catholic. All they know is that they are Catholic and they are just Catholic. I have found that if you talk to them about the Bible, they don't know about it. Then there are those that do know the Bible, but only through interpretation.

A lot of times I cite things for them straight from the Bible and then ask them to interpret it for me. I try to develop a link between Spiritism (Spiritualism) and the Bible and they say, "oh, no, it can't be!" Then I ask "Can't you see the link?" and they just don't know, especially when it has to do with the saints.

I tell them that the church says that you should only

worship God, but that they have saints. And, in Spiritism (Spiritualism), we have the same thing because we have saints, but we pray to God. Sometimes people will ask why we wear the beads and I told them that it is a reminder that I should do certain things. Each bead represents something, that I follow a certain way of life. Then they ask "how is that like the Catholics?"

I start with talking about the priest and how his black uniform is a reminder to him that he is following a certain way of life. Then they ask how come other people are not allowed to touch the beads and I say "You can't put on priests' clothes." Then I just ask a series of questions such as "Are you allowed up to the altar to use the chalice?" Then I explain that there are certain things that each religion follows. Then they are bound to say, "but Spiritism (Spiritualism) is not a religion." Is it a belief in God? Then it is a religion! We've always had saints in the house, like most Catholics, but some of the *centros* we attended didn't have saints or altars.

I am not like my mother in many ways when it comes to believing. She has been indoctrinated by the United States. She thinks the United States is God's gift to mankind and especially to the Puerto Rican people. But I know better. A lot of people know better and know that things could be a little better.

When I was in high school a glimpse of the Vietnam war touched me. We were in an Upward Bound program and one of my friends joined the armed forces and went to Vietnam. He got killed.

I still can picture it in my head, the post card they sent with his picture on it saying that he had been killed. It freaked me out but not enough to keep me out of going there.

Things were so bad here and had built up in me to such an extent that I said, "Man, I am going into the armed forces." So I went into the Air Force. I was a mechanic and my first assignment was Vietnam. I had a good experience there. But when I went to Vietnam I was very naive about what was going on there. In high school at that time who knew what was going on there? It was in social studies that they were supposed to teach you about that. But they were into the medieval periods.

One of the fallacies of high school is that they say they teach you what is going on.   They stick to teaching about the medieval period even though the world is passing you by. I didn't know anything about Vietnam!   So I went. My friends told me, "You see, they're having this war" and I said "What?"   Then I said, "It seems challenging" and I went with a very open mind. I was interested in the war.   I was curious to know what was going on.

While I was there it was funny because I would sit down and watch TV and see the Vietnam war.   I was on a base as an aircraft mechanic.   The hardest and most dangerous job for me was staying away from aircraft propellers and jet intakes.   Rockets would hit the base every once in a while. Otherwise I would sit and watch the G.I.'s fight on TV; it was weird!

In Vietnam I thought there were too many Puerto Ricans there and none of them were recognized and I thought about it and said, "Damn."   We went there.   Blacks were recognized and whites were recognized; everybody was recognized except Puerto Ricans.

I thought it was discrimination because Puerto Ricans were sent there, but those that got the recognition, such as the Medal of Honor, were the typical American.   They pushed what they wanted, the typical American, white or black.   The Chicanos weren't recognized and at that time there weren't that many Mexicans in the United States, especially because of all the immigration there were a lot of Puerto Ricans and Dominicans.   There were some Cubans and a lot of blacks.   There were a lot of whites, but not from the cities.   Some came from the cities but they were mostly from Oklahoma or little towns in Kansas.

The part that gets me mad is that even though I know that everyone is an American, why is it that they have to pick certain groups to be given recognition in the war and leave other groups to just get themselves killed?   The same things happened to Puerto Ricans in Korea.   They wiped us out, and here we go to Vietnam and the same thing happens. You know, no recognition!

So when I came back, I was really pissed!   Then I saw that some of my friends were shooting up.   I said "No man!"   I go out there to fight to keep so - called America as something good and they are letting my brothers and sisters over here get into junk.

All these events had a real impact on my life. That is why to this day I am very radical. I am very conscious of what people do because I support the independence of Puerto Rico. I feel that these things happen because of one's background and access to information. If you don't know anything about a subject then it becomes hard to discuss it.

When I came back from Vietnam, my head went out. I was disillusioned. I could have wiped out anybody. But I never got into a radical group, although my four years in college were very radical. I said to myself, "I went out and I saw my brothers get killed; I went through all this bullshit for this." I saw garbage; I saw Puerto Ricans that didn't know what was happening. I saw all this and said, "Man, this is not good." I went over to Vietnam thinking I was doing something good.

I could have backed away because my brother was stationed in Vietnam too. That's the shit; my brother was in a war zone and I was also in a war zone. There are no other males in the family; the United States got away with that shit. He was on the Coral Sea and I was doing the same type of work in Vietnam that he was doing. He was an aircraft mechanic in the Gulf of Tonkin but he was on a carrier. That's the shit that pissed me off; I said "God damned (*coño*), my brother is here. What if he gets killed and what if I get killed?" My mother would have been left with two sons dead and no one to carry on the family name.

Now, I am a socialist in the sense that I believe that there should be equality in what people get. A lot of things should be socialized, like social services and transportation. You shouldn't have to pay for shit like that. I wouldn't mind if they take out some money from my income to support the bus system. Let me take the bus whenever I want because if we make enough money they can take a little bit more. I don't care as long as I get my medical and my transportation. Things I need I should get free and, you know, things would be O. K.

My religion does not come into play with my politics. We can separate the two because being pro-independence for Puerto Rico and being Spiritist (Spiritualist) doesn't interfere. One is my political belief and the other is my faith, and I have to separate the two. I don't think God would say, "If you believe in Spiritism (Spiritualism) you are going to get independence." It will never get you independence; I think people will get independence.

If you start believing that God will provide independence, then you start believing the same philosophy that the United States tries to indoctrinate people with. It is the philosophy of the survival of the fittest, etc. All that garbage that they try to feed people. God wills it, you get it! If you keep to that mentality, then you get nothing because there is a separation between the two. Political beliefs are based on one's system of living while the other is based on one's faith.

I think that believing in Spiritism (Spiritualism) would be like believing in any other religion. Believe what everybody else believes, helping your neighbor whenever possible, and not doing harm to anybody else. I think that would be taking the Christian philosophy into one's political beliefs. Then one would feel that there should be equality. It goes without saying that then you believe that everyone should have a little piece of the pie.

In another war I would be a conscientious objector; I would never fight another war. Not that I feel war is wrong but in the Vietnam war Puerto Ricans weren't given a fair break as far as being acknowledged was concerned. I feel that way because a large group of people were killed, especially my friends.

The Culture and Family's Impact on Stage I

This first stage presupposes that there are significant individuals in the families of the public and associates who share a belief in spirits. Importantly, this belief in spirits also presupposes that there is an "inherent cultural" rationale for the practice of ancestor worship. Consequently, prior to an individual's arrival at the *centro*, there is a child-rearing process in the home, imposed by significant others and reinforced by the culture, which allows for a belief in spirits.

An individual who arrives at the *centro* for the first time, even if recruited by an important member of the congregation, is considered a member of the public. The public arrive at the *centro* because they need a *causa* divined. A *causa* is a problem with a spiritual etiology. Through the process of divining,[1] the Godfather and the mediums, with the help of the spirits, diagnose the manner in which the *causa* developed.

In entering into participation either as the public or as an associate member, the individual has become involved in the role of believer, even though it is a peripheral role within the *centro*. Those at the centro in this first stage:

1. participate in the services,
2. allow the divination of their *causas*,
3. accept the consultations with the Godfather-Spiritualist for prescriptions (*recetas*) for herbal remedies and rituals.

Those who are associates pay dues on a monthly basis, and also make special contributions to the upkeep of the *centro*. The public contributes an unfixed amount during the passing of the collection box.

Searching for a *Centro*

There are several ways to get individuals involved at the centro. In one way, the public, associates, and mediums refer relatives, friends, or neighbors. In another method, individuals just walk into the *centro* when they feel they need a consultation with Godfather. Some individuals will arrive at the *centro* out of curiosity and wish to see what the services are like before intensifying their participation.

One of the women who worked her way up from the back of the room to the front said that she was just walking through the community when she found the *centro* and decided to see what was going on. She had been on her way to a friend's house when she felt the *centro* was calling her. She decided to leave home early one day and "check the place out" and, upon entering the *centro*, she was impressed. She felt she had never seen such a Spiritist (Spiritualist) altar, nor had she ever seen anything like this *centro* with all the Roman Catholic saints. She was so impressed she decided to bring her daughter to the *centro* so she too could see it.

Another woman says the first time she came to observe what was happening at the *centro* it was her mother who had suggested she visit the *centro*. She watched and became more interested in the place. She wanted to find out the "mechanisms" of the place. She feels this Spiritist (Spiritualist), for all she knew, could have been all "bullshit." If he turns out to be "bullshit" she says she will not be surprised.

One of the godchildren recalling her first time at the *centro* said she wanted to know if the Spiritualist was "for real," so she checked him out. She passed the *centro* several times before entering. She says she is very skeptical about Spiritists (Spiritualists) and remembers behaving like a rock when the Spiritualist called her to the front to work her *causa*. "I am a very hard-headed woman," she says in self-evaluation.

It was only after having her *causa* worked that she developed enough confidence to work her way to the front. It took her two months of just passing the *centro* and thinking about going inside before she entered. Once she entered the *centro* she was impressed by what she saw. But even after the initial contact, it took her about two weeks of thinking it over before she would return to the *centro*. Finding a Spiritualist is a difficult task because they are not all trustworthy. A bad Spiritualist can spiritually stagnate a person.

The Public Scrutinizes the Godfather (*Padrino*)

One informant stays near the back of the *centro*, looking at the ceremonies and only participating in the purification by fire. His major problem is that most of the Spiritists (Spiritualists) who have opened places in the South Bronx have been after people's money. The Spiritists (Spiritualists) were more interested in money than in providing spiritual help. *Centros* have closed down because Spiritists (Spiritualists) are always trying to take advantage of the women by having sexual relations with them as well.

One of the male godchildren remembers staying near the rear of the *centro* for a long time, scrutinizing what was occurring. He feels that when one first arrives at a *centro*, the intention is to sit in the rear pew on Mondays and Thursdays. He remembers saying, "I'll never move to the front, never in my life."

A couple of months later he moved a few pews to the front. He feels that as one gains confidence one begins to move forward. He remembers slowly moving up a few pews until the Spiritist (Spiritualist) informed him it was fine for him to sit in the front pew. His confidence in the Spiritualist was built up when he realized one day that, although he had arrived late, the Spiritualist saved him a seat in the front pew.

An associate feels there is nothing else for individuals to involve themselves in within the community; consequently they come to the *centro*. Then there are those who just want to see what is going on. There are also the women rumor mongers (*bochinchosas*), according to Calibán, who just want to know what is happening.

Recruitment of Individuals into the *Centro*

Recruited Because of a Causa. The godchildren often recruit individuals for the *centro* from among neighbors, friends, or family who need a *causa* "worked." There have been three cases that could be directly linked to the mediums' referral system within a week's time. The first referrals identified were neighbors of the Principal Head Medium and they had a *causa* worked. They later had their newborn child spiritually baptized. The second, an impotent male, was referred by an auxiliary medium. The third *causa* was referred by another auxiliary medium and that *causa* had to do with family-induced sorcery. Sorcery is the main source of *causas* at this *centro*.

There are a number of individuals who search out a *centro* because they have been to a physician, but their symptoms have not been alleviated. The Godfather will treat them for spiritual interference, and then request they continue having their physical problems treated by the physician. Any symptom with material (physical) manifestations will be sent to a physician for treatment; nonetheless, there is a tendency for individuals to go to a physician prior to their arrival at the *centro*. Sorcery is the one etiological category of disease that represents the greatest number of *causas* worked at the *centro*.

One of the auxiliary mediums is a good example of someone who needed intervention since the physicians had diagnosed her as having a heart condition. This spiritual intervention occurred while she was a member of the public. The physician had informed her that her heart valves were not working properly and that she needed to have them repaired. Some people just walk off the street and into the consultation room as she had done. She went back to the physician after a spiritual cleansing (*limpieza espiritual*) and he said there was nothing wrong.

The physician informed her that the electrocardiogram was normal. When her doctor inquired as to what she had been doing to improve her health status, she told him she had been going to a "spiritual place." She says, "I guess that's what's helped me." Another informant admitted going through a similar experience.

Sometimes someone with material problems, is spiritually worked at the *centro*. The Godfather works on the person right before the congregation, as was the case of a woman in her late fifties who walked in off the street. She was having problems in walking caused by combined arthritis and diabetes. The Godfather spoke to her from the center of the room and asked her how she was feeling and she responded, "Fine, thank you." He asked her to stand up before the congregation and then requested she walk up to the front of the room. He informed the congregation she was being held back by spirits and he felt she could be cured that evening. He informed her and the congregation that this ailment was all the more difficult for her because she was a hard worker who deserved better.

The Belief System of the Public and Associates

The attempt to resolve a *causa* is an attempt to deal with spiritually caused problems. These problems are caused by unworked and therefore underdeveloped spirits that roam the earth. The spirits can be worked in numerous ways, but the most salient method is that of working them before a congregation in a *centro*.

The working of a *causa* before the congregation provides a sense of involvement since everyone identifies with the *causa* affecting the individual. Because everyone is a witness to the evil which base spirits can create, it is a means of confirming they are not alone in their problems.

The Material Doctor (Physician) and the Spiritualist

It is the Spiritualist who can intervene and solve a spiritual *causa* which endangers the individual and is the end result of worldly envy. This envy (*envidia*) is directed at one's personal or material happiness. This happiness can be destroyed through material discomforts (physical illness) or through spiritual disruption. Material disruption can be caused by the spirits, but only minor material problems can be worked by the Spiritualist alone. Major material problems need to be worked by both the spiritualist and a physician. The physician specializes in solving material problems.

Spiritualism--The Last Resort

The Spiritualist and the godchildren classify all diseases as either spiritual or material in nature. The Godmother explains that many people come to the *centro* after many months of trying to find a solution to their problems through physicians. They fear doctors perform surgery only to explain afterwards that nothing was wrong. Consequently, people leave the physician's office saying, "I know I have cancer but the doctors can't find it." The Godmother feels Spiritualism is the last resort because only after going to the Roman Catholic Church do people call on a Spiritualist. She feels that people with a *causa* arrive at the *centro* with an attitude of "Let's see how much this is going to cost." They engage the Spiritualist in questions and expect answers, before the Spiritualist has had time to attempt to find out what the person needs.

The Importance of *Consultas* for *Causas* Needing a Physician

The importance of the *consulta* is that it determines the personal rituals needed to safeguard spiritual development. Only after the consultation does the Godfather understand all the factors affecting any individual in spiritual need.

The method used to solve the spiritual problems manifested as material problems (physical) are twofold. The first is a combined Spiritualist and medical intervention; here the physician diagnoses an individual's material problems while the Godfather provides ritual protection. The ritual protection against complication in treatment should suffice in insuring the individual's health.

The second method is to have the Godfather do a spiritual operation to prevent spiritual confusion and the complication of a physician's treatment. The spiritual operation either will eliminate the need for a material operation (surgery) or will facilitate surgical exploration into the individual's material discomfort. The spiritual operation takes place in front of the congregation so that the godchildren can participate.

At the *centro* it is common for people to say they do not feel anything because they are afraid to admit their feelings. They have to be helped into remembering the difference between when they first arrived with a *causa* and how they felt after having their *causa* worked. In this manner a person can begin to understand that, as they are at the table getting their *causa* worked, they are also receiving truth.

La Causa : The Problem Develops

La Causa is an evolved spiritual problem which must be spiritually worked on to prevent its continued growth. It is, nevertheless, a complicated process because individuals may gather several simultaneous *causas* which must be worked. Each *causa* should be worked on independently, on the basis of degree of severity. In the less severe cases, the Spiritualist informs individuals of how it can be worked. Most of the time, a *causa* requires that the Spiritualist begin the curative process and the individual with the *causa* continue the treatment at home with rituals and herbal baths.

Mankind's Desire for Evil

The belief system emphasizes evil as the causative agent of mankind's afflictions and focuses on mankind's ability to do evil. Members of the congregation are horrified by feeling that those committed to evil enjoy it. Generally it is felt that one can never be happy in life practicing evil because nothing condones doing something evil to someone else.

Believers in Spiritualism are taught that the world is influenced by antagonistic spiritual forces. These evil forces can be harnessed by individuals to a greater or lesser extent. Consequently, there are malicious individuals called "sorcerers" who harness these forces and interrupt the happiness that others experience. Envy is the most important catalytic agent for the "malicious" who use base spirits to secure evil. The envious are seen as negatively influencing the progress of individuals to a material or spiritual goal.

Activating Evil: Sorcery (*Brujería*)

There are three major ways in which an envious individual can block the happiness of others.   The first means of blocking others' happiness is with unconscious envious thoughts.   The second means is with people's "tongues" which can be defined as conscious malicious gossip. When these two mechanisms fail to undermine the spiritual or material happiness of an individual, then the consciously arrived at alternative is sorcery.   Sorcery is commonly used by the envious.   Using sorcery as an alternative brings in third parties who specialize in harnessing low-level spirits.

Sorcery: A Vicious Circle

Sorcery becomes a system of activating evil.   It is understood that, in acquiring the services of a sorcerer, one has entered into a vicious circle. The hexed may also have access to a sorcerer, creating a never ending chain of evil events to either party.   One's life could be continuously complicated by these vicious cycles of evil which cast causative agents to afflict mankind.

Malicious Spirits Create *Causas*

Spirits manifest by coming in through windows or being attracted by some noise. These base spirits can attach themselves to those who are defenseless, such as children and spiritually unprotected adults.

The Godfather emphasizes that Puerto Ricans understand that there is a "certain segment" of society which is without human sentiments, unconcerned about the lives of others, and that these individuals dedicate themselves to activating evil spirits.   Naturally, there are others who suffer the burden these individuals create.

Echoes of the Godfather's Sentiments

A member of the public echoes the Godfather's sentiment on the evil which prevails in the Puerto Rican community by saying she is one of those people whose balance easily goes off and needs to be pushed back into gear. She thinks to herself, "I am one of those persons that had to go through a lot of things, so many things. And others don't, but why me?" Many individuals wonder why it is they become the recipients of a *causa*.

Her feeling is that, in order to counter this frustrating situation which is not of one's own making, it is crucial to see Spiritualism as the way out. Once one recognizes a problem and then sees Spiritualism as the solution, one has taken the first step in the believing process. She does not understand why someone would envy her. She believes that this type of envy is a "psychological problem" based on a lack of "self-instruction" (education).

Education

More importantly, people must learn to secure cleaner thoughts. The basis of *causas* is people's reluctance to study, which forces them to be guided by their base impulses; they are unable to take a little time to work for what they want. What plagues this informant is the question of why people are unsatisfied with what they do have and are unable to make the best of what they do have.

Envy: A Causative Agent

Evil becomes so all-encompassing that any problem can then be caused by a malevolent or base spirit. At a party a light-skinned young woman in her teens fell victim to a malicious spirit she had failed to have worked. She fainted and went into an uncontrollable fit. Because she was young and beautiful the etiology was envy, which had activated malicious spirits against her while at the party. Everyone decided it was a seizure (*ataque*) for which the police were asked to intervene. The believers in Spiritualism present at the party understood it was malicious spirits that had attacked the young woman.

Because the young woman had not taken care of herself spiritually, a simple problem caused by envy at a party acquired a life of its own. A person can become crazy (*loco*) as the problems due to poor spiritual protection cause increasing confusion (*envolvimiento*). One informant felt a strong-minded person could survive evil spiritual attacks, but too often a person is overcome.

A *Causa* Can Evolve Into a Psychological Problem

A *causa* can become a mental problem that can be said to psychologi-cally affect an individual. Everyone understands that the spirits can get the best of one. In the end, there is only one solution left for individuals and that is to "work" the spirits and erase the *causa* responsible for the spiritual affliction.

The spirits make people do things they would not do otherwise. These spirits must be worked on and people must be told how it is they can alter their troubled situation. The afflictions must be worked on by people who understand the treatment of *causas*. The *causa* surrounds an individual's existence, attracting more malicious and base spirits. These malicious spirits then create confusion which can only be worked at a *centro* with the help of mediums and a Spiritualist. Otherwise, spiritual confusion can become sufficiently strong to turn an individual into a psychologically disturbed person.

Services Are About to Begin

One informant says the service is called a wake (*velada*) because the people are communicating with the dead. The services begin when the Godfather delivers his first prayer from Kardec's (1969) *El Evangelio Segun el Espiritismo*. The prayers are intended to prepare the congre-gation for spiritual communication. The Godfather often mentions the importance of one's Guardian Angel in the daily affairs of the congrega-tion.

The Godfather explains that he does not exploit the congregation since he never promises people things they cannot receive. He feels that those associates who do not pay their required dues are fooling themselves. The people would pay if he told them they were going to get "villas and castles."

The Godfather tells the congregation he knows they would give up everything they own for the promise of something he could not provide. Then he tells them the saints give nothing unless they are compensated since the saints do not acknowledge one's needs unless the person is willing to pay.

He points to the fact that sorcery in the South Bronx is so common he has found ritually sacrificed animals at his door in an effort to force him out of the building where the *centro* is located. Sorcerers, moreover, have come to the *centro* to challenge his spiritual powers. The saints have to be prepared to withstand these types of shocks to the *centro* and to himself. He knows there are four sorcerers living in the building who suffer a loss in clients because of his presence in the same building.

The Godfather complains that there are times when he waits at the centro for hours to do a consultation and often no one shows up. When people do show up for a consultation, he then can only charge them $5.00 for the baths. Half of the congregation goes to local *botánicas* (herbal magico-religious shop) because it is cheaper to buy items they need. Only half of the congregation buy these items from the Godfather.

At the end of the Godfather's speech, a collection is made to which everyone is expected to contribute. While the collection is proceeding, the Godfather goes into the back room, where private consultations take place, and dresses himself in red Roman Catholic vestments that are placed over his white *Santería* clothing. The godchildren remain in their white clothing with the colored kerchiefs around their waists. The Godfather comes out while taped music plays softly. Slowly the transformation away from Roman Catholicism begins, as he brings out beads to be spiritually blessed while removing the Catholic vestments.

The Godfather walks toward the table where the mediums are sitting. He begins wafting incense over their heads with his left hand. He gives the incense to a male godchild, who then passes it over the heads of members of the congregation. The Godfather returns to the center of the altar area and silently says prayers to himself. He then says out loud to the dead: "We beseech Christ for peace on earth through the dead" ("*muertos por nosotros les pedimos a Cristo por la paz mundial*").

Spiritist Chain of Power: Collective Spirit Possession

Everyone is asked to stand and hold hands. This starts a wild moment in the services because it is here that the first collective spirit possession occurs. Holding hands while standing the Godfather says, "peace and justice" (*paz y justicia*) and then says "strength" (*fuerza*). At the point when he says "strength," most of the congregation falls into a collective spirit possession, which varies in intensity with proximity to the altar. The closer to the alter the more intense the possession.

Individuals make high-pitched, piercing, screaming sounds, and at the moment of collective possession the tape-recorded music goes from traditionally soft conservative religious music to Afro-Cuban popular music praising the Seven African Powers. Everyone sits down and preparations for the purification by fire begin.

Purification by Fire (*Despojo*)

The white table is moved from the center of the room and placed in front of the altar. The congregation lines up in front of a white tile cross on the floor. Florida Water (*Agua de Florida*), which is an aromatic alcohol base bath water, is thrown on the floor and lit with a taper. Individual adults and children walk over the fire, unhurt, and the adults go into spirit possession.

The Godfather touches each of the participants at the back of the neck and on the forehead while they stand in the fire. The Godfather's touch causes spirit possession. Most of the congregation goes through the fire one at a time as the godchildren hold the individuals by the waist to prevent them from falling and hurting themselves while in spirit possession.

After the purification by fire, people are no longer allowed to enter the *centro* and the godchild at the door will not allow anyone in or out without the Godfather's permission. The mediums and the godchildren are the last to participate in this aspect of the purification by fire, especially when they are sick or need extra spiritual protection. During the purification by fire, there is a lot of groaning, moaning, screeching, and hissing as spirits possess the participants.

The Spirits Are Real

What convinced her that the spirits were real, said one informant from the public, was going through the purification. The first time they helped her get through the fire, she felt nothing and she had not expected to feel anything. But on another occasion, she really felt something; it was

> that electricity, I felt a change: If I tell you what it felt like you would think I was sex-oriented. It's a change and it is something different. At first I had a lot of headaches; now it's not like that. Electricity and heaviness came into my arms and into my legs. And then I felt calm.

She enjoyed it and it was exciting. She did not want to speak too much about spirit possession as I interviewed her during the purification ceremony.

Distinguishing Possession During Purification by Fire

There are times when people say they are purifying themselves, but they are not because their purification is more material than spiritual. There are ways to tell the difference. During the purification by fire, water is sprinkled across the congregation, hitting everyone about the head and face. If the water makes the spirit retire from the individual, it means the possession is material. In this manner the Godfather can tell which individuals are more experienced than others in the realm of the spirits. Knowing who is more experienced helps the Godfather in his efforts to recruit godchildren, especially from among members of the public.

Collective Spirit Possession

The most common means of arriving at collective spirit possession among the members of the congregation is by moving both hands over one's head closely and quickly without touching the hair or scalp. This movement is done with forward and back jerking motions, while standing or sitting. This is accompanied by sighing, hissing and gasping.

Their movements bring their heads down to the height of the pew seats in front of them and members in each pew will hold each other during spirit possession to avert an accident.

The holding of individuals who go into frenzied possession near the altar is done mostly by the male godchildren, and male associates. The men place their arms tightly just under the female godchildren's breasts while they jerk their bodies forward and back at the waist, pushing their buttocks back intensely and then forward. Men often hold the women from behind and sometimes from the side, while the women's breasts move through the men's arms. During intense spirit possession, the more experienced women godchildren can push the men up against the wall. Everyone at the font smiles once the collective possession is over.

Spiritual Operations

A symbolic spiritual operation cuts away evil complicating a spiritual or material *causa*. All those present during a spiritual operation have a role. The congregation is asked to pray. The godchildren lead the congregation in prayer, while the mediums assist the Godfather in the spiritual operation.

The auxiliary and apprentice mediums are also involved. One auxiliary medium is more involved than the rest of the godchildren because it is her specialty.

People who have had their *causa* treated in the privacy of the consultation room are afterwards scheduled for a spiritual operation. The operation can take place before the *causa* has been worked during a regularly scheduled service. This, however, is not always the case.

When the *causa* is scheduled to be spiritually operated before the congregation, the individual is introduced to the congregation a week in advance. This introduction enables the entire congregation to spiritually prepare for the operation at home and contribute to the success of the operations through rituals.

Spiritual Operations for Conception

I did not observe operations on men at the *centro*. Operations on women are mostly performed to deal with problems of conception. Of the three operations observed, two were of that character.

The spiritual operation is not performed as a single treatment. It is expected that the individual will complement it with treatment by a physician. Usually the problem is physical, caused by problems, for example, of conception or cancer, the individual comes to the

Photo # 3. Tools for a Spiritual Operation

Photo # 4. The Spiritual Operation

centro after going to a physician. By and large individuals who arrive for spiritual operations feel that the physician is inefficient because he has not brought about the expected results. The spiritual operation is intended to insure that the work of the physician is not undermined by malicious spirits.

Spiritual Operation for Cancer: Cost

One operation at the *centro* dealt with cancer in a young woman. The Godfather operated, asking her to return to her doctor to insure her material well-being. Those people who have not solved their *causa* after a spiritual operation do not return to the *centro*. There is one spiritual operation every two months, with fees ranging up to $300.00.

Rationale for Operation: Malicious Thoughts

One week prior to the young woman's operation, the Spiritualist explained how a *causa* had developed in her. The congregation was informed that there was a high probability, that this young woman had a cancerous growth near her neck. The cancer was caused by her father's malicious spiritual desires to have his wife abort the child when she was pregnant with the young woman, a request the mother rejected. Malicious thoughts, therefore, attached themselves to the young woman as soon as she was born. This is told to the entire congregation in the presence of the mother and the young woman.

Everyone arrives for the spiritual operation prepared to help the Godfather. They bring flowers and candles for the saints and the helpful spirits. Some members bring Florida Water and extra money for the collection box.

The operation begins when the Godfather comes out of the consultation room wearing his Roman Catholic vestments and carrying several swords. He raises them and says that these tools are needed to secure a successful spiritual operation. He then raises the swords at the altar and asks for strength from the Seven African Powers, while praying to each saint in either its Roman Catholic or Yoruba name. He also brings out stainless steel knives and a white sheet.

A spiritual cleansing with a cigar, another form of purification, is done. The woman is asked to sit at the edge of the table and smoke is blown at her from head to toe. She is given a candle and later a Bible to hold. She is asked to lie down on the table used for spirit communication and a white sheet is pulled over her, covering her entire body. A crucifix is placed over her chest, and the swords are placed at the knees, the hips, the lower back, and the shoulder. The stainless steel knives are taken out, placed in Florida Water, and set aflame one at a time. Chisels are brought out and the spiritualist begins the task of symbolically cutting away the cancerous growth.

The Godchildren walk up to the young woman and pull on her hands throwing the invisible evil at water goblets throughout the operation, while the mediums dispose of the contaminated water, and replace it with fresh water. The saints and the Seven African Powers are asked to intercede on behalf of the young woman. The Godfather cuts symbolically into the woman, hitting the hammer and chisel against each other to make a loud hard metallic sound.

After this symbolic cutting, the sheet is cut at the top with scissors, bringing the young woman's head into view. The Godfather takes the knives and begins to cut the evil away from around the neck and head.

He talks out loud with a lit cigar in his mouth, saying this operation will help the material doctors. After using the knives, he breaks them in half and places them in a brown paper bag held by a male godchild. The sheet is removed, torn in half, and also placed in the same paper bag.

The swords remain under the woman while two coconuts, burning at the pointed ends, are hit against each other. When the burning subsides the coconuts are rubbed up and down against the young woman as an act of spiritual purification. The Godfather begins by rubbing the coconut around the head, and works his way down to the feet. After covering all the extremities, he takes the coconuts and also places them in the brown paper bag with the sheet and broken stainless steel knives

The Godfather then ends the operation by asking the young woman to sit up while he blows cigar smoke at her in the final cleansing (*despojo*) process. The congregation prays, and the Godfather and godchildren go into spirit possession. The young woman is seated in a pew among the members of the congregation. When a spiritual operation is performed, the services may take as long as four hours; all other aspects of the services must also be conducted. The bag with the Sheet, Knives and Coconuts is disposed of in a wooded area.

Child Born Due to Spiritual Operation for Infertility

The Ruiz's were having problems because Señora Ruiz was unable to conceive. She had visited a physician for about one year, but to no avail. Señora Ruiz confided in one of the Head Mediums in an act of desperation because it was rumored throughout the housing projects that the medium was a sorcerer. The medium referred the Ruiz's to the *centro.*

The Spiritualist divined in consultation that Señora Ruiz's ability to conceive was spiritually blocked and the pregnancy would be dangerous. A spiritual operation was ordered to insure that the material doctors (physicians) would be capable of positive intervention. He advised Señora Ruiz to remain close to her physicians after the spiritual operation, and to commit herself to the required spiritual rituals.

The rituals would help prevent malicious and envious base spirits from accumulating power over her. Six months later the Godfather informed Señora Ruiz that she had conceived. She immediately went to the physician to confirm her pregnancy but the test results were negative. The Godfather then told her to be patient. Señora Ruiz waited until she developed physical symptoms of pregnancy. She returned to the physician, was retested, and the pregnancy was confirmed. The confirmation that malicious spirits were intervening to prevent the pregnancy, said the Godfather, occurred in the eighth month when the child was prematurely born. He considered an eighth-month birth a dangerous confirmation that malicious spirits were trying to prevent the mother's happiness. Further confirmation was provided by the weight of the child, three-and-one-half pounds. Nevertheless, the parents felt they had been prepared to face these dangers by the Godfather's consultation, the spiritual operation, and the assigned rituals.

The Spirits of the Water

Spirits are attracted to the services by water-filled goblets, which are emptied, each time the spirits are worked on by the mediums. It is through the water that the spirits are locked in. After a *causa* is worked, the contaminated water is poured out into the sink as a means of disposing of the malicious spirits. There is one goblet before each of the mediums even though, as often happens, the mediums share a goblet. However, no two people's *causas* are worked into the same water. The contaminated water is poured out, and fresh water is brought in and placed before the medium. This disposal of water ensures that the residue of malicious spirits can be isolated. More importantly, fresh water is covered with the hand to prevent evil influences that may be in the room from entering into it prior to the working of a *causa*.

There are many precautions taken with water at the *centro*. At no point is someone to drink water without protecting it from spirit contamination. The male godchildren secure the water in goblets for the mediums who remain at the table working *causas*. As soon as someone walks away from the table after having his or her *causa* worked, a male godchild takes the water and empties the evil down the drain.

Working *Causas* and Spirit Possession

The mediums who sit at the table are asked to go into the congregation and call individuals to the front. They ask a member of the public to go forward and to stand near the table and place his hands on the water-filled goblet. The person with the *causa* is asked to confirm or negate the findings of the mediums' divination. Mediums allegedly work without having prior information on the *causa*, although some information is gleaned from those who refer an individual for a consultation with the Godfather.

The working of the *causa* is important to believers. It is here that a person becomes convinced of the power of the mediums and the Godfather. The Godmother says, "I don't know how much it takes to make a person believe, but let me tell you I would jump out of my pants and say they know what I didn't even ask." The members of the *centro* feel that the divining of *causas* can convince individuals about the power of the spirits and the *centro*.

During spirit possession for divining purposes, the mediums work *causas* of spirits searching for enlightenment. The mediums use the following phrases while working *causas* : "peace and justice (*paz y justicia*)" and "enlightenment and progress" (*luz y progreso*). Another phrase used is "strength and power" (*fuerza y poder*).

As the spirits enter a medium, the Godfather says "enter good soul" (*adelante buen ser*). At this point, a medium goes into spirit possession. The spirits begin to communicate with the Godfather through the mediums.

The Godfather asks questions of the spirits, while the medium in contact with the spirit informs the Godfather of the *causa* and how it developed. Further, the spirits inform the Godfather about their desire for enlightenment.

The Godfather asks the individual with the *causa* to confirm or negate - with a yes or no answer - the mediums' findings.

Working a *Causa* : The Insane Daughter

This dialogue between the Godfather and a woman with the causa of an insane daughter took place in 1978.[2] During this session, people walked up from the congregation and had their *causas* worked by the Godfather and mediums. The young woman previously had been up to the altar during the purification by fire. She had rolled around excitedly on the floor. This was her second time in the area where the altar is located.

She was obese, of racially mixed parentage, African-American and Puerto Rican. Her primary language was English; she spoke and understood a limited amount of Spanish. The young woman was brought up by her Hispanic mother. All questions put forth by the Godfather were in Spanish.

The young woman, standing in front of the Godfather, was asked at least two questions to which she responded by asking the medium "What did he say? What did he say?" The medium then repeated the question to the young woman, and again she did not answer. The medium then asked if she spoke Spanish, to which she replied, "Sí." The medium then asked if she spoke English, to which she replied, "Yes." It seemed as though the young woman was willing but unable to answer the questions. At this point, the Godfather addressed the young woman's mother, who was standing next to her. He spoke in very formal Spanish.

> Godfather: When did you, after having this female child, think that she was crazy (*estaba loca*)?
>
> Mother: No. (Meaning either she did not think the daughter was crazy at all, or did not think so until she was older.)
>
> Godfather: You began to think this at about what age?
>
> Mother: At about 10 years of age. (Mediums and congregation at this point in unison say "Proven!", "*Comprobado* !" Some gasping and marveling at the Godfather's pinpointing the problem via the spirits occurs.)
>
> Godfather: To how many Spiritists (Spiritualists) did you take this young woman to have her cured?
>
> Mother: Many.
>
> Godfather: Then you were of the faith? You left the faith! (Here again the audience gasped -- "Proven!", "*Comprobado* !") Mediums to the mother and daughter: Look that way, while pointing to the Crucifix at the altar. (Later, I asked the Godfather why the mediums requested that the mother and the young woman look at the altar, at the same time telling the daughter not to look at the Godfather. He replied that looking at the altar under these situations seems to help these types of *causas*.)
>
> Godfather: You threw statues of the saints out the window. Is that correct (*verdad*)?
>
> Mother: Yes. (Congregation, with feeling: "Proven!" "*Comprobado* !")
>
> Godfather: Do you believe?
>
> Mother: Well....(*Bueno* -- very ambiguous.)
>
> Godfather: But, to help your daughter?
>
> Mother: I don't know.
>
> Godfather: This daughter suffered a frightful experience; they tried to do her a harm. (*Un daño* means specifically rape or sexual abuse.)
>
> Mother: Yes, that is the way it was. (Congregation responds dramatically with "Proven!" "*Comprobado* !"

Godfather: This young girl attempted to kill you. Am I right (*verdad*)?

Mother: Yes. (Congregation gasps, including the Godfather. He now leaned strenuously over the table, looking the mother straight in the eye and asked a further question.)

Godfather: With something pointed, in the kitchen?

Mother: Yes. With a knife.....

Godfather: (completing the mother's sentence): She tried to kill you.

Mother: Yes. (Congregation: "Proven!")

Godfather: This girl hangs out in the streets, doesn't she?

Mother: Yes. (Congregation here is quiet.)

Godfather: You have had to walk the streets looking for her.

Mother: Yes. (Mediums got frenzied and again demaded that the young woman not look at the Godfather and that the mother keep her hands on the water. Both mother and daughter had their hands atop water goblets; the mother seemed to be taking her hands off in apprehension at this point.)

Godfather: And she has been hanging out with many men on the streets.

Mother: Yes.

Godfather: And you live alone. The father no longer lives with you.

Mother: Yes.

Godfather: You threw him out, 8 to 10 years ago, didn't you?

Mother: Yes.

Godfather: Your daughter has the age of 16, 18, or 20 years.

Mother: She is 18.

Godfather: How many psychiatric hospitals have you taken this young girl to?

Mother: Many.

Godfather: Has her condition improved?

Mother: No.

Godfather: I see (in a low keyed voice while shaking his head, with solemn expression).

The session is over and it is implied the mother may return for a consultation. The mother did not move, apparently in a renewed hope that the Godfather would be more committed to her *causa*, while her daughter stared transfixed at the altar. The congregation waited indignantly as shock and disbelief charged the evening air. Everyone was overcome by a mother's suffering, and the revelation of a sexually abused 10 - year - old child.

Private Consultations with the Godfather

Consultations (*consultas*) with the Godfather occur in private every day from 11:00 am until 2:00 pm except Sundays, the members of the congregation are urged to attend services in their local Roman Catholic Church. Extra hours for consultation are added on Saturdays. Individuals are referred for a consultation by members of the congregation. The Godfather can request that a third party who understands the *causa* be brought in to help in developing insight.

Saturday Consultas

There are usually at least two infants at the Saturday *consultas* : parents bring them because they have nowhere else to leave them. The Godfather opens the *centro* by 10:00 am, and generally within 15 minutes there are two or three people. As the day advances, and especially after 1:00 pm, there can be as many as 10 people waiting to see the Godfather.

One Saturday by 11:00 am, there were 4 men and 8 women, all over 30 years old, and 2 female children. On another Saturday, there were 12 women, all over 20 years old; there were 2 men, 2 infants, and a young boy of preschool age. On some weekdays no one arrives for a *consulta*.

The Godfather complained that during the week he often spent his whole day waiting for someone to arrive, but that most people prefer to come for consultations on Saturdays. Those who arrive at the *centro* during the week often need charitable work (*caridad*) because they cannot pay. The Godfather says he often feels like a soul alone (*una alma sola*).

Congregation and the Scheduling of *Consultas*

There are those in the congregation who do not like consultations on Saturdays because it is crowded and the Spiritualist has little time to spend with each of the *causas*. One informant prefers coming during the week. When she is not working she arrives early for her appoint-ment. She avoids coming on Saturdays unless there is an exceptional situation that requires the Godfather's immediate advice and attention. This informant can attend consultations on weekdays, and during school vacations because she is a Board of Education employee. Unlike the rest of the congregation she has extended school holidays.

The Private Consultations

Some participants in consultations marvel at the Godfather's ability to divine *causas* affecting them. One woman declared that once she enters the consultation room, the Godfather can see many things. She said, "Just by sitting there he could look at me and he could see."

She said that it is incredible that he can see what *causa* produced an ailment and tell what type of sorcery causes the problems people have. She believed the Godfather is capable of telling where the sorcery was made, especially if it was done in another country. He can tell, she added, if the sorcery was placed under a tree or buried. The Godfather is powerful because he can see the form of sorcery itself.

The Consultation and *Causas* During the Services

The *consulta* is not unlike the working of a *causa* in front of the con-gregation, except that there are no mediums with the Godfather. The Godfather reported he has many "crazy people" (*gente loca*) in his community, and more and more of them are appearing in the *centro* for help. Some people, he commented, have "the nerve" to challenge his diagnosis. They even "challenge" him directly by asking him to tell them the winning number for "*la bolita*" (illegal lottery), and "to top it all off," he complained, "they do not pay for the consultation." The Godfather said that if the saints would tell him what number to play on a given day, he too would be rich. But the saints only tell you what you

Photo #5. Mother and Daughter Having St. Martin de Porres
Spiritually Cleansed

Photo #6. Family Awaiting a *Spiritual Consultation*

can pay for them to tell you.

On one occasion he had to take money given to the saints and give it to people who demanded he help them pay their rent. He has done this, he observed, even though the congregation itself has problems meeting its own rent. Then, the Godfather continued, if he is unable to please those members of the public, they spread rumors that he is not a good Spiritist (Spiritualist) because he could not give them a winning number. The Godfather, one saturday afternoon, told those present for a *consulta*, about five people, about a woman who demanded he help her by having the saints provide the day's winning number in "*la bolita*". She told him she owed her rent and the saints knew she needed the money. She demanded to know why the saints had not given it to her. The Godfather said he looked up at the altar and to the statue of Saint Lazarus and took the $18.00 left to the saint by a member of the public as payment for a relieved *causa*. He gave her the $18.00. As she was leaving, he told her, "Don't worry, you hit the number!"

Complications with Consultations

Some individuals are weary of Spiritualists who work *causas* with their wives helping them. Those Godfathers who work with their wives are considered to be running a "racket." The Godmother feels that if a husband does the *consultas* and the wife works the table, they are not legitimate in the Spiritist (Spiritualist) work. The Spiritist (Spiritualist) and his wife can confuse each other about the *causa's* development, in which case spiritual blocks are created. These spiritual blocks only tend to further complicate the working of the *causa*. It is important when looking for a Spiritist (Spiritualist) to find one who works the *causa* at the table and the *causa* in the consultation without monetary consideration or personal problems intervening and thus creating a spiritual block.

One will often find that people present at the services during the week are at the consultation on weekends. They attend the services by themselves, but will arrive with their spouses for consultation at the suggestion or insistence of the Godfather.

Marriage Problems and *Consultas*

At one of the services, a man from the public came up with a *causa* that needed to be alleviated. He was concerned with his recent hard luck which had created a series of antagonisms in his marriage. Seeking a consultation, he arrived the following Saturday with his wife, a very good looking and well-dressed middle-class woman. She was nervous and uncomfortable at the *centro*. She fretted at the pew as she waited for her husband to return from finding parking for their luxury car. The Godfather made a special effort to treat them immediately, sensing the uneasiness with which the woman was looking at her nails and kept her legs folded tightly as she awaited her husband's return. As soon as her husband arrived, they were ushered into the consultation ahead of their turn and left swiftly thereafter.

A member of the public came for a consultation because of her mother's request. The Godfather informed the mother that her daughter was in need of spiritual protection. The daughter freely admits that spiritual problems in her marriage were responsible for the distance created between her and her husband. The *causa* was disrupting her marriage. She says that she and her husband were no longer feeling a union between them. The daughter had informed her mother of the problems in her marriage, prior to the consultation with the Godfather but the mother says the Godfather had divined that her daughter was in need of spiritual protection.

The Principal Head Medium feels her first marriage was condemned to failure by the spirits. Her present marriage, nevertheless, represents a spiritual struggle that can be overcome with the help of the Godfather and the *consultas*. She feels the Godfather is an example of how to deal with the spiritual trials (*pruebas*) that confront a family.

The Godfather deals with problems in such an unselfish manner that he becomes a role model for members of the congregation. This lack of selfishness is what enables the Godfather to refer individuals to physicians. It explains also why he does not feel insecure about it. He lets people understand he cannot solve all the problems of the congregation.

Third Party Consultations

Some individuals come to the consultations not for themselves but for loved ones who are in the hospital or sick at home. The Godfather rarely will go to the hospital, since he can send someone with a prepared spiritual object which will help begin the process of eliminating the *causa* and thereby help the material doctors (physicians).

On rare occasions, because the *causa* was serious enough, he has visited members of the congregation in the hospital. He spiritually treated the individual without interference from the hospital officials, but he admitted that going to a hospital for a consultation is rare.

He usually sends beads and prepared holy waters with a parent or a friend of an individual so that the *causa* can be worked on. Once an individual is brought to the *centro* for a consultation, the *causa* can be treated directly if the person is willing.

A Consultation for Spiritual Baptism of a Child

Five people were present as witnesses to the spiritual baptism of the nine-month-old girl of Sr. and Sra. Ruiz. The child was dressed in a blue and white striped cotton pants suit and wore white booties. The parents were tender and felt honored that their *causa* was successfully worked.

Sra. Ruiz and the Godfather came out of the consultation room. The Spiritualist put his Roman Catholic vestments on, while the four people watched. He proceeded to the altar and prayed. He held the child high to the altar. She cried out and the Godfather smiled. Her lungs were clear, she was strong; the conclusion was that the baby was healthy.

The Godfather took two goblets and filled one with water from the faucet at the sink. He brought the water back to the altar and offered it to the Seven African Powers, speaking to the saints/*orishas* in an authoritative voice. He asked the parents to hold their child as he prayed from Kardec. He put <u>El Evangelio Segun El Espiritismo</u> (1969) on the table and held his hands over the parents and child.

The parents held the child's body, as the Principal Head Medium held the child's head. The Godfather poured water over the forehead and it was caught in an empty goblet under the child's head.

She cried and kicked. Prayers were said to the Seven African

Powers who were thanked for securing the safe delivery of the child. The Godfather then thanked each one of the Seven African Powers individually for their involvement.

The Godfather drew crucifixes with white chalk on the arms, the feet, and the palms of the child. He then held the child high at the altar, thanking the Seven African Powers a second time for intervening and securing the well-being of the child. The parents were given a small gold crucifix and a small black hand to ward off the evil eye. They paid $5.00 and left.

On their way out, the Head Medium stopped them and said they should be careful with whom they left their child because it was important to protect the child against the evil eye which could endanger her spiritual well-being. She also told them not to leave the child with anyone, not even a well-known neighbor, because the neighbor may envy the child, causing the newborn spiritual harm. This spiritual baptism was later to be augmented with Roman Catholic godparents who would take care of the more traditional concerns of the child's spiritual well-being.

Three types of Baptism

It is important to remember that there are three types of baptism for Spiritualist believers. The first baptism occurs at birth, taking place at the *Centro Espiritista*. The spiritual baptism does not require godparents. The second is at a local Roman Catholic church. The godparents who participate in the Roman Catholic baptism are chosen from among friends and relatives. Later, there is a third baptism which takes place at the end of Stage II and is a rite of passage for those becoming godchildren. This third baptism occurs in adulthood and requires the individual to become a part of the ritual kinship system represented by the godchildren and headed by the spiritualist Godfather.

Behavior of Children During Services

Most of the time the boys sit on the inside of the pew and the girls sit on the outside to prevent them from playing and disrupting the services. During the quieter parts of the services, one can notice the boys and girls communicating with one another with giggles and smiles. They remain standing for a few seconds when everyone sits down, trying to locate each other in the congregation.

The Male Children

The males are more restless and pay less attention to the proceedings than the females. Male children tend to be cornered at the end of the pew, pinned between an adult and the wall. When the younger boys are taken to the bathroom, everyone moves down the pew. Upon their return they sit on the aisle side of the pew. The young males copy the behavior of the girls who lean into the aisle to watch the mediums at the front table.

Imitative Spirit Possession is Material Possession

The children are allowed to imitate adult spirit-possession behavior. They are stopped, however, when it is felt they could fall into uncontrolled spirit possession. One time a medium walked up the aisle to a 7-year-old girl, placed her hands on the child's shoulder, and forced her to stop imitating the back and forth movements of spirit possession.

At times the mediums encourage the behavior by watching and smiling. They seem to know which children could enter a premature spirit possession. Some children do very well with their body movements and close their eyes to look like miniature adults in spirit possession. Such youngsters, usually about 10 years old, are more practiced and can begin their move from imitating to possession.

The mediums enjoy the young children's presence as they move with the music, swaying back and forth. One male godchild likes to watch the children imitating spirit possession behavior as he travels through the congregation.

The Female Children

The female children, as noted before, are more attentive than the males. The mother of a young female child reinforces spirit possession behavior by kissing her child as she copies the body movements of possession.   The boys appear less prone to imitate adult behavior.

Mothers kiss their baby daughters as the expected behavior of the clapping or spirit possession is achieved.   The parents tend to be more affectionate during services than at other times.   One never sees a mother kiss or caress her male children during the services.

A Young Female Ready for Spirit Possession

One female medium says that a small blondish girl with short hair who comes to the *centro* with her mother has the power eventually to work the table.   She says the child has to be purified by fire although she is only 10 years old. The guides (spirits) take over her body and refuse to withdraw. "One must wait until the spirits feel up to leaving the body." Two or three other children, innocent, and without any understanding of Spiritualism, imitate what they see. All of them have to be purified, although their time for spirit possession has not yet arrived. Children can always be spiritually cleansed, but it is rare that they can actually go into spirit possession, a factor needed for true purification.

Concern for Premature Possession

Some parents encourage their children by showing them how to clap along with the music.   Everyone claps and the children enjoy the clapping most.   Another young girl who is under 10 uses the body movements of the adults in spirit possession.   She can move her body back and forth at the waist, moving both her hands over her head, about three inches from the scalp, with the finger tips pointing upward.   The Head Medium has complained that once this child goes into possession, she will be unable to close out the spirits (*cerrar*) when the services are over.   She considers this a spiritually dangerous situation.

Children Help Their Mothers During Spirit Possession

Female children cooperate by keeping their mothers from hurting themselves.   These children will often prevent their mothers from going too far over and into the pew in front of them as they enter spirit possession.   Children will turn to their mother staying near them, and keep her from going too far forward or backward.

The children are least attentive during the working of the *causas,* and children under 8 tend to fall asleep. Those over 10 carefully watch the mediums as they start moving and shaking at the table in preparation for spirit communication.

Withdrawing and Material Possession

Children begin to withdraw from the *centro* between the ages of 11 and 15, and it is not until their late twenties and early thirties that they return to Spiritualism. During the ages of 11 to 15, they prefer staying home with their brothers and sisters while their mothers go to the *centro.* One can tell which children will eventually return to the *centro* by how well they imitate spirit possession.

Children copying adult behavior during possession are involved in a spirit possession which is considered material. This occurs because they are innocent and not capable of truly understanding spirit possession. By the time they are 15, however, certain children can be found to be quite competent at copying adult behavior.

It is at 15 that guides begin to overwhelm teenagers. Prior to their 15th birthday they are too young to understand how to control their guides and they end up in semi-convulsive states. The more experienced mediums bring children back to consciousness by exorcising their spirit guides for them. Adults who are not prepared for spirit possession will also engage in imitative behavior.

During one three week period there were 23 *causas* worked by the Godfather in front of the congregation. Seven men and 16 women were treated. The *causas* brought for treatment at the *centro* are divided into four all-encompassing categories (see Table 1).

1. Sexually related issues
2. Behavior problems
3. Marital problems
4. Suicidal tendencies

Each of the 23 were checked to determine if they fit one or more of the categories.

Table 1

Causas Worked by the Godfather (Padrino) and Mediums During Services

Causas	Total	Men	Women
1. Sexually related issues	10	3	7
2. Behavior problems	8	2	6
3. Marital problems	6	2	4
4. Suicidal tendencies	6	x	6
Totals	23	7	16

The greatest number of *causas* were reported in the category of sexually related issues. The second most reported *causas* were behavior problems. There were as many *causas* in the category of marital problems as in the category of suicidal tendencies.

Examples of *Causas* in Each Category

One example of a *causa* in the marital problem category worked at the *centro* involved a young man "who laughed at his wife" because he did not believe in the world of spirits even though his wife is a member of the congregation. The Godfather's attempt to deal with her *causa* is being complicated by her husband because of his disbelief. An example of a sexually related problem was the *causa* of the man who "could not ensure an erection." An example of a behavior problem was that of the man who drank excessively and "rolled in the gutter like a bum." A fourth category example dealt with a woman who attempted suicide 8 to 10 times.

There are other examples, a medium was having marital problems with her husband, complicated by failure to have children, with a *causa* as an etiology. The Godfather treated and cured her. Once her causa was treated, she then could evolve into a full medium at the right hand of the Godfather.

One of the women working to become a godchild had problems of sexual preference. Her husband helped in the working of her *causa*. Two male godchildren, representative of the category of behavior problems, did not find work and were "hanging out" in the streets, and, as one said, "deteriorating mentally." None of the godchildren reported suicidal tendencies, although one of the women apprentice mediums reported a desire to commit suicide prior to her involvement in the *centro*.

Leaving for Home and Sealing the Spirit World

After the last *causa* is worked, a final collective spirit possession is done to prevent any accidental spirit possession from reoccurring on the way home or at home. Many of the godchildren often have headaches after leaving the *centro*. Some of the less experienced godchildren fall into uncontrolled spirit possession. The last spirit possession at the *centro* is used to seal off (*cerrar*) the spirit world from one's material manifestation: the body.

Final prayers said, usually a "Hail Mary" or a prayer from one of Kardec's books. There are many warm goodnights (*buenas noches*), kisses, hugs, and handshakes are exchanged as the congregation leaves for home.

ENDNOTES

1 Read (1966, p. 17) defines a diviner as a diagnostician. Thomas (1910-1911) defines divination as "the process of obtaining knowledge of secret or future things by means of oracles, omens, or astrology" (pp. 332-333). The latter definition is more appropriate to this resesrch.

2 Ms. Kathleen Hall, Psychiactric Social Worker, helped in the transcription and translation of this dialogue.

CHAPTER IV

Stage II: Transition to the Role of the Godchild *Ahijado*

Transition Between Periphery & Semiperiphery

Working toward the Spiritualist baptism, is a transitional stage, a position between the associates and the Godchildren. Preparations for the baptism bring individuals into the ritual kinship system of godchildren. Described are the reasons for the use of the beads, and ritual dress. Also, detailed is the manner of preventing the spirits of the dead from becoming an overwhelming entity over one's body and material existence.

Chica, aspiring to be a godchild at the *centro*, is in her early fifties and has two daughters and two sons. One of her sons is Calibán who refuses to intensify his involvement beyond that of an associate in Stage I at the *centro*. The aspiring godchild Chica speaks:

I was born in San Juan and was raised just outside of San Juan in Santurce. My mother was a Spiritist medium. I would go with her to *centros* at night. Almost always it was on Friday or Wednesday nights since all the *centros* in Puerto Rico seem to be open on those two days. That's quite different from what happens in New York. I would go with her and my brother to watch her work the white table.

We suffered from many needs in Puerto Rico. We were very poor. My mother couldn't help me and I was working in a restaurant kitchen. You know how terrible that is. I was a very young woman; maybe I was 17 or 18 years old. Already by the time I was 15 I had my first daughter.

I arrived in this country and lived on welfare. I wasn't by

myself. I couldn't stick to that welfare thing. My brother got me my first room in this country in the same building where he was living. We lived in furnished rooms. We had a small room and two beds. All my children slept in the bigger bed. It was one of those big beds, and all four of them slept in it. My husband and I slept in the small bed. We didn't have anything, not even coats, nothing.

All I work from is spiritual virtue. I am not a healer. I don't feel that is what I am. I don't have those powers. I helped people who came to my house needing spiritual purification (*despojo*).

The Spiritist that I went to in Puerto Rico was very good. She told me that I was going to be in this country a long time. I was to return to Puerto Rico some day. Quickly many spiritual confusions (*envolvimientos espirituales*) developed in my path. She had informed me that my departure to this country was for the purposes of finding something that would help me in my spiritual development. In the end I would be capable of returning to Puerto Rico to work the spirits. But so many things have happened here in the U.S. that what occurred instead is that I've stagnated spiritually.

I am not sure when we started visiting *centros* because I was too young to remember. I didn't know what it was. I do remember that we would go to a gigantic *centro* and my mother would work the white table.

She worked the white table and she was very good at it. I couldn't tell you if there were saints in the *centros,* but in my house there were saints. I don't know about this type of Spiritism (Spiritualism) with the saints; I am presently learning this.

We were lucky because my mother could read and write. But her problem with the spirits was that they would enter her body after she was out of spirit possession. While she was at the white table working the spirits, things were all right, but once she was at home working around the house, let's suppose washing the clothing, and sometimes the spirits would get into her. They would take her over. Sometimes she would go to do something and she would fall to the floor: She would fall to the ground as if dead. She would later awake from spirit possession and wonder what had happened to her. A struggle with her would always ensue after these things occurred because she couldn't understand what had happened. She would ask what it was that she was doing in some other place, when what she remembered last was that she was washing clothing. She would start to cry and she would become very frightened. I imagine that she thought that she had gone out of her mind.

In Puerto Rico all the mediums would get dressed in white. Once when my mother was working the table there was one *causa* she worked that I'll never forget. I'll never forget this because I thought something had happened to my mother. There was one medium working a special *causa* and my mother was next to her working another *causa*. Somehow the spirit communication became entangled and all of a sudden there was another *causa* in the middle. Three *causas* were being worked. The spirits started communicating, and as one would say, the spirits informed the congregation that "there were two that were eating from the same dish." (*Comen del mismo plato*).[1] A woman out of nowhere ran up and grabbed the water-filled goblet used to attract the spirits. She raised it into the air, exploding over my mother and the other mediums. My mother was right next to the medium who was working that woman's *causa*. It had something to do with two friends that were living in the same house and one was stealing the other's husband. There must have been some type of spiritual interference that occurred on one of those women's paths.

All of a sudden all the other mediums jumped up and grabbed the table cloth off the table and rushed toward my mother. To this day I haven't figured out why this goblet blew up in the air. Anyway it cut my mother and all you could see was blood all over the place. I jumped up screaming "What happened?" I thought she was all cut up, but it was a cut across the shoulder, a deep gash. When she came out of spirit possession and saw that gash she was very frightened. She kept wondering what had happened to her.

She bandaged herself and they wanted her to go to the hospital. She didn't want to go. She told everyone that she didn't have to go because she would heal herself in three days. But, you know how people are; they thought she was trying to make less of the entire situation. But she kept saying, "Don't worry, in three days the whole thing will be healed." She left the *centro* and she continued her housework, doing the wash, hanging clothing and dealing with the rest of the household. In three days all you could see were three little dots in the center of where she was cut. There was one very bright spot, and that mark stayed there until her death from cancer a few years back. We continued going to *centros* after that incident, but she developed some distance from working the table late in her life. She remarried and her husband didn't like this type of work and she left it.

I never lived with my father. I always lived with my mother and no one else. I did get to know him and I would go to see him. But there was no fatherly love in him. My father, I don't even want to talk about him because he was calling for me when he died. But they didn't telephone for me from Puerto Rico. They wouldn't call me.

My stepmother didn't call me because of the inheritance. I haven't been able to get anything from that inheritance because they don't want to distribute any of it to me. I went later because he had left a will. He left a house, and of her own accord my stepmother sold it off. I don't know why but I didn't feel like doing her any harm by putting lawyers on the case. But the fact that she is a sorcerer has nothing to do with my not following up the will with a lawyer. She goes to St. Thomas and involves herself in sorcery, but that stuff doesn't make any inroads with me.

I don't remember how I got to my first *centro* in this country. I don't remember if someone told me about it or if I found it by accident, but it was on Koster Avenue in the Bronx. I've been to many *centros* on Koster Avenue. There used to be one there and I used to work the table. I worked the table and I don't even know how, but I did it. Maybe I am coming on the same thing as my mother (family spiritual chain). They say that when this belief in spirits occurs in one's mother that it takes the son or daughter down the spiritual path. That's what they've told me. I am not one to say if it's true or if it isn't. I was put at the table because the spirits would take over my body.

They had saints at the Koster Avenue *centro*. The Spiritist (Spiritualist) gave us baths and he did the spiritual purification as done in this *centro* here. The purification is done without undergarments. He would give me the spiritual cleansing (*despojo*) bath. I would put on an old dress and he would pour water over me. Later after the bath he would tell me to go change my clothing. I would bring clean clothes and change into them. The old clothing had to be thrown out. Anyone could get the baths.

But there was this spirit that would overpower me and force me into tearing my clothes off. All that kind of stuff. At that other *centro* they would work with that spirit to prevent it from coming into to me so that it wouldn't leave me naked.

I left that *centro* and I never returned. I never returned; I don't know the motive but I never returned. It was a very good *centro* but I withdrew from the place. Later I met some of the people from that *centro* and they told me that the Spiritist (Spiritualist) had been paralyzed. They cut off one of his legs; I just didn't return. He didn't give beads. He would work the table and he would provide prescriptions (*recetas*). He would put *Santería* records on during the services. This was going on around 1965. It was a Puerto Rican family that ran the *centro* made up of the Spiritist (Spiritualist), his wife, and their daughter. They were the leaders at the *centro*. They were the first to have worked at the *centro*. And it was the first *centro* I went to in this country.

My sons and their friends went into the armed services. One of my sons went into the Navy and I put the beads around his neck myself. I cleaned them with coconut water and Florida Water (name-brand toilet water). I put the beads on the altar for a few days. I liked those beads; that's why I bought them. I had them on myself. And I put them on my son. He was in the Navy.

My other son got beads also. He went into the Air Force and was in Vietnam. One was a mechanic with the Air Force and came back almost a sergeant. I don't know how I did it but I put the beads on myself. My son's friend wanted me to place beads on him too so I also gave him a set that I was wearing. He was a young man who lived in the building. He wanted something so that when he went to Vietnam nothing would happen to him. I placed beads like these on him. I placed the green beads of Saint Martha on him. I put the beads on my son and his friend and they went into the service. After returning, my son's friend still kept the beads I gave him, even today.

went into the service. After returning, my son's friend still kept the beads I gave him, even today.

Another time I started reading cards. I told one man what he had told his wife. I had never seen her. And he said, "How do you know these things?" I told him I didn't know anything. So, I left the reading of cards. I have them in my house. I don't touch them either, because everything I told him occurred. And then I got scared. When I say something and it occurs, it scares me.

Now since I've been at this *centro* I haven't dared do anything like that again. The Godfather (*Padrino*) told me during a *consulta* the types of things that I had been doing in my house. And I told the Godfather that if someone comes to my house with pain I do the passing of the hand (*pases*). In this manner the pain goes away. The Godfather here has prohibited that kind of practice.

I met the man who later became my husband in Puerto Rico when I was about 15 years old. He was a merchant marine. His family was also involved in this spiritual work but it wasn't that important to them. I was nothing to them also. As far as I was concerned he too felt I was nothing. He would come back from trips abroad and I would do him a lot of favors. A lot of personal things occurred and I was pregnant, although we never really had sexual contact.

According to others, my first pregnancy was intended as a punishment for my mother. Something like this happening to me without having had sexual contact! I was pregnant and I had my eldest daughter. He left on a trip and didn't return for nine months. I was supposed to force my father into helping me with $20.00 a week, but I didn't want anything from my father. I did what I had to do because I didn't want anyone to force my father to give me anything. So, I went to talk to my stepmother and my father forced me to marry.

Once my husband saw the child, he stole her. I had to chase all over San Juan to have him give me my child. My daughter was not 40 days old. He beat me and stole her. I decided to go to the beach area of Ponce to his family's house looking for my child. It was a terrible life. My mother-in-law helped me find my child and I returned to San Juan. But his family abandoned him. His mother felt that it was my fault because I did not attend to her son. But often gone six, seven, and sometimes nine months. But I did receive help from him. He would send money for me and my children.

That was my life until he got sick and we were sent to this country. I arrived here when I was 25 years old and by that time I had four children. At 25 I went and spoke to the doctors. I explained that I was not interested in knowing any other man. I also told them I wasn't going to have any children from any other man. Those were my feelings. My husband stayed home taking care of the children while I went into the hospital and was operated on to prevent conception. I signed for the operation after my second male child. They operated. I don't know what they did but according to the doctors I still have all my organs. I am not missing one organ. Don't ask me to explain because I cannot; all I know is that I haven't had a menstrual cycle since I was 25 years old. So, I don't know what it is to menstruate as an older women.

My husband wrote a lot because for a time he was a singer. And he would write down everything that he dreamed. My husband saw my spiritual development and he might have been scared that I was a sorcerer. Maybe he noticed what it was I was carrying along with me spiritually from my mother. He must have noticed that I changed and that he was still in the same underdeveloped spiritual condition. Maybe it was that. So he saw me as an enemy and as soon as he entered the house the spirits would overwhelm him. No one could fight him when the spirits grabbed him. The cops had to knock him out, to get him out of the house once. They had to control him because he would beat me and the cops. I told them to either put him in jail or I'd kill him. I showed them that I had four children in the house and they took him to prison.

Every time I went to court I would tell the judge that I wouldn't take him out of jail. Something was telling me not to do it. So then the judge told me that the man was sick with tuberculosis and he said, "We cannot leave that gentlemen here." I told the judge, "I won't allow you to let him out of jail unless you give me an order that he never enters my apartment." I had children; let him leave. Five years later he died of a heart attack.

I had a terrible life always running and fleeing from home

with my children. One time while we were living in the project he accused me of having sexual relations with his son and he beat me. He knows about working the spirits at the table; he was crazy, and he felt I was taking his spiritual protection away from him. Since he drank so much he made himself crazy. I imagine that on the spiritual side he was consumed (*envuelto*). Or something like that.

When I went to my husband's house after he died I saw that he had saints and a series of colored water and another series of things all over the house on the floors. I didn't bring any of that stuff home. I didn't even touch that stuff. He had an altar and he had a bunch of things on that altar. I didn't care about that. In any case, he died with a shot of whiskey in his hand just as he had said he was going to do. When he went to drink it he fell backwards. They called an ambulance but before he got to the hospital he was dead. Since then I have been struggling with my children and they have all been sent to school.

He has been dead eight years. Life was a Calvary since I married that man. He was a man that drank a lot. In Puerto Rico, my mother could control him with her spiritual powers. She could dominate him. He would beat me up and she would get in between us.

He was a believer. He prayed and was religious. He told me that he had to die here in this country. He had a revelation that he was a priest and that he had to die drinking. That is the way he died, drinking. There was nothing anyone could do to take that out of his mind. He dreamed it and he died drinking. Thank God I had a job; I've been there 14 years now; at least there is a spiritual affinity with the nuns where I work. To them I am something; to me it seems that way. So thank God!

Since I have been in this country, this is the first time I have gotten to know Spiritism (Spiritualism). My mother used nothing on her body, although the spirits would overwhelm her. Now I am getting to learn about the saints and the beads. I do this to help people. It looks like my spiritual path is advanced because the Godfather gave me beads about a month after I was here. It's been a year since I first arrived here at the *centro*. I didn't think it had been that long.

I found this *centro* while passing by here on my way to

my son's place. I felt that this *centro* was calling me. I left home early and I said to myself, "I am going to check that place out." I was very much impressed by the place. I can never explain it to myself but I was impressed by the place. For one, I had never seen such an altar at any *centro*. I felt as if I were sleep walking when I saw that altar. I have my own altar, but I've never seen anything like this.

I was so impressed with this *centro* that I brought my daughters and my sons here. I like the way things are worked here. I like the way I have been developing spiritually here in this *centro*. I would like to finish developing what it is that I have brought spiritually. I want to develop those things that have been provided to me spiritually through my work. I come to work the table as a medium and I am going to do it.

It is the Godfather that informs the individual of what it is one has spiritually. But it is you who must acknowledge your spiritual guides. You must begin to develop them and the Godfather, once he sees your effort, helps you by giving you those things that ensure progress.

For example, I had been told that it would be necessary for me to have an operation. I came for a consultation (*consulta*) and the Godfather told me that I needed a spiritual operation. He sent me back to the doctor and the doctors explained that I didn't have anything. They told me that I was perfectly okay. I returned to the *centro* and I informed the Godfather of how his diagnosis was confirmed (*comprobado*). I am well and I am going to become a godchild. I came here to find out what was happening and he told me to trust my spiritual guides. The guides would take hold of me in the house but I didn't know what that meant. I just remember that I would pray a lot.

I keep a black madonna in the house on my altar. She is a large madonna, and I have a smaller one in front. That's the way I have them. I have a third madonna to the side of both of these. I received this small black figurine playing the flute; I placed it in front of all three. He is sort of sitting. I had one saint in green and another series of saints representing the Seven African Powers.

I've seen a baptism and the Godfather will do mine later. I do remember seeing that he takes the beads off and waits before he puts the new ones on. Later he takes the new ones out of coconut water and he wipes one's forehead with the coconut water. He does many things. I was surprised and I liked it; I was very much impressed. That day I saw the baptism the spirits made me feel the currents (*fluidos*) of their presence.

My brother visited me and he wanted me to place some beads on him. I wouldn't dare. He wants to get a set of beads of the Seven African Powers. He has a lot of problems because he too was a merchant marine like my husband and he was blackballed in the union. He lost everything. He lives in Manhattan near 14th Street.

The second stage at the *centro espiritista* represents the transitional period associates go through in preparation for baptism into the godchildren.

In general, individuals in the process of going from associate to preparation for baptism in Stage II have been participating in the congregation, or the periphery of the *centro*, for a minimum of two months. They are usually associates who have proven themselves capable of keeping their dues up to date and ensuring their spiritual purity.

This transitional Stage II is a trail (*prueba*) which tests one's faith in the spirit world. The trial requires rituals, ceremonial clothing and the addition of beads. This is done in preparation for baptism into stage III. This stage II begins the process of bringing the individual out of stage I and into stage III.

It is in this Stage II that a groping for deeper understanding of the *causas* which affected one's life begins. It is hoped greater insight into the self can be gained. One who intensifies involvement into Stage II usually has a family spiritual chain (*cadena espiritual*) which has predestined this individual to do the work of the white table.

The Godfather identifies those with a family spiritual chain during group spirit possession, when sprinkling water over the congregation distinguishes those who can and cannot go into spirit possession. It is during the consultations that he informs those in Stage I that they are more experienced in spirit possession and that they have a family spiritual chain which requires their continual development in the arena of Spiritualism.

It is nonetheless the need to have a *causa* diagnosed or treated which initially brings the individual to the *centro,* although once the Godfather has remedied their *causa* satisfactorily there is no means of guaranteeing that an individual will remain. The Godfather's ability to instill trust insures the desire of individuals to attempt to become godchildren and involve themselves in this transitional Stage II. This transition becomes the means of integrating oneself into the social fabric of the *centro espiritista* and into a more pronounced role. The interview with Chica provides an inkling of an individual's self-perception as she involves herself in Stage II.

The Factors that Make for a Godchild

First, it is understood that a family background in Spiritism is most helpful in becoming a godchild. Second, the ability to accept the existence of the world of spirits. Third, one must have confidence that what one is doing is correct for oneself and ultimately good for those in need of having their *causas* worked. Last, one must be certain that purity is maintained on a spiritual level and that the material world will not create conditions which would be counterproductive to the spiritual world one is seeking to enlighten.

Individuals arrive at the *centro* because of trials which test their belief. These trials must become part of the person's world view. In this manner, they take their development seriously; otherwise the spirits begin to block their path to development. A woman went through a process of trials prior to becoming a godchild. Although she had succeeded in overcoming her *causa* (trial) her baptism was cancelled because she did not attend the services on a regular basis.

The first step in becoming a godchild is the baptism into the core grouping of godchildren - the ritual kinship system. It is there that the individual is instructed on establishing communication with the different levels of the dead. However, before the baptism, one has to prepare oneself.

One notices which individuals are to be baptized by the number of necklaces they wear. Children under 12 are never baptized and do not wear the different colored beads. Young children usually wear one string of white beads, but the adults wear many more beads, which can symbolize the possibility of baptism, although it could also indicate associate membership. Often associates do not become godchildren, but wear the many colored beads representing saints for protection from malicious forces. The beads have to be spiritually cleansed and purified and can never be touched by individuals not spiritually pure.

Chica is troubled about her progress toward becoming a godchild. The nuns at her job always try to touch her beads. She tells the nuns not to touch her beads, but they do it anyway. The nuns see them as prayer beads. They do not see them as beads needed for self-protection in becoming a godchild. She does not say anything because she does not want them to know that she is a practitioner of Spiritism (Spiritualism). She becomes concerned that her beads have been spiritually contaminated by the nuns touching them. She brings them to the Godfather to have them cleansed and spiritually purified. Part of her preparation toward becoming a godchild is the acceptance of the concept of spiritual protection as a means of remaining spiritually pure for continued advancement.

The Family Spiritual Chain

When the present Head Medium first arrived at the *centro*, the Godfather was enthusiastic because the saints needed someone with her experience to ensure a higher level of spirit communication. She was an important addition since she came from a long line of spiritual believers. He explained that she had to be spiritually cleansed as soon as possible to secure her integration into the godchildren and later into the mediums. Her spiritual operation was very important for her because it relieved her of her *causa*, which allowed her to conceive. Once her *causa* was worked she was ready to be baptized into the godchildren without waiting the long period of time that most others wait.

The old Head Medium welcomed the new medium to her position at the table since having her at the table would help her own spiritual development. She was to work people's *causas* and was seated at the table without being baptized because the saints requested it. She is the only person to have come to the *centro* and work the table, and not be baptized until afterwards. She feels what helped her was prior experience in working the dead.

One month later, the Godfather baptized her as his Principal Head Medium. She was pregnant by the time of the baptism, a result of the spiritual operation to remove a *causa* interfering with her ability to conceive.

The Godfather had divined that the Principal Medium and her sister could start having their *causas* worked simultaneously since they had arrived together at the *centro*. Care must be taken to protect the family chain of worshipping the dead. However, the Principal Medium's sister was apprehensive of working the dead so she had to wait for her spiritual baptism prior to taking her place at the table. Her stumbling block was fear, which manifested itself as a lack of confidence. More-over, she had many more *causas* that needed working, and they had gained strength because of a history of leaving *centros* before her many *causas* had been relieved.

When the sisters first arrived at the *centro* in 1976, there were only four mediums at the table. This shortage prevented work on the many *causas* people brought to the *centro*.

The Godfather decided the sisters would participate in the ritual of becoming a godchild at the same time. The Godfather informed them that this belief in the spirits is a family chain which they must not break.

One of the apprentice mediums now between baptism and medium-ship says that the most important thing is to feel confident in what one believes. She sees confidence as the most important factor for baptism into the godchildren, although having Spiritism in the family helps. She feels that, once one is baptized, one feels it inside. It is not something tangible that people can point to, see, or touch. Baptism provides the necessary confidence to walk down the streets and not fear anything or anybody.

Dressing in White

She continues by saying that since one feels that no one can harm you, you have the feeling that people relate to you because you're powerful. When one is dressed in white people look at you with respect. Some people hate what it means when they see godchildren dressed in white and wearing beads. Others too notice that hate and scorn. The object, however, is to gain the confidence one needs to be capable of spirit communication. Those aspiring to become godchildren begin wearing white before they are baptized and can usually be spotted among the public sitting in the second row or guarding the rear door.

Preparing for Baptism

The Godfather says he baptizes everyone the saints tell him to baptize during spirit possession. It is outside of his ability to exclude anyone who comes to the *centro* for help, and the saints can request that anyone be baptized. He cannot exclude anyone from baptism by charging exorbitant fees.

Nevertheless, the Head Medium feels that not everyone can be baptized because it is more complicated than just a ritual. She feels it depends on what a person brings with him or her spiritually in the form of experience. Everyone comes with spiritual work to do at the table (*trabajar la mesa*). Not all those who want to become godchildren can work with the dead, since there are those persons who come to cure (*curanderia*). Therefore, it all depends on the individual and the individual's experience.

The Godfather will communicate with the saints and they inform him of who must be baptized. The saints provide the reasons, different for each individual, for the baptism. The Godfather meets in private consultation with the perspective godchild and if the individual says yes, then he or she is prepared for baptism. The first set of beads is provided in preparation. These necklaces serve to prepare the person by ensuring his or her purity, and also start the development of the spiritual protectors which will later help in spirit communication.

A young woman in preparation to be a godchild said she was informed by the Godfather that she was ready to become a godchild in the near future. The Godfather was told by the saints that it was the young woman's turn to be baptized. Nevertheless, she expressed some reservations because, during the fall of 1979 and spring of 1980, 20 new people were baptized by the Godfather and only one of them remains a godchild.

She has taken the loss of godchildren seriously. She fully expects that the secret ceremony, which only members of the *centro* are allowed to attend, will follow the same routine as past baptisms. She will dress in white, and the beads she has been wearing will be exchanged for new ones.   She will wear her new beads for the first time on the day of the ceremony.   The beads will have been purified in the inside of a coconut.   Then the Godfather will take out the beads dripping in coconut milk and place them around her neck.   The rest of the coconut milk will be used to baptize the individual by placing the liquid at the forehead and the back of the neck.   This baptism can occur for up to 10 people at a time.

At this Stage individuals begin to realize the importance of their grandparents' and parents' belief in spirits.   Therefore, the deceased from previous generations demand that family members who live continue the belief in spirits and pass it on to future generations.   Implied, although never directly stated, is that the ancestors need to secure their own development up the spiritual hierarchy.   It is understood that there are familial failures with the belief system that need to be redressed by family members who are alive.

It is only through continued development up the hierarchy of spirits that an ancestor can be prevented from falling into darkness.   In the same vein, only through development into a medium does one's own spirits become enlightened and develop up the hierarchy.   But development into a medium presupposes having previously experienced the role of godchild.

It takes a long time for an individual to go from identifying a *causa* that needs working to becoming a godchild.   The time period is determined by what the person brings spiritually to the *centro*.   Most people with spiritual experience are given the beads within one month, whereas others do not receive theirs for years. Kerchiefs are also given.   Each kerchief is a different color and represents a different saint.

One aspiring godchild remembers receiving two out of the seven beads representing the Seven African Powers.   It took her six months to get them.   Her third set of beads took her another six months.   She still has four sets of beads to go.   She says it will take her longer than the others to get those beads.   She understands that one can be at the *centro* an entire year and end up with only one set of beads.

It is through the saints that the Godfather knows who deserves beads. It seems to depend upon what an individual brings to Spiritualism from his or her past.   Other factors take on significance such as frequency and promptness of attendance at the *centro* and the quality of participation.

The beads are given first; the kerchiefs, worn around the waist, are given once the individual is a godchild. They are used to help the individual blossom spiritually. They are not used for spirit communication, but to attract spirit protectors and secure continued spiritual development. They prepare individuals for what will happen. In this manner, a godchild is strong enough so the dead (*muertos*) can be brought down to be "worked" at the table. The beads and kerchiefs provide a means, a power to attract the dead.

Not all godchildren, no matter their family chain, are capable of sitting at the table to work the dead. The beads are not the only considerations and do not automatically lead to mediumship. There are other factors that can interfere with the process.

Many things have to be learned from the process of becoming a godchild. Among them is learning how to distinguish between the spiritual and the material. The guides, which are spirits that help in communication with the dead, must be distinguished from other types of spirits. "Spirits are so much more intelligent than most mediums," says the Godfather to an aspiring godchild who feels that she is failing.

The youngest of the aspiring godchildren has been wearing beads (*collares*) for a year. The Godfather called her to the front and had her take them off. She was asked to turn around, face the altar, and keep her back to the congregation. The Godfather took her beads and hid them. He then asked her to turn around and find them somewhere in the *centro*. She recalls being bewildered by the task. But in one motion she walked to the back of the room, near the entrance, reached above the refrigerator, and found them on the shelf where the rocks that are used to attract the African Powers are kept.

She realized she had trusted her instincts. She did not know what to do with herself since she felt so happy to have passed her trial (*prueba*). She is becoming more confident and trusting of the Godfather. She feels it will facilitate her integration into the godchildren.

This confidence is important. She has heard from the godchildren that it feels terrific to help individuals who arrive at the *centro* with *causas* to be worked. The godchildren who are apprentice mediums inform her that there is a sense of relief in one's self when one does a good job of working someone's *causa*. It is a beautiful experience.

One aspiring godchild feels she is a beginner.   She says Spiritualism is "like Karate" where there are "stages of development."   She feels it is somewhat like the "stages of development" individuals go through in their lives.   She points to one of the godchildren as an example of one who is highly developed, saying that she is that way because she developed her sense of how to deal with the dead in her childhood.

Situations where individuals have their baptism cancelled are uncommon at the *centro*.   All individuals undergo trials which are either economic or personal.   Attendance prior to baptism is considered mandatory.   The spiritual trials begin with attendance and later advance to other areas of spiritual development.

An individual cannot be allowed to continue to baptism while ignoring his or her spiritual progress because the guides and protector spirits will not be properly prepared. If this lack of preparedness occurs and the individual is baptized into the godchildren, the entire *centro* can have its work blocked.   It will weaken the *centro* and in the process weaken the prospective godchild.   This weakening of the prospective godchild will make him or her vulnerable to complicated *causas*. If the individual should withdraw from the *centro* halfway through the preparation for baptism, it would create the possibility of multiple *causas* evolving which can spiritually consume (*envolver*) an individual.

When an individual fails to deal with the complications of trials, the Godfather points it out publicly during services.   He informs them that they will not be baptized because they have not been sufficiently serious in their duties to the belief system.   Everyone takes notice of the failing individual.

The most obvious infraction is that of absence.   All godchildren are expected to attend the services at least once a week.   The only reason accepted for not participating in the services is illness or employment hours which conflict with services.

The one factor that never comes up as preventing baptism is that of an individual not paying associate dues.   Often people fall months behind in their dues because they are not working or working part time.

The Belief System of Those in Transition

One aspect of the *centro* that attracts many Spiritist (Spiritualist) worshippers is the impressive size of the altar. Chica was impressed to such a degree that she had her son and daughters visit. Most meaningful to her is that she feels that the Godfather is not out to take advantage of her either monetarily or sexually because he waited a month before asking her to buy her first beads.

She does not feel rushed into things, even though the Godfather feels her spiritual path is more developed then others who arrive at the *centro*. She has been given the bead necklaces because she had previously worked as a medium and has a family chain that brings her to Spiritism (Spiritualism). She hopes to succeed this time in developing her spiritual guides and protectors, which she attempted to develop in the past. She is thankful the Godfather, unlike other Spiritists (Spiritualist), helps individuals understand the belief system and its complexities. She gets personal attention and her questions about the belief system are answered.

Another woman is very happy with the help the Godfather provides. She feels now that he helps her in interpreting her dreams, she can begin to understand what is spiritually preventing her development. She did not feel anything at first, but now it is different. At other *centros* she had attended, they never told her what was troubling her. Further, they would never inform her of how she could help herself spiritually. She feels good that the Godfather helps people who are really interested. He told her that if you are not interested, you shouldn't waste your time. Nevertheless, if one believes and is just learning, he helps. He helps people by opening their minds and enabling them to retain better what he is teaching.

Chica remembers being very scared of the Godfather when she first arrived. But he gave her the type of attention she needed. She remembers he told her to light her candles and to start building her altar. She felt better as she intensified her rituals. She now understands it takes a long time to work the evil of envy out of one's system. There is no way to get that evil out without spending time praying and burning candles. One must stand before the altar and plead for faith.

She feels "envy" caused her original problems and had attached itself to her like leprosy, sucking her blood away.   Chica felt her mother's curse had been placed on her when young, and this curse could only be alleviated by having her complex *causa* worked at a *centro.*

When her *causa* was worked at the *centro,* she was informed that an evil spirit was maliciously manipulating her.   She understands that during the first consultation, the Godfather is not supposed to tell an individual the complexities which pertains to his or her *causa.*   Each person can handle just so much.   In her case, she understands why the Godfather withheld information, saying that her emotional constitution is not one that can withstand a lot of things hitting her all at once.   She feels too much information about her *causa* could overwhelm her.

The Godfather worked on her *causa* until it made her sick.   He knew what the problem was, but he did not tell her, making her think to herself that she did not have anything wrong.   She originally felt that the Godfather was unable to find anything.   She now says he knew she had other problems, but he was not letting her know.   If he had told her about the complexities of her *causas* at the first meeting, she would have gone crazy.   The important thing about the Godfather is that he was willing to tell her the things she needed to know in a positive manner.   He reassured her that things would get better.

Chica feels that the first thing a person has to do is to have his or her problem identified as spiritual and acknowledge that the *causa* must be spiritually treated.   The person must also be willing to build up spiritual protectors (*protectores*).   The first step is identifying the *causa* ; the second step is having the *causa* relieved (*trabajar la causa*).   The third and last step is ritual clothing and buying the beads thereby building protectors.   This third aspect, the building of protectors, is very complicated since the Godfather has to determine what is spiritually necessary for an individual's protection.

In Chica's case, it was necessary to have her protection built up because of her health-related problems.   The Godfather then started safeguarding her health by means of a spiritual operation.   Herbal baths had to be taken, and an altar had to be built for the spiritual protection of the home.

Learning to Control the Spirits

One prospective godchild, a woman in her forties, feels things are different now since she is working her way into the godchildren. She has started sensing things she could not feel before. She was informed by the Godfather that she will be baptized. She senses more of the spirit world and she is more capable of differentiating spirits. Sensing these things is nothing she can see or feel tangibly. It is something that at a certain point one can just feel inside.

The Godfather knows who brings spiritual powers to be developed. He says that one's spiritual protection dictates how one is judged. Many people bring influences of the dead from high level spiritual hierarchies. It is possible to tell which persons can develop their higher level spirits by analyzing which type of material problems they encounter. These material manifestations (problems) can cause physical discomforts.

Controlling the Spirit Protectors

The first level of possession is communicating with the spirit protectors while beginning to sense the presence of the saints. It is important to learn to control the spirit protectors. Sometimes in the beginning all the protectors, about a dozen, try to penetrate the body at once, causing convulsions.

The protector spirits compete to enter a body, causing great spiritual confusion. The Godfather teaches one how to control spirit possession and prevent all the protectors from attempting to enter one's body at the same time. He says that there is a method to prevent an individual from being "screwed up" by teaching them how to allow one protector at a time an opportunity to penetrate the body.

Another problem is "closing" (*cerrando*) the protectors out from the body. Sometimes they refuse to leave. At first, apprentices cannot "close" them out, and the future godchildren go home with headaches and feelings of nausea. This discomfort does not occur once the Godfather teaches the individual how to "close" out the protectors. It is a mental effort of control of the dead.

A younger more educated informant was willing to speak about the erotic sensations which protector spirits gave her as they penetrated her body.   It is like that moment of anxiety, that strange feeling as if something sexual is about to occur.   It is erotic but it changed as the protectors stopped penetrating her body all at once.   It is more in control now and she can enjoy the penetration one protector at a time.

Sensing the Saints

She now is at a higher level of penetration and can identify the saints which enter her body, something she could not do in the past.   She can feel St. Lazarus, since he takes hold of her arms and bends them while penetrating her.   She feels him doing the same thing with her legs.   She feels his presence in all her joints.

She is now trying to identify another saint penetrating her body, and is keeping herself spiritually pure so she can communicate with that saint.   This saint will help her see things better.   She can feel.   Now, she is working at seeing the penetration.   She needs help from this saint to bring light (enlightenment) to what she feels.   She senses that the saint has already helped her see the spirit world more clearly.   It is a female saint, but this is all she knows at this time.

Distinguishing Protectors and Guides

Many fear the spirits because they enter the body unexpectedly.   The apprentices, especially those who are least experienced, are taught to recognize the signs of oncoming possession.   Such as hair standing on end along the arms and the side of the head.

Sometimes they begin to speak directly to the spirits.   A future godchild is not sure if it is appropriate to speak directly to the spirits. She does not know if the Godfather would approve, although he has said everyone develops differently.   She has not been told by the Godfather that what she is doing is incorrect.   The Godfather must divine during possession the best method for conducting communication with these spirit guides.

Guides

Still Chica felt that it was not her main concern to develop her protectors because she had been through this once before at another *centro*. What she is developing, with the Godfather's help, is her guides. She feels this part of the development to be very difficult because one must develop the spiritual guides by one's own process of spiritual purification. The Godfather helps her to identify the spiritual guides so that she wouldn't confuse them with other spiritual entities. The Godfather informs the prospective godchild as to whether her communication is with a protector or a guide. In this manner, one begins to understand the differences.

Toward the end of the period of preparation one begins to feel the saints enter the body. Chica remembers the whole side of her body going limp. The difficult problem with the saints is the process of learning to control them as they penetrate the body. They can start penetrating one's body even at home when least expected. She is learning what to do during those occasions and how to ask the saints to withdraw. She now understands this Spiritism (Spiritualism) is more difficult to deal with, and is a completely new experience, unlike anything she had done as a medium.

Many feel they work hard and deserve to be godchildren. Others want to work the table, but feel it will take them a year to get there. Chica still must wait her turn at baptism which she expects to occur in the summer of 1980. She understands, once baptized, that she will have a greater opportunity to learn because she will be sitting among the godchildren at the *centro*. Unlike other informants she does not picture herself among the mediums at the table working *causas*.

The protectors, guides, and lastly, the saints, represent the ascending order of possession for a medium. The saints are the last to be developed because they are the highest in the hierarchy.

Saints and Their Affinity

The issue of different affinities must be considered in the belief system. Each saint calls on an individual. As an example, each saint enters (*montarse*) each individual differently and needs to be ritually satisfied to a greater or lesser degree. If everyone were to share an altar in a family, there would be confusion as to which person's saint is being satisfied with offerings of fruits and flowers. One's affinity also affects the size of the altar or shrine in the home.

There is a "calling" about how big one's shrine should be. Each saint will make different demands and determining their affinity such as the color of the flowers, types of foods, plaster images, and rituals. The Godfather does not tell anyone which images of saints to buy, although it is understood one begins with the Seven African Powers. The home altar is a collective representation of an individual's affinities symbolizing the family's ancestors and the incorporation of a new generation.

Securing Progress at the *Centro*

In order to secure continued progress at the *centro*, one must keep up the rituals, as well as attendance and participation in the *centro's* activities. At points when things are not going well either in the home, on a personal or on an economic level, the Godfather is very supportive. Spiritual development, however, cannot be abandoned because of material problems.

One informant progressing to the level of godchild keeps up her rituals and comes to the *centro* at least once a week. She is interested in some day becoming a godchild. She does not feel it will happen soon. She understands that she has always had spiritual powers but these powers were not developed while young. Now that she is being helped, she might be capable of catching up and becoming a godchild. If one is truly interested, the Godfather will help; otherwise, he will be unable to help. She thinks it is pivotal that the Godfather inform the individual about his or her abilities.

Another aspiring godchild says she understands why others improve so much faster than she does. She is learning more than she originally expected. However, she is still unable to sit down and tell (divination) what type of *causas* a person brings with her or him. Yet, one aspiring godchild can go into full spirit possession, while another has only started to control her spirits as they penetrate.

Divining Confirmed

The youngest of the aspiring godchildren says that now that she is having her divining confirmed at the *centro*, she feels more comfortable. Sitting up close to the mediums and having her sense of the *causas* confirmed makes her feel as elated as when she passes one of her college exams.

She knows when she is successful because it feels good. She says she feels good because she gets to sense things and then has them confirmed by the mediums. She feels even better when what she has divined on the side lines is similar to what the mediums have divined while in possession at the table. She can sense when the divining is "right on the dot."

She reminds herself, that she has always been able to feel her way around situations, especially when something is not right. She says she can just feel it. She now sees that the Godfather is helping her because in the past she had feelings but only used them to "get by." If she did not feel like doing something she would not do it. Conversely, if she felt something was right she would do it. Now she will learn to go further with her senses.

New Prohibitions

The aspiring godchildren have been prohibited from working the spirits for friends at home now that they are to join the godchildren. Chica, who was interviewed at the beginning of this chapter, is one of those who used to do spiritual readings (*pases*) and help build individual protection by providing beads. *Pases* are symbolic hand movements over the body used to read the spiritual aura. She has been explicitly informed by the Godfather that she is no longer to do *pases* or give away sets of beads. If she continues these rituals, it could unintentionally lead to complications which will confuse her spiritual development. Chica is in her early fifties and is a small woman under 120 pounds, but she has lifted a 150 pound man on her back in her apartment to cleanse him of evil while in spirit possession. She has also served others needing spiritual cleansing in her home, among them family and friends that needed protection while in Vietnam. She will no longer work the dead in her home; it is prohibited.

ENDNOTES

[1] *"Comen del mismo plato"* is an idiom which expresses that there are two women who are either knowingly or unknowingly involved in a sexual liaison with the same man.   It can either be extramarital affairs, or single women.   It is directed at women and I have never heard it used in reference to men.

CHAPTER V

The Semiperiphery

This chapter represents those who have been baptized and have begun to work the spirits of the dead. This difficult task forces many to leave the *centro* prior to either working the dead or some time soon after. The reasons for leaving the *centro* at this point are given as are the complicated issues which often prevent a Godchild from progressing up the hierarchy of the mediums which is the core of the *centro*. The interview which follows directly below reflects the concerns of the only male Godchild who as an apprentice medium has progressed to speaking to the spirits of the dead.

M iñe, a 32 year old, Afro-Puerto Rican, is the only male to develop sufficiently to sit at the table as an apprentice medium. He has no relatives who attend the services and is loyal to the Godfather who he views as a father figure. The Only Male Godchild Miñe Speaks:

> I was born in this country and lived somewhere on 103rd Street and Columbus or Amsterdam, down in Manhattan. I was living there for a couple of years. I moved to 116th Street between Lenox and Fifth Avenue. I went to public school there for about three years. Later, I went to Catholic school for the rest of my education. I lived in that area for 10 to 15 years.
> My life is not a complicated one. I continued in Catholic school and I believed in the saints and in the miracles of

saints. I carry a medal of Jesus and a crucifix on me at all times. It is a burden to me to see the blood shed from Him in pictures or in movies. I have always believed in Him. You know I have never said to myself, "I won't believe that you and the Virgin don't exist if you don't help me." What I have done is to believe all the more in Christ and the Miraculous Virgin. That was until I started understanding Spiritism (Spiritualism) a little bit.

I was brought up a Catholic and I always felt there was a Catholic Church somewhere around the corner where I could go and sit down if I had to shed a tear. Fine, I would shed a tear for whatever things I did wrong. It did not matter if it occurred a year, a month, or a day ago. You know. My life goes on. I found out about the saints from my mother and from Catholic School. I found out about the miraculous Virgin. My mother introduced me to the saints. There are some saints who I carry in my heart and who will defend me. But I knew about the rest of the saints. I knew stories about the saints because I used to love to read them. The times I wanted to find out about a saint's life, I would sit down and read. Especially if I wanted to know if the saints had been involved with God, or if they ever felt a love for God, or if I wanted to know why they became saints.

I would say to myself, "If I am in this service I want to know what it is that I am here for." I know that I am here to do good, to defend people, all the people that I can defend. I asked in prayer if there was more to it. I was asking these questions when I was young. I wanted to know why. You know, I never turned my back on the Church. It is true that I haven't gone often lately, not even to confession, but I haven't turned my back on the Church.

My mother came with a star.[1] She comes from Loiza Aldea in Puerto Rico.[2] From my understanding, when someone comes with a star, according to what my mother told me, that means that one has come to work with saints. That was what she told me when I was a kid. My father was also born in Loiza Aldea. He understands it but he does not practice it. You know.

From what I heard, my grandmother didn't believe in physicians. She died at the age of 70. She never wanted to believe in doctors. When she was sick she wanted to cure herself with Spiritism. She had been brought up with

Spiritism; she had come with her star as well. I came to practice this through my mother's side. As you know, Loiza Aldea has a lot of Spiritists and sorcerers. You might know about the Feast of St. James (*Fiesta de Santiago*)[3] because people get dressed like sorcerers, and the African music and so forth is well known.

The only ones who practiced Spiritism were my mother and my grandmother. I used to go with them to *centros* when I was a kid. They used to go to a *centro* on 117th Street and Park Avenue. I think that years ago it was well known because of the manner in which the President of the table and the mediums worked. I went there about three times. I told my mother that I wasn't going there any longer because I didn't like it. I was too scared. You had to go down to the basement to see the mediums but all I could see was candles. I don't remember saints or anything like that at that *centro*. It was dark in there and I would say "no way, José!" I used to be very afraid of it. My mother would carefully explain what they were up to and how people used the mediums and so forth. But my knowledge of all that is a blank.

I never got involved with that *centro*. I went three times and I didn't go back to that *centro* on 117th Street. I didn't want to be bothered. I didn't feel it was for me. I decided I wouldn't go for it because it wasn't really me and I didn't like it. It didn't have saints and those types of things.

I was without a job for a year. Can you believe that for a whole year I was without a job? But I was getting unemployment insurance. Luckily, I was living with my mother and I didn't have to give her that much.

It was in 1977 that my mother went to the Godfather at the *centro* to speak to him about the problem that I was having. The Godfather told my mother that he wanted to see me whenever I had a chance. I went to see him. We spoke and then my mother and I spoke to him. He gave me a warm spot in my heart and he gave me a warm smile. We rapped and he explained what was happening to me. I started going there every day. I used to sit down with him and he explained things to me. He used to tell me to keep working on my betterment and he said, "I hope to God that you continue working on your development."

I started out by cleaning the *centro*. He wanted me to

clean up and I said, "no problem with me." I used to go there on Saturdays. I would sit down. I would do errands and buy stuff at the *botánica*. I would buy whatever he needed for the herbal baths. I would go and buy him coffee and things like that. I used to wash and mop the *centro*. I used to sweep it on Mondays and Thursdays. Afterwards, I would go to the services. You can say that I started at the *centro* as the porter.

After that, I continued at the *centro* and I liked it. He recognized what I was bringing with me spiritually. He would explain a few things to me about Spiritism (Spiritualism). But once in a while I wasn't too involved so I would just go there on either Monday or Thursday. When I started, I was always in the back of the *centro*. I would never move to the front. I would have never done it in my life. I never thought it was going to bother me, but I was afraid. Well, I moved up a few benches after a few months.

I started liking the Godfather and everybody else. The Godfather told me that one day I would be at the front with the godchildren. I would say "if God's willing to let me." I felt that if I were to go to the front that I would not argue with the situation. Then after that I started going to the *consultas* on Saturdays and he started giving me confidence. He would ask me to spend Saturdays with him. I would say okay and spend Saturdays with him and he would explain things.

After a while I began to feel more comfortable and confident. I would try never to be late. I would always try to be early, but when I came late he would sit me in the first pews and everything. He would put me through the purification through fire and do to me what he does to everybody else. They worked a few of the *causas* that I had. Even if I were 5 or 10 minutes late, he would always save me a spot.

He put one set of beads (*collar*) on me, but even if you've been a godchild somewhere else he puts one set of beads on because God wants it that way. Sometimes people get up to 15 sets of beads, but they turn their back on Spiritism (Spiritualism). Because you turn your back on religion, you're going to suffer, but it will only be a warning. You'll have to go back and start all over from the beginning with the first set of beads. You never know. In the end, after starting all over, you could be stronger than before. If you started with one and went to 15 sets of beads, the Godfather might recognize even more of your spiritual powers causing him to give you up to 20 sets of beads. You could be even stronger because you've been warned and you suffered.

It is like how God never gave anyone the cross to carry for him. The only one that carried it was Simon and that was due to the fact that Simon was doing charitable work. Simon wanted to help. God did not give it to the other apostles. He did not give it to them. He could have given it to the other apostles and walked freely to the top of the mountain. But he didn't. Now if it's true, when you start off on these things, your guides will tell you if it's okay.

I was baptized. The Godfather was very happy when it happened. My Godmother was also very happy. They were preparing for me and I didn't know it, and I didn't know that it had to do with what I used to see. It had to do with the godsons and goddaughters. I asked him to explain all these things to me. He said, "You've come to carry the cross and you're going to carry it for the rest of your life." That was heavy. To walk around until they've recognized your spiritual strength and then find out that these things count for working the white table and to wear white. To be able to do good.

The Godfather used to explain things to me little by little. I am a newcomer, so he would never explain anything difficult to me. He would tell me what it was that I could do or not do when I worked my first dead soul (*un muerto*). You have got to be careful about how you work the dead. He had to explain the reasons for success. In this fashion I could open my eyes and my arms to helping everybody. He explained that I was not too familiar with all this and that he had to sit down with me and tell me. He told me things for two or three minutes. I would say, "Yes, sir," but I was trying to impart what he was saying into my life.

He would always tell me to continue coming. I saw everybody getting dressed in white, so before I was baptized I started dressing in white. I did this for six or six-and-a-half months. I could not believe myself. I said, "I am not a Godson. I am just a member. How come I am dressing in white?" Me, I could take the clothes off and I don't know why I didn't. I couldn't take the white clothes off and I was wearing them all the time.

I never asked the Godfather why but he knew about it. He must have known. Nevertheless, I missed my appointed day for a baptism and the Godfather and Godmother were very angry at me. He told me that it would take about three years for the saints to reconsider me. I had to take care of some financial business that was very important. Sometimes there is need for punishment even though God doesn't like to do it. But that other thing came first and I had to take care of it. So I said, "Okay, I understand it is going to take at least three years for me to be baptized."

But on All Saints Day, during that week, the Godfather told me that I was going to be baptized. "I thought I had to wait three years," I told him. But all I had to do was wait about three months: August, September, and October. I said to myself, "My God, the saints have accepted me." The Godfather said that the saints wanted me in the *centro* and that they have their reasons. I said to myself, "Me, Miñe, I don't believe that after only three months after missing my scheduled baptism I am going to be baptized." All together it took me about a year to be baptized.

Now I wasn't going to argue, okay? I got baptized the week of All Saints Day. That was the week of All Saints and All Souls. It was the week of the saints. I didn't know that they would accept me. I don't know the reason. It was only three months and week of waiting. I was very lucky.

I said to my mother, "Mommy, look." And she said, "Miñe, my God, I don't believe it." I continued at the *centro*, but I still made my little errors. My baptism was a private thing. I had to go there on a Saturday. I went and I was nervous. I didn't know what was happening. How was I supposed to know what I was getting myself into?

All these things were new to me. It was lovely and beautiful, but it was heavy and strong. But it was my understanding that these things were involving me for the rest of my life. That's the way I looked at it and that's the way I felt. The Godfather is always looking out for my back because he wants to know if I hurt somewhere. If I am hurting he wants to know why; it is that I feel that way. And if he has to handle me, well, he'll do it too. For others, he sits down and he talks to them. With me he is more direct and tells me to my face. He'll punch me in the eye in a second.

I make sure that my Godfather is safe when he works the

table with the mediums. I work the table when there are other godsons there. I don't like working the table if there aren't any other men there. I have to keep my eye on him, especially when working the table. A lot of people say that the Godfather puts his trust in me. But at the same time he's always watching. But it hurts me to know that he's got no one watching over him. That's what's killing me.

If I could spread my blessings, I would give them to the persons who deserve it. They would never leave the *centro* and the Godfather would never leave his godchildren. Even if I was able to leave without punishment, I wouldn't. It would be like going crazy to leave. Now I love sitting down and saying, "All right self, here we go."

But, you know, deep down inside the Godfather hurts. Sometimes he sits down and he is so exhausted dealing with people day after day. As you know, he sheds his tears also. Just like everybody else. If he has to shed his tears for you in front of a million people, he'll do it. That won't bother him as long as you've received your blessing from Christ. I understand so he trusts me. To my understanding, he is my Godfather.

He has told me that there would be people that I was going to help out. They would come up to me and I would help them out. He said, "You'll do that at your altar." So he told me that I was going to cry and that if I had to give blood in a cup that I would do it. I would give it for that person, only to have that person turn his back on me. He said, "you're going to feel very hurt!"

We are a family and we don't consider ourselves like John Doe and Susan and so forth. You know, if the Godfather has to tell me something because the saints have told him, well, you know, he'll do it. If the saints have to punish me, then he'll tell me and everybody will know. Everybody at the table will know before or after the services. He might make a special meeting to deal with these things. Sometimes he tells us to explain to people what it is we've done wrong at the *centro*.

Because it is a family, I might ask one of the mediums about what it is she thinks I did. I would ask her why she feels that I feel a certain way. She might give me some details about what she thinks and how the Godfather might see it. Sometimes in meetings when the godchildren get together,we talk that way and the Godfather will sit and listen. He observes everything. He studies me.

I might ask the Head Medium or any other medium. I might ask one of the male godchildren. I might have to ask for an opinion or advice. We're all in a family so we don't hide anything. Now, the only time we will hide something is if it has to do with our personal life. In that case, it is something that only my Godfather knows about. He does not want us to talk about how we went for a drink with our friend John Doe. He doesn't want to know because it is something personal and not something that concerns us all. We sit down and we'll talk. We'll have soda and we'll rap, you know, so on and so forth.

As with Christ, who was told by the Holy Spirit that he hadn't failed because he knew what was going to happen, we feel the same way here at the *centro*. The same way that Christ had to suffer, we have to suffer all the more. When we have problems we sit and talk about them and get advice. The Godfather is there to watch over us. You come to the Godfather and tell him that you have a toothache. You know you're not going to be able to sleep and the Godfather is going to be right there to help you. He is just like a father; just like Our Father was with His Son. So, he gives you good advice and provides an understanding. He tells us what we need. Like the Father, the Godfather doesn't want us to suffer. We are taught to learn from our mistakes. So, if something comes up that is bad, we sit and talk about it because he needs us. We need his love and his understanding. Once in a while he needs our little advice too.

A successful medium can get up and answer questions that are put to her. Well, as you know, the one that started all this was Christ. He asked Him for permission and his Father gave Him permission. He also gave Him the rights and gave Him an understanding. The understanding was given so that He didn't fall back because there is a lot of evil in this world. There is a lot of temptation. The Holy Spirit is the purity and the one that brings everything. We have to become pure. And, you know, the same way that He fell and fell three times and kept going. He wants the godchildren to continue the same way.

My first experience as a medium was three or four months ago. I used to sit right there in the front with the godchildren and so forth. I used to help out the Godfather while he was communicating with the spirits during the *causas.* One day as he was working a *causa,* he asked me what I felt just out of the blue, just like that. He was asking us for proof of what was spiritually ailing this woman. I was just sitting there and answered, "Boom, boom, boom." And he said, "That's correct." He smiled and I didn't know what was going on. I said to myself, "Ay, what's going on, baby, tell me?" After that I started getting myself involved by saying something every now and then. Little by little, I started putting in my things during the working of the *causas.* He started helping me and I started feeling and seeing things. Later, I started seeing this and feeling that about a *causa.* But, you know, it was a very slow process.

I don't come like the rest of the mediums. Because if there are 40 mediums, maybe 39 of them have been in this since childhood. They have been feeling and seeing things since the age of five or six. You see, I am the only one who hasn't been feeling these things since childhood. So my process has to be very slow and I have to be sure of what I am doing.

The Guardian Angel guides you. He takes you and helps you as a medium. You might want to give proofs 2 to 15 times, but you may not be correct. Maybe you have to do it 15 or 20 times only to find that it is the 16th or 21st time that you are correct in giving a proof. Sometimes people don't do things properly and they leave with a headache. You've tried everything from A to Z, but still the following morning you wake up with a headache. You say, "This is chaotic," and then you try one more time and you're right on the head.

Then you say, right on (*vaya*)! Then you're lucky. You've hit it at the 16th or 21st try. And then you're going to leave. But the thing is that anywhere that you go you're going to have the same Guardian Angel. You will also have the same protectors. There is no reason for leaving. If you stayed, you might improve. I am in the *centro* because it's looking good for me.

The first time I sat at the table, I just walked in the door and I said to everyone, "Hello." Then they told me to sit down at the table. Almost two years after I was baptized I was told to sit at the table for the first time. I thought it would be one of those things that wouldn't bother me. Everyone went, "Miñe at the table....whooo!" I was bringing my guides up and bringing my spiritual things up (the spiritual hierarchy). I said, "Well, fine." I sat at the table and so forth. But it was scary because it was no joke. I was kind of nervous. I sat in the middle on the left side, between the Head Medium of the left side and one of the auxiliary mediums. It was very surprising and everybody was surprised. But they wanted me to have a little taste of it.

Every time I have sat at the table it has not been the same. There was one incident that got a little out of hand. I had so many things going through my mind as I sat. The Godfather put me there knowing all the things that I had on my mind. I felt real bad one day. When he said to me "Sit down," I said, "What?" But he said to sit down and I sat down. But he noticed that there was something wrong with me. You know. I felt kind of funny but I had to remove all that from my mind. I had to remove everything that was bothering me from my mind. I had to do that from the time that they started working the *causas* until they finished.

I felt funny that time, yes. But every time I sit there I get a different feeling. I might get a feeling of happiness or I might get a feeling of anger. I might get the feeling that I am getting nauseous. I get a different feeling every time I sit there working the *causas*. You know, every time I sit there, to tell you the truth, sometimes I like it and sometimes I don't. God forgive me.

To me, a good medium reaches a level of comfort with the spirits. He's one that gives everything and that level is his home, he feels comfortable at the table. He will tell you, "Let's go heal a wound of someone with leprosy." He will say "Let's do it." He would never say, "Let's not do it because we might get sick." He treats *causas* because he is used to doing it already himself. He will treat the leprosy. I feel I have to follow the Godfather. You learn to live and you learn to suffer.

I like to work on anybody and I get those feelings. But sometimes when I am at the table I have to ask permission to stand up. I walk over and help the Godfather because he doesn't call on anyone else. I help with the water, the incense, and the collection. He puts his trust in me. He puts his love in me, you know.

I am not a 100% medium, not even a 99% medium. I am the only male apprentice there and I consider myself a 10 percenter. But this 10% is trying to struggle hard, and am the only man there but I have experience at the table now. I am the best of all the men, but maybe that's because I do show my appreciation for the way they worked my *causa*. I want to spread the morale so that everyone will be happy. I want to help everybody so that they don't suffer. I am at the *centro* ; I see it and I feel the suffering. I want to shed a tear for Him without it hurting me at all. I have recently gotten to the point that I can get deep inside myself.

Sometimes I am so tired. I am a bit beat. I have so many things on my mind. Sometimes I feel like I should just stay home, but then I say to myself, "I am going to my second job." I just can't leave the *centro*. That goes for everybody from the Godfather to everyone else at the *centro*. As long as there is something to see there I am going to stay. The mediums have given a lot of themselves. And, a lot of other people have given us help also. I cannot go further in my rating of myself because I cannot get that 100%, but I shall.

I don't want to go anywhere else because what I have developed at this *centro* isn't mine. These things belong to God. The Godfather helps you to develop them. You develop them because you deserve it. If you just walk away you'll be less happy.

The godchildren are carrying their things from the bottom of their hearts. When they work the table we feel their presence. Even if the medium is sick at home we still feel she is with us at the table. These blessings that people bring have been recognized by the Godfather and will always remain there, once recognized. Even when people have to leave the *centro*, we don't forget them because they tried their best. Even if the person pulled their thoughts [a conscious withdrawal from the session] while here on Mondays and Thursdays, they tried and their thoughts came through. When you have a good thought about everything and about all the godchildren, it works.

Once in a while working the table, I got sick. I had to rush home. They rushed me home because my house had gone out (he fainted). Once in a blue moon my house goes out. I knew the time when it happened. Up to the second.

It becomes a habit to work *causas*, just like going to

school and knowing that the bell is going to ring. You have to serve the saints. Sometimes the Godfather has to ask persons to leave the godchildren because they are not developing spiritually. Another reason for asking persons not to participate is their health (material problem) which prevents them from developing. I wouldn't want to leave and I don't want that to happen. I don't want to go anywhere else.

Sometimes we have a medium we call Lady Godiva because she is a rumormonger (*bochinchera*). She will sit down at the table on Mondays and Thursdays, but all of a sudden she wants to do things on her own. The Godfather gives her those things and you can't work the table as if you were in your house. Some people feel that because they have helped three people's *causas* that is all they have to do. You never have helped enough people. People come and then all of a sudden, they are gone.

All I can tell you is that the people at the *centro* are the best. Ay, yes, if some day I leave the *centro* the saints are going to bring me back the hard way. Wherever I go, they're going to find me and they are going to bring me back the hard way. They are going to bring me back the hard way to the same place.

You [the researcher] look like a saint, the one that used to write a lot. Yeah, he used to sit and write and write. He used to go crazy writing.

In this Stage III the godchildren represent the semiperiphery of the *centro*, whereas the periphery is composed of Stage I which includes the public and associates while Stage II is Transitional. The godchildren are apprentice mediums. The mediums of Stage IV are the upper rung of the godchildren.

Among the godchildren there are several members who have been in the *centro* for at least three years. The average number of godchildren present at services is 18, which includes 15 women and 3 men. The three male godchildren serve as assistants to the workings of the core grouping of mediums at the table; yet all three are present for services every Monday and Thursday. Their roles are distinct and different from the rest of the godchildren because they are not women. The men are more readily socialized into physically oriented roles needed at the *centro*.

The role of a godchild is to secure spiritual protection for others. To this end, they must be baptized into the grouping of godchildren. Two types of baptism can take place at the *centro*. The first of these is spiritual baptism of the young into the Spiritist (Spiritualist) belief system. This baptism must later be reinforced by a traditional Roman Catholic baptism, in which the godparents of the child are chosen by the parents. The third baptism is that of individuals into the godchildren. This baptism into Stage III usually takes place after the individual is 16 years old. It must be emphasized that not all godchildren become mediums since it requires persistence and confidence in one's belief in spirits, especially for divining (*meditación espiritual*). Withdrawing from the godchildren is seen as betrayal and defection from the "family."

All the godchildren acknowledge that only those who speak up and say what they see and feel while *causas* are being worked will become mediums. Often the first sign of one's ability to become a godchild and an apprentice medium is the sensing, feeling, and the discerning of spirits during the purification by fire. All future godchildren are informed that they must speak up if they discern during the services, especially while *causas* are being worked, the sorcery or malicious spirits involved. The godchildren instruct future godchildren in expressing what these feelings are while the dead are worked.

Preparing the Spiritual

The Godmother was asked what she liked most about this particular *centro*. She said the *centro* has been a school to many in the congregation. She says, the Godfather has informed the godchildren he will not be among them forever and their role is to ensure that the belief system flourishes. She sees the main purpose of Spiritism (Spiritualism) as teaching individuals that there is good and evil among all mankind. Also, through helping others one is helping oneself. Her feeling is that the more one learns about Spiritism (Spiritualism) the more competent one is in helping others in need of having their *causas* worked.

The Godmother emphasizes that the training of godchildren is intended to ensure that individuals continue the work of helping others with *causas*. A good Godfather must always be ready to have someone continue the work of the spirits. The Godmother says that if the

Godfather leaves "somebody else can take over." The Godmother says that when individuals first are recognized as being spiritual the Godfather informs them that they have something beautiful to be spiritually developed.

The importance of getting instructions on rituals and learning how to communicate with the dead should not be taken lightly. These instructions prepare each godchild to enter the *centro* ready to communicate with the spirits. If one is not ritually prepared, a spiritual block will occur.

One woman godchild feels something might go wrong with her "spiritual eye" which helps her in reading *causas* if she does not prepare herself with care at home. Not only can spiritual preparation affect one's "spiritual eye," but also a poor material life, such as excessive drinking. If the "spiritual eye" is affected, then one is unable to learn to see causas clearly. If one makes a mistake in the perception of a *causa*, mistakes will be made during the working of the *causa* at the table. A poor "spiritual eye" is detrimental to providing prescriptions (*recetas*) because one is incapable of correctly relieving the *causa*.

Special Sessions for Godchildren

The material problems of the godchildren are treated during private sessions. These special sessions are arranged by the Godfather. If a godchild has a material problem, all the godchildren are called for a session at the *centro*. Special sessions occur irregularly. The godchildren sit down and discuss questionable behaviors during these private sessions. The Godfather mediates these sessions, helping to clarify the spiritual side of what might look at first glance like something material in origin.

The baptism allows an individual to participate in these group sessions. The major concern in these sessions is to dissect those things which are spiritual and those that are material. Godchildren are more then mere acquaintances. People, once baptized, learn to speak plainly and are not afraid to say what needs to be said.

The godchildren must know what is going on among the mediums at the table. The mediums must know what the saints and the spirits they are working with want. The mediums cannot keep problems to themselves. They must open themselves up and speak out, otherwise blocks evolve among the godchildren which then affect their work at the table. Therefore, when the *centro* closes down for the evening, it is sometimes necessary to call the godchildren in for a closed meeting. In this manner, any problems encountered during the services can be worked on immediately. By preventing material concerns from interrupting the spiritual work, this ensures that everything functions correctly at the *centro*.

Material problems between mediums are also explained so that feelings between the mediums do not get out of hand. This type of material problem has occurred when there is jealousy between mediums. The Godfather has been forced to handle the problem before it surfaced while working the dead. He often explains what occurred materially, and how it surfaced during the working of a *causa*.

The godchildren become an extension of one's family. Raúl, a male godchild, says it is like being in your own home, you ask what is going wrong and discuss it. The spiritual progression of the group must be protected. Conflicts such as jealousy or other material (nonspiritual) problems must be confronted openly. It is a family.

Private sessions are intended for the purpose of having the godchildren ask advice of the Godfather as well as each other. The Godfather listens attentively while individuals explain their personal problems because he might better understand what might be interfering with a godchild's spiritual development. The Godfather provides the opportunity for individual godchildren to relate better to one another.

Once baptized, an emotional commitment to the godchildren is made. Miñe, the male apprentice medium, says sometimes he feels tired and would rather stay home. But, he says to himself, he is going to his "second job" at the *centro*. He feels he is important to the group. He passes the collection box during the services. And he cleans up the *centro* after services. The rest of the godchildren do not directly help the Godfather. He feels he must be there to help the Spiritualist with his burdens. He says, "I always have to be looking over his back, you know!"

Another Godchild explains that even when she was in the hospital, she could see with her "spiritual eye" everything going on during the services. She felt she was present at the *centro*. Miñe concurs, saying absence at the services does not mean people are forgotten by the godchildren. Baptism means you have entered a family and your presence is felt even during your absence.

An individual who has been baptized into the godchildren can come into conflict with the group even though one is innocently trying to enter the group. Jealousy is called a material block because it is not intentional, while envy is a spiritual block because it harnesses evil. It is up to the Godfather to distinguish between the material block and the spiritual block in specific cases.

One godchild is very happy at this centro because it is unlike the other *centros*. At other *centros*, the Godfather would refuse to involve himself with the godchildren. She remembers the godchildren at the other *centro* as constantly fighting. Moreover, the Spiritist, by not interesting himself in his godchildren, made it impossible for the godchildren to work together. Envy and jealousy became helplessly intertwined, and *causas* were poorly worked at the table. She left that *centro* and feels lucky to have found a new one where the Godfather is interested in the welfare of the godchildren.

The Women Godchildren (*Ahijadas*)

Becoming a godchild solves and, at the same time, creates problems for the godchildren. On the one hand, they have solved the problem of finding a place to participate in the helping of individuals with *causas*. They are learning how to ensure that their own spirits will find a higher place in the hierarchy of spirits when they die. All too often, on the other hand, it creates problems. Godchildren suffer scorn because they wear white on the streets of their neighborhood. Many women godchildren fear people who ridicule them for their spiritualist beliefs because it serves to create blocks.

Others have taken to dressing at the centro in the consultation room. In this manner, they hope to avoid rumors and ridicule in their neighborhoods. Anyone who dresses in the white of a godchild is immediately perceived as a sorcerer. Most people do not view a spiritual person as someone who solves the ill effects of sorcery, envy, and ensuing *causas*. Only those who understand the commitment to Spiritualism look at the believer dressed in white with respect.

One female godchild's progression to the table was quick. She had felt and seen spirits from the time she first arrived at the *centro*. She spent three weeks sitting with the rest of the godchildren and was called to the table as an apprentice medium to work her first spirit of the dead (*muerto*). She now feels only those not afraid of the dead are chosen to become godchildren. She presently wears her white clothing and her colored kerchiefs around her waist as she comes to the *centro* for the services. She felt nervous the first time she sat down at the table. She now feels that this is natural when experiencing something for the first time.

Mercedes, a godchild, recalls her fear and loneliness before she was baptized and became a member of the godchildren. She remembers spirits surrounding her in her bedroom after her three children were in bed. Spirit visitations are different depending upon whence they come (their division). There are Black Spirits from the Congo division and American Indian Spirits. The Indians are tall and wear a head dress. The spirits from the Congo division are nine feet tall and wear only a loin cloth. The fact that they were wearing colorful clothing was a good omen, but their size frightened her. Before she was a member of the godchildren, she would wake up in the morning and feel exhausted. Now, since she has been working at the *centro* as a godchild, she sleeps better and is no longer disturbed by the spirits at night.

Mercedes says that learning to communicate with the dead is the most important development, but that the longer one is involved in a *centro* the more one can learn to control the communication. She feels what she has learned is very good. The time and effort one puts into learning are the determinants in the communication process. It has also helped her especially in dealing with different kinds of people. This *centro* is different because it helps her to learn how to deal with people. "This is unlike other *centros* that are not concerned with one's learning," she said.

The Male Godchild or Apprentice Medium

There are only three males involved in the godchildren, and only one out of the three has sufficiently developed to the level of apprentice medium. From Associates onward, the differences between the males and females become more clearly defined since fewer males develop to the level of Medium in Stage IV.

The female godchildren warn the males at the *centro* not to be overconfident about their Spiritualist ability because women are better at securing enlightenment from the spirits. Those men who do become godchildren think highly of the Spiritist belief system, although they are less likely to become apprentice mediums and work the spirits at the table. Often the men are intimidated and overwhelmed by the belief system and the power it provides women for divining, foretelling, and sorcery.

Only one other male besides the Godfather has sat at the table since the *centro* opened. A male godchild can be asked by the Godfather to sit at the table and be an apprentice medium, but it depends on his participation in other aspects of the *centro*. These other aspects include the manner in which the godchild shows his belief in the spirits. Before someone can sit at the table and work *causas*, it is necessary that the saints communicate this desire to the Godfather. The Godfather does not make this decision on his own.

The Male Apprentice Medium

The role of the male godchildren is to display a commitment to helping those who are having their *causas* worked. During the working of a *causa*, Miñe tenderly wipes the tears off an old woman who cries because her son does not want her living with him. At other times Miñe has held women who fainted while having their *causas* worked. In these situations, it is always Miñe who steps forward and comforts individuals during consultation.

After two years as a godchild, Miñe was given the opportunity to show how well he is developing his spirit guides (*cuadro*) and protectors. Miñe is the first male in five years to work as an apprentice medium. One apprentice woman medium who has known Miñe for years says he is the most articulate of the male godchildren when communicating with the dead.

There are many men who are associates, but most could not become godchildren because they lack confidence. The only male willing to have his divining confirmed by the Godfather is Miñe, and he is progressing slowly in his divining. He takes the risk of having his divining judged on the basis of the facts surrounding a *causa*. There aren't many male godchildren like Miñe, who are willing to handle the complexities of divining.

Miñe has been given permission by the saints to sit at the table four times. He has given satisfactory proof that he knows the type of *causas* which have affected individuals. Since he has taken the initiative and been successful, he is now taking further steps to enlighten his spirit guides. These steps will secure his ability to enlighten the spirits of others suffering from *causas*.

The Principal Head Medium says that men take longer to learn to read *causas* than women because it is difficult for men to show their commitment and love. But with time, the men begin to express their love and show their commitment to spiritualism. At present, the best thing most of the men can do is to guard the mediums and prevent them from accidentally hurting themselves during spirit possession. They can also help in preventing members of the congregation from hurting themselves during collective possession and purification through fire.

Slowly, men too come near the table to work it. It can take years for the Godfather to determine if a male will progress sufficiently to handle the spirits. Miñe was unable to continue when he sat down at the table the first time. The Godfather cannot allow any apprentice to continue trying without the saints' permission; otherwise the saints will express their dissatisfaction.

The first time Miñe sat at the table, he was not very articulate. The second time, however, he was more experienced and did somewhat better. The most important sitting for an apprentice medium is the second because it is a better indicator of how well he or she will do.

There are only two males capable of working the spirits of the dead at the *centro* : Miñe, as an apprentice medium; and the Godfather, who has been working the table for 20 years.

The Godchild Guarding the Door

Raúl is a tall thin Afro-Puerto Rican in his late twenties. He is strikingly muscular and dresses in the white clothes of the godchildren. He has been a member of the congregation for six months and has been given the job of guarding the door. He provides an ominous presence at the door. An apprentice medium reflecting on the role which Raúl fulfills says "he is at the door; he is the door man here and I guess that's it."

Raúl's role is more complicated than it appears because the Godfather must have absolute trust in him. It is always an Afro-Latin male who guards the entrance, and most of the time it is Raúl. He takes his instructions from the Godfather, who gives them through hand gestures, from the front altar area to the rear of the *centro* where Raúl is located. Only during the purification by fire does he leave the rear of the *centro*. No one else is allowed to open the door at that time.

There are two reasons for keeping the door guarded by a male godchild and purpose of the guard is to avoid unnecessary incidents. First, it is necessary to prevent unwanted strangers from wandering into the *centro*. These strangers might be out to do spiritual harm to the Godfather. Second, it prevents individuals from opening the doors during the services allowing malicious (base spirits) from the street to enter the *centro*. Moreover, these malicious spirits can confuse *causas* being worked by the mediums, especially after everyone has been purified through fire.

An incident occurred in the winter of 1979, when services were stopped at the half way point. During the services, the Godfather asked a woman to establish her "spiritual credentials". The woman prostrated herself before the Godfather and said she had arrived to learn from the "chosen one." The Godfather asked all the godchildren to stand up and hold their hands up high. The woman began to explain that she had arrived to learn. The Godfather called her a liar, saying her interest was in damaging the work of the centro. He told her he was fighting the type of sorcery (*brujeria*) she unleashes.

Everyone in the centro reeled in fear as the woman was recognized as a sorcerer. The Godfather threw water at the sorcerer, she backed away shrieking. The Godfather stood in front of her and stared down at her while the entire congregation prayed. As he sprinkled water at her, he asked that the door be opened. Raúl, the male godchild, opened the door and ushered the sorcerer out. From the street, the sorcerer began to laugh in a high-pitched voice that spread chills up everyone's back. The Godfather said that she came to create spiritual blocks by spreading base spirits and confusing the work of the *centro.*

The Problems of the Male Godchildren

Most of the time there are good reasons why the men do not say anything. Often it has to do with self-doubts about their belief in spirits. The Head Medium sees the least active male godchild as an example of the problem of self-doubt in the spirit world. Most female godchildren are disinclined to speak about the male godchildren, since they are not developing at the speed with which the women develop. The women have also questioned the Godfather about the men's lack of spiritual development. The Godfather's suspicion is that men are less spiritually inclined than women.

Raúl feels it is a man's problem that they are not spiritually advanced. He says it is more difficult for men even when they come from a family that has been involved in Spiritism for generations and have been at *centros* since childhood. Raúl has been unable to secure spiritual development because he does not have the necessary faith. He arrived on earth to work the table but has never sat down to diving the spirits, consequently preventing his development. He has gone through many trials (*pruebas*), but has not intensified his involvement at the *centro* beyond making the entrance secure. After years in Spiritism (Spiritualism) he "still has his doubts," says the Head Medium, acknowledging Raúl's problem. Yet, he can see (divine) and can give proofs (*dar pruebas*), but his doubts prevent him from developing into a medium.

There seem to be other considerations besides commitment to Spiritism, which is material in origin, and affect the male godchild. The Head Medium, Altagracia, feels that male godchild Manolo is someone who could be an advanced medium, but he is not advancing because his wife does not believe in Spiritism (Spiritualism). The struggles between them are due to his participation in the *centro*, and have become a block to his spiritual development. This blockage occurs even though he has inherited a family spiritual chain (a family history of Spiritism). He participates in the services, but his commitment is ambiguous. His wife undermines his development because her interests are material, such as her college education. Manolo does not feel he will be capable of balancing his participation at the *centro* and his wife's demands that he abandon Spiritism (Spiritualism). His greatest problems are accommodating his wife's desires while at the same time performing his spiritual rituals at home, and adjusting his work schedule for participation at the *centro*.

Consequently, Manolo does not participate in all the activities of the *centro*, limiting himself to the services. Often he wears black socks, when they should be white along with the rest of the clothing of the godchildren. Miñe feels that maybe it is because he hurries from his job to the *centro* that prevents him from being properly dressed. But between his wife's demands and his not following the dress code of the godchildren, he is not viewed as taking the belief system seriously. His behavior can cause a block to the *centro's* work. Miñe is concerned that a block could create a dangerous spiritual situation for the Godfather, whom he assists.

Most of the godchildren have decided to ignore Manolo as much as possible, at least until he can resolve his block to his spiritual development. It seems unlikely he will leave his wife. Two of the women godchildren left husbands because they didn't want them to work the spirits. They are presently mediums at the *centro*. These two women have an especially negative view of Manolo and his lack of commitment to spiritualism.

In general, the women godchildren feel men are unlikely to commit themselves to spiritualism at the same level women do. Their rationale for the failure of men to become apprentice mediums has to do with and their unwillingness to balance their search for material wealth with faith.

"Men are not confident in their beliefs and men are hard-headed, causing them to find it difficult to understand the work of the spirits," says one woman godchild. Also, "men feel funny because there is a majority of women at the *centro*," says another woman godchild. Men are more conscious of what they are saying, especially when working *causas*. They are also afraid of offending women while working *causas*.

Miñe admits that of the men at the centro, he is probably the most competent since he is the only male to be placed at the table as an apprentice medium. He feels this is possible because he has been willing to show his appreciation to the saints who have provided him with power. He never thought Spiritism (Spiritualism) would be so important to him and that he would feel like remaining involved for the rest of his life. He says this power is something new to him.

Learning how to work the spirits is viewed as complicated and difficult. Miñe has given more time and energy to working the spirits than any other male godchild at the *centro*. The Godfather says that Miñe is struggling hard, as a male, to become an apprentice medium. Miñe has no blocks set against him in his family because his wife and mother are believers.

A Full Crew of Godchildren is Necessary

Miñe does not like sitting at the table as an apprentice medium when there isn't a "full crew" of godchildren at the *centro*. When few godchildren are present Miñe feels that his first job is to guarantee the spiritual safety of the Godfather. Miñe does this by standing behind the Godfather during services, thus assuring that the Godfather is not thrown from his chair if his spirit protectors should fail. Miñe especially does not like working the table when there are no other men at the *centro* who can keep an eye on the Godfather and his needs. Miñe refills the goblets with fresh water after each *causa* is worked, a task he cannot do when sitting at the table. Miñe sticks to his job as assistant to the Godfather. He has been put in the position of having to get up from the table in between *causas* because there are no men he trusts, except the door-keeper, Raúl, to prevent the Godfather from falling backwards while in spirit possession. The Godfather does not call on others for help because he trusts Miñe's judgment and understands Miñe is showing his appreciation to the saints for his progress.

It is understood that during the services, the Godfather puts his trust in Miñe. His association with the Godfather has become so obvious that members of the public started calling him "little Godfather" (*Padrinito*). Miñe says it is true the Godfather puts his trust in him, "but he is always watching."

The four times Miñe has sat at the table he received different feelings from the spirits. The first time he sat at the table he had too many fears going through his head. He felt unsuccessful because he was overwhelmed by the new experience. He was feeling uncomfortable while removing all thoughts about this world from his mind, it became difficult for him to enter spiritual meditation (divination). In self evaluation he said that his first attempt at being a medium was "real bad."

Even though Miñe is the only male to become an apprentice medium, his development has been slow because he has to be reassured at each step. He remembers how after that first time at the table he just walked out the door in a daze without thinking about what he had been through. He noticed, however, that many members of the congregation were saying "There goes Miñe," in admiration.

It took three months before he was asked to sit at the table again. He was placed to the right of the Godfather. Sitting to the right of the Godfather, as an apprentice medium, is considered important because it allows one to be close to the Principal Head Medium. By sitting in that place, one can develop into a Principal Head Medium at the right hand of the Godfather. He had to wait six months before he sat at the table for the third time, and another six months for the fourth time. It has taken Miñe more than a year and a half to be seated at the table four times.

Doubts about the spiritual world are usually caused by material (worldly) concerns. Men are also frightened of divining *causas* that would "offend" women members of the public. They will often say that they feel "out of place" because they are out numbered by women. What emerges eventually is their lack of confidence in their abilities and trust in the spirits.

<u>Reasons for Leaving the Godchildren</u>

There are several reasons given for leaving the godchildren. Among them are lack of commitment to Spiritualism, distrust of the Godfather, and excessive time demands. They feel that if an individual was truly committed in the first place to spiritualism, there would be little likelihood of leaving.

The godchild's commitment is essential for success at the *centro*, but not all godchildren succeed and remain. Many fail to continue because the rituals are too difficult or their spouses object. In other cases, the amount of time required to become a godchild was considered excessive.

When godchildren drop out, but are not forgotten, their spiritual powers once recognized by the Godfather become a blessing granted by God which they always carry. Their presence is felt at the *centro* long after they've left.

Miñe is deeply disturbed by godchildren who leave, and he doesn't understand what forces them to leave. Miñe wants his "cross to always be brighter," which is the burden he bears for helping individuals with *causas*. He wants his bright cross to guard his back against evil.

One godchild said she didn't understand what could be gained by leaving the godchildren and abandoning spiritual work. Another godchild thought that some abandon the belief system because the Godfather had given them an insufficient number of bead necklaces. Others among the godchildren, especially the mediums, are envied because they have received as many as 15 different beads representing the 15 different spirits with which they communicate.

Those individuals who "turn their backs" on the belief system place themselves in a position of suffering with no means of alleviating their pain. Every time one "turns his back" on Spiritism (Spiritualism), he suffers twice as much. The first time a godchild turns his back on his obligation to help someone who is suffering, the spirits create a *causa* in this person's life to test his belief. The second time a godchild turns his back on Spiritism (Spiritualism) by leaving, this is another trial, a warning, that is more difficult for the godchild to eliminate. It is possible that the Godfather will find unrecognized powers in a godchild and that there are more than originally brought by the individual. This, however, occurs over time. If a godchild who has left a *centro* later returns, it could make him spiritually stronger than had been originally recognized. This returned individual's trial then becomes an object of group lessons to the rest of the godchildren about the evils encountered if one leaves.

Failing to follow the rituals and instructions

Some godchildren fail because they do not listen to the Godfather's instructions. According to one godchild, it is simple to follow instructions, such as saying prayers, but if instructions are not followed, that can start problems in a godchild. The Godfather gives reading material to the godchildren, and some do not study it. If the Godfather sees there is something wrong spiritually, he will inform the godchild and provide prayer and ritual instructions. One must follow the instructions to prevent falling behind in one's development as a godchild.

Many godchildren cannot withstand the trials that occur after baptism. They are unable to fulfill their commitment to participate in the activities of the *centro*. This failure causes the godchild to develop distance from the rest of the godchildren. One godchild feels it is only after baptism that one can tell how successful a new godchild will be. If godchildren are not committed to their beliefs, they cannot show their faith and love. Their willingness to "sing out" (*cantor*) the proofs involved in a *causa* is an indicator of their commitment to Spiritism (spiritualism).

One can tell which godchildren will not succeed by their lack of participation in consultations. One can also tell if godchildren are following the instructions of the Godfather because it is their only way to build protectors. The new godchildren must light candles daily. They must ritually place foods requested by the saints at their altar. In this manner they learn spiritual cleanliness, as well as build up spiritual power. But if the godchildren do not keep their commitment, their spiritual growth will stagnate. It is important that the other godchildren lend these stagnating individuals a hand because the dead need their help in the search for enlightenment.

Lack of Confidence in the Godfather

If the Godfather has confidence in the godchild, he can help him learn. If a godchild distrusts (*desconfía*) the godfather, there is no need for him to remain a godchild because it creates blocks to his learning process. Distrust on either part creates a block which, in the long run, is counter productive to participation at the *centro*.

One godchild who dropped out refused initially to discuss her reasons. After an absence from the *centro* of over a year, I made an arrangement to see her. She is a tall woman raised in the United States from mixed European parentage. Short hair and tall, she dressed simply but stylishly and wore African styled jewelry. She was a believer. She spoke about her experiences. She feared the Godfather was unscrupulous. She was afraid to be alone with him in the consultation room and distrusted his intentions, even when the Godmother was present in the *centro*.

He had begun to read her spiritual currents by passing his hands about two inches from her legs and it made her uneasy. As the

Godfather moved his hands down her legs, she was unable to allow the spiritual reading to go any further. Before she departed, in 1979, she was considered the best candidate among the godchildren for apprentice mediumship. A block prevented her spiritual enlightenment because she had misgivings about the Godfather.

Anyone who establishes a block eventually leaves, according to the Head Medium. One can tell which godchildren are not comfortable because they sit on the edges of their seats, looking at the table and not saying anything. These godchildren do not see anything. They neither see the *causa* nor do they give proofs about the type of *causas* being worked at the *centro*.

The one thing they can do is spiritually cleanse themselves during purification through fire. The only manner in which a godchild can advance is through developing his or her ability to provide proof of a *causa* and of its development. Otherwise, spiritual protectors begin to wither away and go into darkness. Consequently, unassertive godchildren go into underdevelopment, darkness, and later stagnation. Once this occurs they leave the godchildren and the *centro*.

Insufficient Learning and Progress

Some leave because they feel they've learned enough to work the spirits in their homes. But, according to Miñe, one of the male mediums, those who want to work the spirits at home are nothing but "Lady Godivas". They just want to put on a show, not realizing that their powers were given to them by someone else. Miñe feels the Godfather develops those powers for individuals. What is unusual, says Miñe, is they leave without warning; they just leave "all of a sudden....boom!"

The gist of the problem with some godchildren is they are not satisfied with their progress at the *centro*. They also do not feel comfortable with the pace at which they are enlightening their spirits.

The godchildren who remain understand the impatience, but realize from experience that new godchildren want to progress fast. It is the *centro*, in the end, which determines whether an individual godchild is going to learn. The experienced ones say that even when godchildren are interested in learning, *centros* are often unwilling to teach them. This occurs because individual Spiritists fear competition. Many godchildren try to involve themselves in Spiritism, but are not provided instructions on how to prepare themselves for spiritual cleanliness and purity. It takes the right type of *centro* to learn Spiritism.

According to Raúl, a major problem in learning about Spiritism (Spiritualism) these days is that everyone who wants to be a godchild thinks he or she knows everything about Spiritism (Spiritualism). They arrive at the *centro* and say they have been mediums and can work the dead. But, in reality, they are unable to do anything. The learning process takes time. At first, one starts to feel things and then one begins to see things. This seeing and feeling is the "whole bit," says Miñe, and is a slow process even for those who have been sensing and seeing since they were young. It takes time at the table to learn to communicate with the spirits. A female godchild reflecting on her spiritually given patience says she is learning to communicate with the spirits and now has her own altar. But, as a godchild, it will be a long time before she will have learned enough about *causas* to become an apprentice medium. Pride is the most dangerous of the factors leading to a person's stagnation in development as a godchild. Pride blocks the learning process.

If a person does not bring a clean spirit, they prolong the suffering of those searching for relief arriving at the *centro* for help with a *causa*. This prolongation of suffering can occur when a godchild is inexperienced. Well-intentioned godchildren, who have not been properly taught the working of a *causa*, can contribute to the spiritual overwhelming (*envolvimiento*) of an individual. Instead of curing, one could make a *causa* worse or place the person with a *causa* in an unnecessary and complicated trial. If the individual becomes spiritually overwhelmed, it could lead to insanity.

To prevent harmful occurrences during the services, there are two rules which a godchild must follow in helping to secure spiritual cleanliness. The first rule is that godchildren must work out their personal problems so they do not affect the working of *causas* during services. The second rule godchildren must learn is to keep their world balanced between the spiritual and the material.

The Belief System of the Godchildren

The godchildren in Stage III are in the semiperiphery of the *centro.*
They are informed that they have to forget personal problems at the
door of the *centro.* They are taught to put their material and emotional
problems aside. In that manner, with a clear mind, they can learn from
what the mediums do at the table. The *centro* is like a school to the
godchildren because one learns from the Godfather. The godchildren
are searching for a way to learn about the spirits, as well as for their own
spiritual enlightenment and development.

It is to the godchild's advantage to pray and perform duties in the
spiritual arena. It is only through the process of involving oneself in
spiritual duties that one can secure success. The spirits and saints ask for
proof of the godchild's belief. If the godchild proves his belief through
the rituals, then, when going through the trials, he or she will be
protected. Each trial the godchild goes through helps the godchild's
spirits go further up the hierarchy. In turn, they help the godchildren's
protectors and guides become stronger.

One godchild says she failed to develop an understanding of the
spirits because she was not able to find a Godfather willing to teach her.
She felt she had wasted a lot of time because she could not work the
spirits of the dead. But this trial of not finding a Spiritist teacher was
more material in origin than spiritual. A *centro* must be a school. If not,
there is a material problem. If it is not a school, learning does not occur
and the spirits cannot be enlightened by the godchildren. The material
problem is usually jealousy.

The Godmother says that a *centro* has to have power to attract
people. Training is needed to develop power. Through training, the
godchildren understand their rituals and develop their powers which
were initially unknown even to themselves.

The Guardian Angel and Instructions

It is important that the Guardian Angel be developed and his powers
used to secure the spiritual development of each godchild. Faith in the
truth is essential for positive results because there are those who come to
the *centro* to ridicule what is going on. The godchildren waste their

time when they work these types of *causas* because they are filled with falseness.

One must guard against converting material problems into spiritual problems. The Guardian Angle is the entity that helps distinguish the differences between spirits. It is also one's protector while in the world of the dead. More importantly, one must be taught how not to confuse the two. A godchild says, "The spiritual is something you have to be very careful with." The godchild learns to trust spirits that appear at the right side of someone needing a *causa* worked, and the Guardian Angle is used for this purpose.

Roman Catholic Saints

The *centro* emphasizes the importance of one's knowing the saints' days and the manner in which saints manifest (*montar*) themselves during possession in mediums. Godchildren are expected to distinguish the saints by the different physical sensations during possession. The most distinguishing aspect of possession by saints is through identification with a given saint's life. When asked about the saints, the godchildren feel they have always been interested in the lives of the saints. They enjoy reading about the saints and many feel the lives of the saints are important in understanding the saints' role in Spiritism (Spirituism). The Catholic saints become symbolic models and are called interchangeably by their names from Yorubaland, e.g., Changó, or their Roman Catholic equivalent, e.g., Santa Barbara. By understanding the saints, one can better serve people with *causas*. It is the saints' manifestation as highly evolved spirits that inform an individual of how well he or she has been working *causas*. The Godfather hands out biographies of saints. These biographies detail professions as well as which type of *causas* occupy a particular saint's interest. The Godfather discusses the physical manifestations that belong to the different saints. The biographies also contain the feast days for each of the saints as listed in Catholic calendars.

The godchildren feel more comfortable in places where there are saints because they sense "good vibrations," unlike in Spiritist centers where there are no saints. One godchild feels better when she goes to a Spiritist (Spiritualist) service than when she goes to a mass at a Roman

Catholic Church. She feels better because in Spiritism (Spiritualism) one has to pay attention to learn. In the Roman Catholic Church, "you just attend a mass." In the Roman Catholic Church all that occurs is the praising of God, which she can do at home.

All the godchildren feel the Roman Catholic Church is important in their lives. Unlike the Roman Catholic Church, which does not view Spiritualism as a religion, the godchildren do view Spiritualism as a religion. They find no contradiction between the Roman Catholic Church, its saints and their own belief in God, the Seven African Powers, and the manner in which spiritualists empower the saints. The religious beliefs of the Church of Rome and Spiritualism are viewed as similar and Rome's rejection a trial of one's faith in the world of the dead.

ENDNOTES

1   This means that she was born to work the spirits of the dead.

2   The Afro-Latin community of Loiza Aldea on the northwest corner of Puerto Rico is a stronghold of African culture on the Island.

3   The impact of the "whitening process" in Puerto Rico can be seen by the fact that the patron saint of Loiza Aldea, the stronghold of African culture, is Saint James, The Moor Killer (*Santiago Mata Moro*). In the Hispanic Caribbean, blacks are called *Morenos*.

CHAPTER VI

Stage IV: From Godchild to Practicing Medium

The Core

What is a *causa* and how is it divined? This chapter explains the feelings involved in sensing the spirits of the dead. Spirits penetrate the body, but only after one has developed faculties and insured the development of guides. It is difficult to control these penetrating spirits. The spirits come in different temperatures and the mediums can sense their presence. One must sense these spirits through the spiritual eye and learn to listen to one's spiritual protectors. But one's personal life can block everything on the path to spiritual development. The Gods (Saints) must be fed ritually. Women are at the forefront of helping because men are selfish and materially oriented. But, the *Centro* can be outgrown by a well developed medium and she may be forced to establish her own *Centro*.

Altagracia is a 37 - year - old Puerto Rican woman with two teen-age sons and a four - year - old daughter. She is the Principal Head Medium to the Godfather and sits at his right hand at the table. Altagracia speaks:

I have been in the United States since I was three years old. When we came here my mother was very young, my sister was a year and a half old, and my brother was four months old. My mother never put us into the position of having to attend Catholic Church. She told us as long as we had faith in God, that's what mattered. She still tells us the same thing. As long as we have faith in God and love for God, He would help us. She told us to be good children, parents, and men and women. As she saw it, the person who was a good son would be a good father and would be a good husband. Then God would insure their success.

My Sister and I follow the same spiritual path since we both started in Spiritism at the same time, when we were young. My sister later withdrew from Spiritism because of some fears she had developed. She has always been a very quiet and reserved person, even as a youngster.

In my house everyone believed in Spiritism. My father, my mother, their parents before them. Everybody on both sides of the family. They all believed in it but no one really got into it. They would go to certain places if something wasn't right according to them. But none of them ever became as involved in this in the same manner that I have. Especially my mother who never wanted to go to *centros*.

My father was the one who wanted to go to *centros* or *templos*. All you had to tell him was where there was a good spiritual meeting and he would go see what the place was like. He used to go to *centros* even when he was a young man. Although he was born to be a medium, he never really developed it.

I was 15 when my father first took me to a *centro*. At that time all I would do was giggle during the services. Then I would start laughing out loud because I felt funny all over. I would start to scream. Then I would start to cry. I would not want to be at the *centro*. When I wanted to leave the *centro*, my father would force me to stay because he wanted me to know what was going on. According to the Spiritist (Spiritualist) I had something dragging my development down. The Spiritist (Spiritualist) said that he could help me and they started to spiritually work on me for a month or two.

I started to feel spiritual currents (*fluidos*) after the Spiritist (Spiritualist) worked on me. I noticed that when the Spiritist (Spiritualist) took my hands, or when the Spiritist (Spiritualist) took his bandanna and hit me, that I would feel as if I wanted to dance. I wanted to jump up and down. About two months later I started to sense my first spiritual guides. But I couldn't speak in tongues, so my father gave me lessons in the house by first praying to the saints. Later he just told me to speak in tongues. My father would ask the spirits what they wanted from me so that they could help me speak in tongues. In this way they helped me move forward spiritually.

After about six months in the *centro*, I turned 16 years of age. So after six months I was sat down at the table for the first time to work *causas* as an apprentice. I was at that *centro* for another year after I worked that first *causa*.

We moved out of Brooklyn and into the Bronx. In the Bronx my father and I went to another *centro*. He and the Spiritist (Spiritualist) had been raised together in the same town in Puerto Rico. There I continued my development. He would give me instructions on how to establish communication with the spirit guides. He would explain what I was supposed to feel. Little by little I would learn to distinguish the different types of currents representing the guides. I also learned which guide's currents belonged to a person's *causa*.

The problem remained one of securing the proofs (*evidencias*) that went with the *causa*. I practiced in the house. I spoke to the saints and lit my candles. I would go to the *centro* three times a week with my father until the Spiritist (Spiritualist) couldn't open the *centro* any longer because he was returning to Puerto Rico. I was forced into spiritual withdrawal.

A while later my father found another *centro*, but I didn't like what I saw going on there. I started looking for a *centro* for myself. I was about 17 then. I went to another *centro* and the Spiritist (Spiritualist) became a friend of mine. She is now the Godmother (through Roman Catholic baptism) of one of my children. I went to her and she helped me by explaining the different things about Spiritism. It was more or less what I had already learned, with some new insights. I continued as her helper for several years until she moved away.

About the same time my father returned to Puerto Rico. My father started our development into Spiritism in the family and things were no longer taking place as they used to. Before he left, he used to hold prayer meetings in the house in which we all participated. We would all sit and pray, brothers, sisters, my mother, and some aunts.

Although my mother was a Catholic, she believed some things in Spiritism because she would tell us that there were people that were into doing evil to others just for the hell of it. Some people use Spiritism (Spiritualism) to frighten-people by saying "you give me this or else." Which means they are going to do some sorcery (*brujería*) to you if you don't give them something material. The spiritual blessing is something that has to be given because it is granted to you by the saints. When the saints feel you are ready, they will give you something you want to achieve. It does not come when you want it, but when the saints feel like giving it to you. You have to go through a lot of trials.

I realized that I had to keep myself spiritually clean. The many *centros* that we went to didn't do much for us. If we went for a consultation, the first thing the Spiritist would tell me is that I could help him more than he could help me. Often they wouldn't see me for a consultation and would tell me, "I can't help you!" I sensed that there was something interfering because I could see it in my dreams.

I didn't return to a *centro* for another three years. I began to notice that when I did go to a *centro* there was something odd occurring in me. But I had no help from a Spiritist to help me figure out what was bothering me. Upon my arrival at some *centros*, they would recognize me as spiritually developed and would sit me at the table. They said that I was a very good medium. I would go once and the next time they would sit me at the table to work the spirits. But they would do this without understanding if I had any *causas* nor did they know what I was about.

They would tell me that something had happened to me that kept me strong enough to deal with these problems. Nothing had happened, but I was concerned. Sometimes spirits would present themselves and hit me because my protectors weren't developed. I allowed these things to further knock down my ability to protect myself.

I was never prepared spiritually nor was I ever told how to build protectors. I was not told if I was in need of herbal baths. The things that I did, I did them myself in my house. I was able to do it because I have always had an altar. I would light my candles and I would pray to the saints to help me understand what was going on around me. The saints would give prescriptions for baths. It was the only way to ensure protection. I would also build protection for my family.

I had to work hard as if I were a man. I needed jobs to support my kids. I didn't have anybody's aid. I finally met up with a man who seemed to show that I could have some peace of mind and possibly some fulfillment in the future. It turned out that he had more problems than me.

I need patience just to deal with my husband and his spiritual problems. I don't know if I could last a lifetime with him because of his kids and his former wife. I can't deal with it. The saints haven't told me any different, nor have they told me that our marriage will break up. So I have to keep holding on and taking what has to come and be calm. I have to pray to God that I get what I want. But, as I have already informed the Godfather, it is patience I need which is taking me years to get hold of.

My husband is not one that will go to the *centros*, but once his daughter starts, there may be problems. He doesn't believe. As a joke, I tell him to be careful what he thinks since he has two witches in the house: me and his daughter. He just looks at me from top to bottom. But he doesn't say anything because I have explained it to him, that his daughter comes to practice the same thing that I do.

In 1976 I had an accident on the job. I fell down the stairs and hurt myself. After that I had to spend more time at home. I couldn't go out anywhere. I began to notice things in my apartment which I felt weren't very good. Right there and then, I wanted to go to the *centro*. But I didn't know of one. I needed to go somewhere where someone could tell me what was going on and what I was spiritually good for. Since I couldn't find any place, I just continued treating myself at home. I would say prayers and go to church. I would speak to my spirit guides to provide me with help while I lit my candles.

My mother-in-law called me one August and told me that she had heard of a good *centro* and that the Spiritist (Spiritualist) who ran it was very nice. But she was concerned about going alone and she wanted me to go with her. That's how I found this *centro*. When I arrived, I entered the consultation room and the Godfather recognized my spiritual powers immediately. He recognized that I had certain works (sorcery) aimed at my being. These *causas* were created to prevent my spiritual advancement. In one case, a *causa* had been developed aimed at having me do away with my own life.

The confirmation of what he was saying had already occurred to me in a dream. I saw myself running down the street naked. I saw myself crazy. I did feel at first that I was asleep and he confirmed that too. He told me that I should increase my attendance at the *centro*.

But I couldn't find anyone to go to the *centro* with me. I didn't feel safe going at night by myself to the *centro*. I was living a long distance from the *centro* and I had to take a bus through many areas. I wanted someone to go with me, even if it was only to accompany me. My mother-in-law only wanted a consultation and didn't return. Neither my brother nor my sister wanted to go with me.

Some time later, my father-in-law decided to go to the *centro* on a regular basis. Then one of my sister-in-laws said that she would like to go to the *centro*. She had been to many *centros* and this one she liked. I started getting rides to the *centro* with them. We all liked the manner in which the sessions were conducted at the *centro* and the manner in which they worked the spirits and *causas*. I thought then that I would love this place. Later, my sister needed a consultation because of a series of conflicts in her marriage, which later ended in her divorce.

There weren't many *causas* worked at that time since only four mediums worked the table. The Godfather was the fifth person at the table. There were many people who came to the *centro*, many who at some point had worked the table themselves.

But many of them were involved in other things that weren't really Spiritism (Spiritualism). They truly don't carry Spiritism (Spiritualism) for a clean purpose. They don't take it the way they are supposed to. The saints do not give people permission to use them for those types of works (sorcery). If people do these things, they become spiritually consumed (*envuelto*) and more problems evolve in their spiritual existence.

That was what was happening to me. Things were being done that weren't for the good or in the true Spiritist sense. The Godfather confirmed this for me when he helped me recall a dream in which I saw my own burial and everything. He was not very pleased that I wasn't working the table because I had been born on this earth for that purpose. But he said that he would give a helping hand. His feeling was, since I had started working the table from youth, there should be no reason for my staying away from working the table. I was given a consultation, my sister-in-law was given a consultation and later, my sister was given a consultation.

My sister and I would go to the *centro*. We started going regularly. We were part of the public and it took about a month and a half before they worked my first *causa*. I later received certain herbal baths especially made for me. I was also given some herbal water to cleanse the house of malicious spirits.

My first *causa* the Godfather took care of by spiritual cleansing. But later, because I was having problems conceiving, they told me that my next *causa* had to be worked through a spiritual operation of my womb.

Back in 1971, physicians wanted to operate on me because they had found a series of stains in my womb. Further, the womb would get swollen as if I were pregnant, but I was not pregnant. The physicians couldn't explain it. I was a woman who was young and generally in good health. It was difficult for the physicians to explain. I looked like I could have at least 20 children. They ended up giving me about 100 pills to help me conceive but nothing would happen. I could not conceive and the swelling wouldn't go down either.

Six years later, I submitted to a spiritual operation here at the *centro*. So there I was in the *centro*, and I had to get a spiritual operation. I needed those things in my womb taken out now since they had already worked my first *causa*. After the operation, the Godfather informed me, because of the strength of my faith in Spiritism, and because of the time I had already spent in Spiritism, that the saints had requested I be sat at the table. Therefore, the saints asked that I be baptized. The Godfather's saints thought I would be a very good medium. I had the interest and the faith.

For many people at the *centro* it was strange because I was new and they didn't know me. They didn't understand that I had arrived with many years of practice in Spiritism. Also, I had already worked the dead. I was not just starting and they didn't understand how the saints could want me at the table before I was baptized. But before I had sat down, I had already been spiritually cleansed (*de-*

spojada). Several months later I was baptized together with my sister.

I wasn't immediately put at the front of the table as the Principal Head Medium. That was a good sign. I had to work my way up. I felt it was the first time since I was 15 that someone took interest to see what was stopping my development. In other words, the Godfather said, "Let's see what you're dragging behind you that's not letting you go forward."

The Godfather explained what they had already told us at other *centros* - that our situation was due to our family's spiritual chain. In this chain, our entire family has come to work the table. They didn't put my sister to work the table at first. She was a godchild for a while before she worked the table. Those not at the table are the godchildren, while those at the table are mediums.

By the time my sister and I were baptized I was already pregnant and had it confirmed by the Godfather during a consultation. He checked me out in the consultation room and told me there was a pregnancy on the way. The Saint Virgin of Mercedes was providing me with a blessing. So that by the time I was baptized, I was already pregnant.

People that come to Spiritism must come with faith and love. That's when it is possible to advance. And that's what makes possible people getting something they want. But without faith and love, they fall behind and their condition deteriorates.

There is only one way to advance and that is through the development of the ability to detail proofs (*evidencia*). The harder you work at developing your spiritual guides and protectors, the greater the number of proofs you can give as a medium. The protectors and guides must be satisfied at home so that you can use them to help you at the *centro*. In this manner one begins to find out what is in the individual *causas*.

The godchild who wants to become a medium must want to be taught. The spiritual guides must be developed and later the protectors have to be developed. That's another spiritual level. After a while you can arrive at the point where you can sit at the table. Then you have the programs at the table by relieving *causas*. After a while you can begin to work the dead.

Working the dead is another step that has to be taken. Many mediums are afraid of letting the dead pass through them. This fear itself can make a medium regress. If this fear is not dealt with, they then begin to establish blocks (*cruces*) at the table. What they have done is block their protectors, preventing their continued work. It is a fear they put into their minds often unconsciously while in the spiritual arena.

This unconscious fear is the same one that makes people fall out of the Spiritist community. While working the dead, they've created a block. This prevents the individual medium from concentrating on her own development, and prevents the development of spiritual protection. Consequently, this prevents the medium's body from being taken over by the dead. Sometimes the medium is rolling on the floor; that's caused by an inability to control the dead through the medium's protectors.

There are many trials for the godchildren, and many see it through to the end. They themselves develop the distance if they cannot deal with their trials. Maybe you can tell after people are baptized which ones are going to develop distance from the *centro*. But you can also tell by their love, faith, and the enthusiasm with which they arrive at the *centro* who is really going to succeed.

One can tell which godchildren are taking this seriously by the manner in which they are willing to sit at the front and say their proofs of *causas*. One has to also notice how serious the godchildren take the consultations. It is during the consultations that the Godfather understands if the godchild is lighting his candles. Also, that's when he understands if they are putting offerings on their altars for the saints, especially those saints whom they want to attract to themselves as enlightened spirits of the dead. Those who are serious go to the Godfather regularly for consultations and continue moving forward from apprentice mediums.

One has to listen to what the Godfather says. When you have your protectors, they let you know when something isn't right. Further, these protectors not only let you know that something isn't right, they also tell you what to do. When I see things I can't handle, I immediately go for a consultation and check out what is happening. The Godfather sits down and explains what is going down. He explains what has to be done and I say, "Let's get to it".

Once things are explained, you cannot have doubts. Once you have doubts, it closes you off from a solution. If you start to think why is this happening to you, then you start to blame the saints, the protectors, and the guides. If you blame them, especially if you've been working the spirits, you have closed yourself off from the help they can offer.

These things have to be explained in sessions to the godchildren. Usually the Head Mediums and an auxiliary medium have to explain things while the Godfather listens. We explain the importance of baptism to the godchildren who are going to be baptized. It is something sacred. It is not something that you can fool around with. Those wanting to become godchildren better make damn sure this is a step they want to take because it is not an easy road.

Once a godchild, you have to ask permission of the saints before leaving your home to go to the *centro*. You must pray before leaving the *centro*. The problem is that upon your arrival you must be protected. There are all those people present and they bring with them all sorts of spiritual things to the godchildren, so we are prepared to deal with it correctly from the time we leave our homes. He explains these things especially to the new people.

Part of the instructions to the godchildren has to do with how to secure correct spiritual preparation. People have to be taught how to prepare those things which protect them. They should never just put on their necklaces (beads) and run out the door to the *centro*. Something could happen as they come through the door. My Guardian Angel wouldn't be prepared to enter the door and it couldn't protect me.

My sister, the left Head Medium, her specialty is spiritual operations. She loves them and that's what she has come to do at the table. Prior to coming to this *centro*, she wasn't very good because she had some fear about spirits. But little, by little, at these meetings with the Godfather, he explained those things we have to do at the table. He also told us what can be done and what cannot be done. Little by little, people come to understand what is allowed.

You see, not everyone can become a godchild because it is like everything else in Spiritism (Spiritualism). Everyone comes to a certain point, but not everyone comes to deal with the dead directly. And not everyone comes to cure (*curanderia*). It all depends on the individual person and her experiences. It is later, after consultations with the person, that one comes to understand what saints an individual brings with him. If the Godfather's saints ask that this person be baptized, and if the person agrees, the person is given necklaces. Then later they are taught how to develop their protectors.

My sister is an example of someone who had to develop little by little. She had to make herself feel more comfortable in the chairs where the godchildren are located, and later at the table. She continued to learn until she was no longer an auxiliary medium. She continued growing until she wasn't afraid.

They started her process a little slower than they did mine, but once they saw that her guides were developing they helped her develop her ability to give proofs. She was showing interest and faith. This kept helping her. She was raising herself more into the area of Spiritism (Spiritualism). All this took place a few months after being baptized.

They sat her down at the table for the first time, even though they knew she was still afraid, because they felt she had faith. After sitting at the table for the first time, because she couldn't resist it, she was placed at the table every time she came to the *centro*. Her initial fear was due to her concern that she hadn't really come to work the table and speak with the spirits.

Here the situation for her was good because they would explain things to her. And with those instructions she could get an understanding that there was no need for fear because she was at the *centro* to do this same thing that I was doing. She was as involved in this as I was. Just like me and my brother, she had arrived to work this, and she couldn't do anything about it. She had to continue that family path. Once she cleared her own path, she could help others clear theirs. She would eventually be able to help those who were in worse condition than she.

My sister had once before started to work with spirits, but had abandoned it completely. This happened when she was younger. She was so afraid of it she couldn't stand it. She had developed resistance over the years that she had to work out of her system.   So when she started, they had to work the *causas* that were causing resistance on her part.

I have never developed a resistance to the spiritual world. For me, it was different.   I developed two specialties.   One is, I have come to work the dead (*muertera*) and the other is I have come to do curing (*curandería*).   I am between these two, but mostly, I have come to work the dead.   The other Head Medium is here for the same thing that I am here for.   But my sister, she focuses more on curing through spiritual operations.   The mediums give instructions to the godchildren on how to determine what it is they have come to work.

People who don't develop, create blocks (*cruces*) for the spiritual development of everyone at the *centro*.   But this is unconscious.   Sometimes people arrive at the *centro* to purposely create blocks that prevent the mediums and the Godfather from helping individuals with their *causas*.   In this manner, they have created blocks that are intended to prove the Godfather a liar.   This happens in front of the people at the *centro* so that the *centro* can be destroyed through distrust.   He would then have to close the *centro*. But if one has been preparing the protectors, then there is no reason to fear because the protectors will hit the individual and knock him to the ground, especially if he is a sorcerer (*brujo*).

The blocks have to be prevented because there are many people who come with faith to the *centro*.   They are looking for help and the Spiritist (Spiritualist) must be ready to provide that help.   Then there are many who cause unconscious blocks because they are interested only in getting the winning number.   Some come to attempt to control their husbands so that things will be cool at home.   There are a lot of blocks; some are mental.   Then there are those that arrive to create the downfall of the *centro*.   There are many who cannot stand the Godfather and work to see his downfall.

Sometimes we have sorcerers who come to the centro. They block those things being worked at the *centro*.   They block the medium's guides and the protectors.   The Godfather has protectors whom he leaves by the door as guards. When the sorcerers enter, that's who they first come into contact with and it weakens them.

These sorcerers are more interested in knocking the *centro* down; in tearing the Godfather down; in tearing everything down. They are also interested in creating the downfall of the mediums because people are envious.

People come to the *centro* and see the way things are done here. They like the way the mediums work the *causas*. They like the Godfather's protectors because they like the way he works their *causas*. The sorcerers think that by doing certain things they can spiritually undermine him by taking away those powers he has. When they arrive, they come to insult him and to do him harm.

My husband is very afraid of these spiritual things. I asked him to accompany me here once for Santa Barbara's feast some time in December. That man left the *centro* crazy. He had a headache and a half. He has powers. He comes to work this also. Yet, with all they have thrown at him (sorcery), he doesn't want to acknowledge the fact that he should be working the spirits. He told me he doesn't want to get involved in it. He doesn't say anything else. He is outside of it, and as long as he is not in it, he doesn't give a damn. He just doesn't want to be bothered with it.

That's a common way for men to relate to this. In general, men take longer to get themselves involved in Spiritism. Men, they understand, but they are involved at the *centro* in other ways than are women. The men are best at guarding the door and guarding the mediums to make sure they don't fall backward during trance (spirit possession). All the men who have been baptized have not been sat down at the table. The Godfather tries to sit men at the table, but only when the saints order it. It also depends on who then gets seated where at the table. He tries to sit them down in a certain seat on a given day. People are seated at the table so they can continue to give their proofs and in that way continue forward. They can take further steps into mediumship.

My brother started when he was small, at the same time I did. At the sessions my father used to give at the house, my brother, as small as he was, would give proofs. He was 9 or 10 years old when I saw this. Even after I was married, he would go with me to the temples (*centros*). He would sit there and tell me what he was seeing. He would tell me that person has this type of *causa*. But he never really wanted to get involved in it all the way.

My brother has gone through much turmoil and many trials. This happens because he has arrived on this earth to work the table and he refuses. He still has his doubts about Spiritism. It is not like you do it or you just don't do it. It does not work like that. You have to have love of God and resignation. You must be at peace with yourself, and you have to know how to deal with Spiritism [Spiritualism] to keep up. Otherwise, the saints will have your head.

I explain it that way to my children. They have to pray before going to bed. They have to give thanks to God they are alive and they have to thank God they can eat, walk, and hear.

School is good, but it is different. Up until now, school has not interfered with their belief in Spiritism (Spiritualism), even though they are in Catholic school. Two of them are in Catholic school, the eldest in Catholic high school. A problem has come up because of gym class. The older son wears his beaded necklaces and the Hispanics goof on him, calling him a sorcerer. At the beginning he would get angry.

So, to avoid a fight, he decided not to wear his beads to school on the days that he has to go to gym. The nuns and priests have said nothing. And he has the saints' permission to leave the beads at home. He puts them on top of his saint. The rest of the week, he wears his beads to school.

I suppose one day they may call me into school, because if they see the necklaces (beads) on him they may send for me and talk to me about it. I might have to take the two of them out of school. You know the Catholic Church doesn't believe in this, although the Godfather does tell people to believe and go to the Catholic Church.

I carry the necklaces with me at all times. I explain it to my children. And I ask them to tell me if they think that I am evil. I ask them if they believe in what I am doing, and I ask them if they see me as a sorcerer. The older one looks at me and says he believes what I am doing is good. I tell them I am taking them through the same path I took. I tell them I arrived to work the table and I have been doing it. And I tell them they have come to do the same thing, all three of them. No matter what spiritual line they come to work, such as curing or working the dead, they have come to work the table.

I want to give my children an understanding of this from the present moment. In this manner, they can see what they have and what they are going to do. If they adapt themselves to it now, they won't be bothered, especially my older son. If someone were to call him a sorcerer, he is to continue walking and keep his mouth shut.

I take my older son to the *centro* because he is ahead of my other two kids. I take him so he can see what I am doing. This way, he wonders what I am doing and begins to ask me questions. I explain what I am doing at the *centro*.

I cannot keep my son up late at the *centro* because he has to be up early to get to school since the school is a distance from the house. So when school is in session, I don't bother him. But once school is out in the summer, then I have him come with me to the *centro*. Maybe I end up taking him to the *centro* about once a month during the academic year.

I teach them at home to respect the power of the saints. I teach them to knock their knees together three times as they enter school so Elegguá will remove obstacles in front of them. In this manner, Elegguá is called to guard them by moving them or removing the obstacle.

I am concerned with youth because they are not taught to have faith. At least in Catholic schools they receive a Christian education. There, they learn to love God and understand what He means. They receive a spiritual teaching from me, and then they receive understanding of faith from the Catholic school. I hope with these two influences, when they take their own paths, at least the fundamentals will remain with them. They are taught a love of God, and that those willing to do harm exist.

They understand, by doing charitable work and being good Christians, they are being humanitarians. They have already taken a concrete step in the right direction. Check it out. My kids are all baptized in the Catholic church. The two boys have had their Holy Communion and their Confirmation. I hope the girl will follow the same steps and the path into Spiritism (Spiritualism).

I do not allow my husband to interfere with my daughter's spiritual development. She will be sent to Catholic school. Kids need that because of the way this generation is today. In the teaching of Spiritism (Spiritualism) to my daughter, my husband is not going to get involved.

Now my daughter is imitating me. She will continue imitating me until she is about five. She will begin to understand a little better once she is older. She will begin to understand what I am doing when we are here praying alone in the house.

She already speaks to the saints in a manner that is similar to the way I speak to them. She does the same thing I do; that already is a form of instruction. But true instructions will have to wait until she understands what is good and bad. I have begun to teach her the meaning of those things that she brings with her, because of the family chain. Once she understands this, then she will truly take her first steps. Then it will be time to ensure she continually gets to the *centro*.

My father says that I am the man and the woman of the family. I can always be counted on. Being a woman and having been sick often in my life has taught me to keep pushing, to keep going. Because of this, I have had to push others in my family, especially my father. So now he says I am the bitch in the family, but he doesn't mean it. That's his term because that's the way he is, and he can count on me. He introduces me by saying, "This is the older of my daughters and she is the bitch of the house."

After baptism the new godchildren in Stage IV are apprentice Mediums. They are refining the spiritual powers they have been granted. One godchild said that as an apprentice medium, she was given peace of mind. It is now the godchild's turn to provide peace of mind to others by working on *causas*, and they do this by becoming mediums. They get a feeling of helping out the members of the public by sitting at the table as diviners. Further, by helping out the members of the public with their *causas*, the mediums are learning about their errors and how one problem can lead to another, complicating one's spiritual life.

In order to advance from an apprentice medium to an auxiliary and finally to Head Medium, one must be capable of communicating with highly evolved and enlightened spirits and saints at home as well as in the *centro*.   An apprentice medium who remains afraid to speak to the saints and the spirits in her home will not progress to the next level of divining *causas*, but will remain as a godchild.   Often the apprentice will feel that the atmosphere at the *centro* is more conducive to communicating with spirits and saints.   Apprentices feel safe in the *centro*, much safer than at home.

At home, they start by sitting at their altars and praying for guidance and comfort.   They speak to the saints and spirits.   They sense their presence and at the same time fear their presence.   The auxiliary mediums reassure the apprentices, informing them that they should not worry because their protectors are developing.

Most apprentice mediums also fear working the spirits of people they do not know at the *centro*.   They often feel they are publicly meddling in people's personal affairs.   The Godmother will attempt, in every way possible, to prevent "tragedies" from occurring by circulating in the crowd and watching for disgruntled husbands.   Mediums working *causas* publicly at the *centro* are cautious because they fear that intimate personal *causas*, once revealed, can cause a family tragedy.   Spiritual cleanliness helps a medium in sensing when it is correct to speak openly about the personal problems contributing to a *causa*.   The mediums, not wanting to be confronted by an angry husband who might be sitting in the congregation, will often request that the person with the *causa* return for a consultation.   (The Godmother says there are things one must keep one's mouth shut about or risk getting "your block knocked off; you know when to shut up!")

Situations where there is a fear of speaking up about a *causa* complicate the spiritual work of the mediums because they begin to focus their attention on material concerns instead of the spiritual *causa* needing work.

One can tell which mediums are the better ones by how relaxed they are during the period of preparation for spiritual meditation.   Only through their ability to relax are the mediums capable of securing the transmission of their thoughts (*transmición de pensamiento*) to the spirit world, and it is only through the transmission of thought during spirit possession that a medium establishes enlightened spirit communication.

Enlightened spirits make themselves known in various ways.   Noises are often heard while in possession, during an unconscious state, and these signs help the medium understand that the spirit is going to help her in working a *causa*.

An apprentice is taught that there are two types of things a medium must be capable of doing while in spirit possession. First, she must be capable of sensing the physical aspects of the *causa*. Second, she must have the ability to see the details of a *causa's* origin. If the medium senses pain or swelling, this *causa* has something to do with pain or swelling. Then she describes what the source of the *causa* can be and what type of person is responsible for its development.

"The first is 'out there,' while the second is what was done to that person to create the *causa*," explains an auxiliary. In other words, the second action is getting to the source of the *causa* in a "more heavy" manner than just saying that the person's eyes itch or she has back pain. The ultimate step in being a medium is to see more than one feels, to see what created the *causa* in the first place.

Mediums are unconscious of what they are saying. All they remember is the point prior to the spirit's guide entering their bodies. The mediums learn about the backgrounds of the persons with the *causas* once they are in spirit possession. The guides are especially important because of the signals the mediums receive from them. They see spirits around a person with a *causa* and how the spirits badger him. These spirits inform the medium about the *causa*.

The mediums can distinguish the different problems they encounter as part of a *causa* by sensing cold, heat, nervousness, depression, and tension during spirit possession. This helps them ask individuals with *causas* whether they have the same feelings as the mediums.

To work a *causa*, it is important that the guides (*guias*) are fully developed since it is only through the development of these spiritual guides that one can work the *causas* without creating blocks. It is a matter of helping the spirit guides so they can help the medium.

Faculties and Guides

The development of guides is different from the development of the faculties (*facultades*) used to communicate with the spirit world. Faculties are a sensitivity to the spirit world usually recognized in childhood.   It is strengthened by teachings from relatives who believe. These faculties help individuals become aware of sensitivity to spirit guides.   Later one must decipher the difference between spirit guides and spirit protectors.   Spirit protectors guarantee that mediums are spiritually secure when working *causas*.   It takes an indefinite period of time to secure that the spirit guides take over one's body and at the same time insure the protectors.   Distinguishing the difference is a difficult process.

One can sense the manner in which the stronger guides start taking over the body.   In the meantime, one has to develop spirit protectors which can be saints or spirits from the upper levels of the hierarchy. Guides do not cause harm if one is sure of one's belief in spirits; otherwise, if one has second thoughts, there is a warning against in-volvement with guides.

The Guardian Angel develops, along with the guides and protectors, to aid and safeguard one's movement in Spiritism. One must pray to the Guardian Angel to keep one's safety in mind as one focuses on the malicious spirits in an individual with a *causa*. Once a person becomes a medium, withdrawal from the work of the spirits becomes difficult. There are signs if one's development begins to cease.   There are pains, headaches, and psychological problems.   Malicious spirits begin to take over the medium's material existence, as the protectors lose their power and the Guardian Angel is no longer gathering strength.

Spiritism (Spiritualism) provides trials that "shake" the spiritual be-liefs of individuals.   Spiritism (Spiritualism) is so powerful, according to the Head Medium, that one must be ready to forbear the harsh trials. One must attach importance to these trials and learn patience because these trials are aimed at creating doubts in the belief, and work against spiritual growth.

Transmission of thought helps the mediums develop their communi-cation skills with spirits of enlightenment; otherwise they could be closed out of the spirit world during possession. Thus, the session of spiritual meditation during the services becomes necessary for transmis-sion of thought. The entire congregation (the public, associates, the godchildren and the mediums) is involved, thereby insuring transmis-sion of thought by the mediums.   Spirits of enlightenment, besides being contacted by transmission of thought, help the mediums to keep in touch with the *centro* even when absent. Consequently, when a medium is sick and is spending several days in the hospital, she can communicate with the activities going on in the *centro* through her ability to transmit her thoughts. An apprentice medium and an auxiliary medium both were absent and saw themselves at the *centro*, as if they were actually participating. Even though the apprentice medium was home ill and the auxiliary medium was hospitalized, they both experienced the services from afar through their transmission of thought. Their presence was also felt by the mediums at the *centro* although they both weren't physically present at the *centro*.

The working of a *causa* is viewed as a form of charity. Performing charitable works is important to the development of the medium's spirits. The more *causas* a medium works the greater the possibility that the medium's spirits will not remain at the malicious level after her death. What makes the mediums' work charitable is that people do not respect the importance of communication with the world of the dead. Because the mediums respect the spirits of the dead by working *causas*, their own spirits surpass the malicious level by developing insight into what retards spirit evolution. The lack of respect for the medium's work, combined with working the *causas* of unappreciative individuals, are the preconditions for securing that one's spirit will be enlightened, experienced, and brought out of darkness.

Often people with *causas* do not thank the mediums for their work, but the mediums cannot get angry because they will create blocks. The mediums must be trained to have patience, and to understand the charitable character of their work. It is crucial that the mediums not react with anger when they work *causas* that belong to the unappreciative, since their spiritual growth will be stagnated. This stagnation occurs through an accumulation of blocks. The development of blocks further establishes an inability to relieve *causas*. Blocks and poorly worked *causas* will in time turn into the medium's own *causa*. It is essential, therefore, that the medium understands that charity can sometimes go unrewarded and that blocks caused by a grudge against a person can lead to a medium developing an unwanted *causa*. If this *causa* goes untreated, it can spiritually consume the medium. If the medium is consumed by darkness, it will create a dangerous situation for the material and spiritual health of the medium. It will also endanger those at the table who work with the medium.

The Arrangement of the Mediums

An even number of mediums, usually eight, always work the table, otherwise six or four of the more practiced mediums work *causas*. If there are an insufficient number of the more practiced mediums (auxiliary & head mediums), then some godchildren are chosen to be apprentice mediums and sit at the far end of the table. This would then move an auxiliary into the position of head medium at the near end of the table closest to the altar. The spiritual hierarchy is always physically represented by the mediums at the table where the most practiced and enlightened mediums head communication with the spirit world.

There are always two Head Mediums present with the Principal Head Medium on the right-hand side and another on the left-hand side. There are two auxiliary mediums at the end of the table with four apprentice mediums, two on each side in the middle. The Godfather is the President of the table in the Spiritist tradition, coordinating the work of the mediums by advising them in the task of divining the causas brought to be relieved.

There are 18 godchildren, 4 of whom are chosen as practicing apprentice mediums. These four apprentice mediums are chosen just before the services begin. Of the godchildren, only those working the table are called mediums, while the term "godchild" is used to refer to anyone near the altar dressed in white, except the Godfather and Godmother. The Godmother always dresses in darker colors and stands to the sidelines. She is neither a godchild nor a medium. This *centro* considers it a block if husband and wife work the dead together. She is nevertheless always present safeguarding the Godfather's reputation, and hindering any rumor, especially about solicitous behavior toward women with *causas* during private consultations.

The mediums are ranked on the basis of experience and ability. It is while working the table that one can observe the differentiation among apprentice medium, auxiliary mediums, and head medium. This process of precise divining is practiced while the mediums are working *causas* from the public during spiritual meditation. The godchildren who are confident can whisper their divination to a Head Medium or can whisper them into the Godfather's ear. He will confirm or negate the Godchildren's divining of the spiritual *causa* by saying publicly "confirmed good soul" (*confirmada buen ser*). Sometimes when divining is correct, a godchild will be told, "that's correct," emphatically in English for all to hear. This encourages and reinforces the godchildren who are working to become apprentice mediums to speak out and attempt divining *causas*.

The Spirits of the Dead and *Causas*

The mediums must see by divining what created a *causa*, and tell the individual its origin. If the *causa* is created by sorcery, the medium must be capable of describing the sorcery in her spiritual mind's eye. The Head Mediums are distinguished by their ability to provide information as to where the object used in the sorcery can be located. A good medium must be capable of telling how the *causa* evolved, what was used in the sorcery to ensure its development, and where one can find or has found the object used in the sorcery. Oftentimes an individual with a *causa* has found it and was not aware it was sorcery.

One apprentice medium had to revert to godchild because she had not been progressing. She said she could feel the *causas*. She could sense the problem because she could feel the aches and pains. She could sense the spirits because she could feel the hot and cold sensations down her arms and neck. She could determine the affect of the *causa* on the individual, but she could not go beyond that to seeing the material origin of the *causa*. Hot and cold sensations are the distinguishing factors of spirits. People can sense the spirits even if they have never been involved in Spiritism. This is a result of a spiritual chain caused by dead loved ones. Some spirits do not wish to be recognized and enlightened. These spirits which do not want to be recognized are more difficult to work. Each medium can contribute in some way to a spirit's enlightenment, but what has to be determined is how a given medium can contribute at the *centro*.

One apprentice medium who regularly sits at the table says that when a member of the public begins to walk toward her, she can feel his or her *causa*. She says that at the point when someone walks up to the table, one begins to sense what the individual brings as a *causa*. She says "I can sense things and things start clicking." The preliminary feelings help her to start concentrating. After these initial feelings, she begins to sense as she enters a spirit possession whether she is doing a good job. She goes into spirit possession slowly, closing her eyes and becoming more involved as she provides proof of the *causa* affecting the individual.

Temperature Variations and The Spirits

Mediums must learn to distinguish the different spirits. There are spirits which arrive as traitors or are out to confuse the mediums. Spirits which arrive as hot sensations are felt to be spirits coming to confuse. Cold sensations come from spirits which bring a dead person's *causa*, through another individual, sometimes a relative, to be worked at the table. This *causa* is from a spirit in need of enlightenment and one which can betray the medium in her effort to work the *causa*. The medium can be confused while attempting spirit possession by sensing cold and falling victim to a betraying spirit, or by sensing hot and being confused. Only through experience can one learn to distinguish the spirits.

The mediums find most troublesome the feeling of cold spirits which are viewed as spirits of light and intelligence. The mediums feel that betraying spirits must be forced into enlightenment against their will. Cold spirits can also be out to confuse the medium's judgment.

The cooler a spirit, the greater the possibility the spirit is genuinely looking for enlightenment and will help in resolving a *causa*. The colder a spirit, the more likely it's bringing a *causa* to be worked that belongs to someone already dead. The hot spirits do not bring *causas* to the mediums to be worked.

These differences in temperatures are felt through variations in currents (*fluidos*). The faculties (*facultades*) to sense currents (*fluidos*) begins as trials (*pruebas*), often in childhood, which help in the development of mediums.

Keeping the Table Balanced

Keeping the table spiritually balanced requires the most powerful medium to be at the right-hand side of the President of the table, who is the Godfather. Under no circumstances are the mediums ever changed from the right side to the left side during services. Mediums are placed indefinitely on a given side of the table and tend to remain on that side.

If a change must be made, an auxiliary medium will become Head Medium, and the best one of the apprentice mediums will become an auxiliary medium. In other words, if a Head Medium is out for any reason an auxiliary medium becomes the Head Medium, while a more advanced apprentice medium temporarily experiences auxiliary mediumship.

From among the godchildren, one person who has shown spiritual development in the belief system is chosen to sit at the table as a temporary apprentice medium. It is rarely the apprentice medium's first time at the table since an endless stream of inexperienced mediums would create an inconsistency. Consistency is essential for positive results during spirit communication, and also reinforces the social hierarchy of the mediums.

All the mediums are ostensibly working their way up to the Godfather's place as President of the table. Those who prove themselves competent at spirit communication get to sit at the table. Those with the most enlightened spirits are the Head Mediums and are seated next to the Godfather. The three at the head of the table are considered the better spirit communicators. The Head Mediums have a family history of Spiritism.

Difficulties in Balancing

Once the left-hand Head Medium was absent because her husband would not allow her to leave the house for the *centro*. Her absence is highly unusual. There have been absences of mediums making it difficult to balance the table and causing the Godfather to reshuffle the seating several times before he was satisfied.

The Godfather walked around the room and looked at each of the godchildren. He asked one of the left auxiliary mediums to move to the

Photo #7. Medium in Spirit Possession

spot of the left-hand Head Medium.   He then was not sure which of the two apprentice mediums on the left he would place at the end as an auxiliary medium.   The problem is one of balancing the table so that material concerns, such as jealousy, do not develop among the mediums and negatively affect spirit communication.   If worldly concerns have developed, material forces would block the spiritual communication. This could endanger the services and the medium's spiritual growth.

Altagracia, the Head Medium to the right, and Frances, Head Medium to the left, have different styles of communicating with the spirits while working a *causa*.   Yet, they share certain similar mannerisms while speaking with the spirits of the dead.   They both attract an individual's attention with their body movements and by what they say while going into spirit possession.   Their movements are so intense that they startle the members of the public watching them work the *causa*.   Further, their emphatic hand gestures while going into spirit possession captures the attention of those having their *causas* worked.

The differences are more telling then are the similarities.   Frances, the Head Medium on the left side of the Godfather, begins spirit posses- sion by saying, "Look, look at what they are saying" (*Mira, mira lo que dicen*), which implies that the spirits are telling her something scandal- ous.   It also implies that immediate contact has been made by the medium with the spirit world and she is being informed about the *causa*. Moreover, at the same time she is speaking and swinging wildly in her chair, she is hitting the water-filled goblet with the palms of her hands. The public and godchildren are impressed with her ability to get right to the source of *causas*.

Altagracia on the right side is recognized as the best of the mediums because her method of securing an individual's attention while working a causa is highly physical.   She twists, whirling around from side to side, pounding on the water-filled goblet.   Everyone is surprised by the emotional energy she puts into working the *causa*.   Each person's *causa* when worked by her is seen as an extremely dangerous one.

Altagracia is respected because she gives the most detailed proofs. More importantly, she is articulate with spirits in English and Spanish and she knows how to communicate with the spirits by using the appropriate words to draw them from hiding.   She understands the *causa* and its treatment. Altagracia is capable of helping the rest of the mediums communicate because of the extensive number of protectors she carries. It is her power manifested through her 16 different saint protectors that makes her so important in spiritual communication.

Most of the time information about a person has to be cautiously detailed when working a *causa*. Often, when the Head Mediums feel a *causa* is sensitive, before anyone responds to the *causa*, the medium will speak into the Godfather's ear requesting a review of what she senses in an individual's *causa*.

If the Godfather feels it is an important question it is asked with care by the mediums since a jealous husband could be in the congregation. A jealous husband could create a very dangerous situation for a wife attempting to have her causa relieved. Altagracia has often gotten up from the table and approached someone with a *causa* and whispered a question into her ear. She has returned to the table and whispered the answer in the Godfather's ear while he shakes his head approvingly or disapprovingly. Individuals with complicated familial *causas* are often protected from what the Godmother feels could turn into a tragedy by airing it during services when the public is listening.

The medium must be ready to prevent a "tragedy" from developing because the dead have personal information about an individual's *causa*. The dead also tell the mediums the type of spirits "dragged" around by the individual causing his or her *causa* to accumulate malicious power. Handling information about the complications of a *causa* does not inhibit Altagracia. She feels she can handle *causas* without an incident developing among members of the public, unlike the apprentice mediums, she does not get nervous when dealing with *causas* that have to do with infidelity.

The important thing in being a medium is that one cannot have doubt in the spirit world. A person with doubts can be closed off from the spirit hierarchy. One must feel comfortable to speak out while in spirit possession about what one sees involved in a *causa* through the spiritual eye. At the same time, one must listen to the spiritual protectors which secure one's own development while relieving the *causas*. Listening to one's protectors allows the best means of dealing with the expressing an individual's *causa* in front of the public.

Altagracia had been thrown to the floor by her own powerful spirit which she had not sufficiently developed when she was an apprentice medium. She has not been thrown to the floor again by new developing spirits looking for enlightenment. She is nevertheless often in pain because of the intensity with which she works *causas*. Also, Altagracia can be attacked by malicious spirits sent by envious individuals to harm her because she is powerful. Her protectors must be strengthened through consultations with the Godfather for prayers and rituals at her altar to counteract these malicious spirits.

Altagracia says there is nothing to be feared in malicious spirits if one ritually gives candles, food, and prayers to the protectors and guides. At home one prepares the protectors and guides by lighting candles and providing foods which the saints and spirits demand. These foods give the spiritual protectors and spirit guides strength to safeguard the mediums.

The Personal Life of the Mediums Can Create Blocks (*Cruces*)

Personal problems can evolve into a *causa*. This is particularly likely for the mediums, especially since their husbands generally are not interested in Spiritualism. The two Head Mediums have had to confront their husbands' demand that they stop their practice of Spiritualism.

One of the auxiliary mediums also told of having the same problem with her husband. Nevertheless, the truce which the Head Mediums and their nonbeliever husbands have arranged is that as long as there is no discussion of Spiritism (Spiritualism) between them at home there is no need for a block to evolve.

Still, an auxiliary medium's marriage ended in divorce because she and her husband could not work out an understanding between them. Once she started her involvement in Spiritism (Spiritualism), everything she had ignored in her home came into the open. She felt the material-problems clearing themselves up before her eyes. "I was having problems at home, and I was thinking of killing my husband. I got rid of him after coming to the *centro*; everything took its own course and that's what really helped." She says, "I find I am better off. I'm more calm and my life is going smoother. The worries I used to have before, the headaches I used to have, and the tension (are gone). Without him, I live with my kids. We're happy!" Both Head Mediums' husbands decided to remain with their wives, knowing they practice at the *centro*.

The husbands are fearful that interference could negatively affect their personal lives. Altagracia warned her husband on several occasions that interfering in her beliefs could cause blocks. She blamed her husband's car troubles on his interference with her role as a medium saying that it undermined her power.

Causing spiritual blocks on a conscious or unconscious level must be dealt with since they can develop strength. If a block develops strength, it begins to attract and involve malicious spirits reinforcing the block, it can develop into an all encompassing *causa*. Consequently, the auxiliary medium was forced to eliminate the block to her spiritual development. In the process, she found it was her husband. In Altagracia's case, the husband refuses to interfere, fearing spiritual retaliation against him because he created a block to his wife's participation at the *centro*.

A block, once developed into a *causa*, evolves into a trial of one's belief in the spirit world. One must decide to deal constructively with the *causa*, or fail the trial which, although it has spiritual roots, may affect the material being on a personal or familial level. Altagracia says that there are many types of trials. Sometimes certain things should be dealt with because of their material make-up, even though it has nothing to do with the spiritual make-up. But material problems, such as back pains, headaches, and physical discomfort, when not properly worked spiritually, can evolve into a *causa*. She says that wearing beads can be seen as a trial. In the summer, she is forced to wear blouses with high collars for fear someone might notice her beads. The beads alone make many people in her community think she is a sorcerer. Some people, upon seeing Altagracia's beads, try to touch them. If the beads are touched, they lose their protective powers.

To avoid raising suspicion, it is best not to wear the beads on hot summer days. Instead, she feels forced to leave the beads home, but she must first ask the saints' permission. She places a rosary inside her brassiere instead of wearing her beads. She has been wearing beads for 10 years. If she goes out without them, she feels something is missing, even if she carries a rosary, she feels naked.

One cannot work the table as a medium until the blocks which can evolve into a personal *causa* are worked out of one's life. Otherwise, a dangerous situation is created at the table where *causas* and blocks are confused among the mediums while in spirit possession. Further, this confusion complicates the *causa* being worked on between the medium and the individual from among the public or the associate who is searching for relief.

Women Make Better Mediums

One general feeling at the *centro* is that women are more concerned with the spiritual needs of a family because they are more spiritually developed than men. Women are viewed as better at developing their spiritual powers because they are more devoted. Further, women are viewed as more interested in helping people. One apprentice medium during a group session was asked if she thought material things were bad and she said, "It's not that I am not interested in the material too, I am, of course." She feels man cannot live by bread alone, and Spiritism (Spiritualism) is also an important part of her life. She figures "there has to be some balance between the spiritual and the material, because if one has too much of the material and not enough of the spiritual, then one is not balanced." The Head Mediums agreed.

The Head Mediums explained that men are out of the home too often, and do not get to know about the evil that can develop in the home. It is the woman who must go about trying to find spirituality. The men do not want to get involved. But the women can feel when there is some malicious spirit interfering with their material happiness.

Generally, it is the women who take notice of the problems encountered by their husbands. If a woman senses her husband wants to leave her, she becomes suspicious and says to herself that it may be something that has been "thrown at her" (sorcery). At that point she will go to a *centro* to have a *causa* relieved to ensure the marriage is not further impaired. Men in general are viewed as not thinking about these spiritual facets. More often, men become resigned to whatever is going to occur. Men are less likely to ask themselves if something spiritual is causing their problems.

Altagracia says her husband is an example of a spiritually disinterested man because, although she tells him that he must calm down and understand the spiritual explanation, he is unwilling to attempt to work with enlightened spirits. Sometimes, after a careful explanation of the spiritual reasons for his problems, he says "bullshit!" He believes in his own way and says that he does not want to get involved in going to the *centro*. The men who try finding the spiritual reasons for their *causa* do not often go beyond those reasons. They rarely develop to the point where their *causa* can be ritually worked by the spirits. It is not that women are more important, but generally women search for solutions to problems. Since it is women who are the ones looking for solutions to spiritual problems, they are the ones who develop their guides and protectors.

<u>Outgrowing the *Centro*</u>

The Head Mediums are concerned that some time in the near future they will be forced to open their own *centros*. The Godfather understands that they will have to leave the *centro* if the saints demand they establish themselves as Presidents of a table, since it is impossible to have more than one president in one *centro*.

Altagracia hopes her protectors do not request she open a *centro*. She feels, unlike the Godfather, that she does not have the patience to handle all the problems one encounters as president of a *centro*. She hopes she will have the strength of character to withstand the unappreciative behavior of the public. She says, "Materially, I have an anger that's a real bitch." She does not feel she is capable of putting up with the disrespect the Godfather encounters without telling half the public in the *centro* to go "to hell." All that the Godfather tells Altagracia is that one must be patient and develop greater self-control.

Altagracia says she will have to control herself before the saints and protectors ask her to establish a *centro*. She must develop patience; otherwise she will create blocks which will be counterproductive to the work of her *centro*. As President of a table, she will come in touch with many different types of people from all walks of life. Some days she will have to deal with decent people. She will also have to deal with people who are "just plain dirt," and people who represent "low life." She does not want to deal with that level of society, but she might be forced to do it as a trial by her protectors. On a material level, she is not interested in establishing a *centro* and fears people from the "low life." The other Head Medium says she could not handle the pressures of owning a *centro* and the lack of respect people exhibit after one helps them with their *causa.* Respect is not the only problem. There is also the problem of the manner in which certain individuals from the public don't pay for the charitable work done for them.

Altagracia feels that if, upon working her first *causa* as the owner of a *centro* she was treated disrespectfully, it would make her forget to be patient. She would call them "mother fuckers" right away. The Godfather, while she speaks, looks at her disapprovingly. She looks at the Godfather and says with a big smirk, "God bless him for his patience." The Godfather looks up and catches her sarcastic remark like a fly ball. He then instantaneously responds by saying that one day he is going to throw her into the "shit pile." A recent Americanism he has learned. They both laugh. Altagracia will never reach the higher levels of spiritual development open to her without patience.

Many mediums might want to start up *centros,* but because of the material problems involved they decide against it. "I am one of them; I refuse to deal with these things," says Altagracia, while the other Head Medium agrees. "If the saints demanded it, I would have to do it."

The mediums truly believe that Spiritualism repairs people's lives by teaching them how to deal with people and problems. Initially everything seems difficult, especially when one first starts at the *centro.* Slowly one comes to understand the Spiritist (Spiritualism) belief system. One eventually comes to the realization, "maybe I'll be able to do something with my life," as one auxiliary medium asserted.

An apprentice medium said that Spiritism (Spiritualism) is like nursing. It reminded her of her youth, when she wanted to become a doctor and was accepted into college. At a later point she wanted to take up nursing instead, but now, although she never actually went to college, she leans more toward the spiritual curing of material *causas* than anything else while working the dead. As an apprentice medium, she also feels that this is a way of dealing with the psychological state of members of the public, to her it is like being a psychiatrist or psychologist.

It is expected that a person will believe in Spiritism (Spiritualism) after having a *causa* worked. They have no other choice but to believe, says the Godmother (*Madrina*), because the medium does not know the individual except through the *causa*. The medium is able to tell so much about an individual with a causa. They are bound to believe.

CHAPTER VII

Stage V: The Role of the Godfather (*Padrino*)

Managing the Ensemble of Individuals in the Core

The Godfather manages the individuals who make up the participants at the *centro*. He involves himself in the life of each of the members of the *centro* while understanding the differences between those who need attention in the public and those needing help among the mediums. He explains his concerns for himself in a system which uses sorcery while also explaining the methods used in combating it. The use of group sessions and private consultations is explained.

T he Godfather, in his early fifties, was born in Mayaguez, Puerto Rico. He is married to the Godmother and they have four children. He was besieged by personal problems just before this interview, but viewed the entire situation as yet another trial intended to test his faith in the saints and spirits. Hurt, anguished and often times angry, he kept to himself the issues that contributed to the rumored disputes between him and the Godmother. The interview with the Godfather follows:

I am the only member of my family to work the spirits. I was brought into the world spiritually. This spiritual aspect serves to orient the person. During the period of my own development many years back, I looked for the fundamentals of spiritual development as I learned about Spiritism (Spiritualism).

I never knew the process of how the spirits would arrive in the body or, better, how the body receives the spirits. I went about understanding how these occur through various signs. The spirits give signs which are composed of different feelings in the body. Such signs can be heat flashes; pinches (*pellizcos*), or sensations in parts of the body, such as the arms or legs, falling asleep. There can be 20 million variations which detail the coming of the spirits in the fingers, hands, legs, and heart. Each of these inform the medium that a spirit is appropriating his or her body.

A person must familiarize himself with the souls (spirits). Further, a person must familiarize himself with that saint which provides individual material and spiritual faith. Each individual can understand the saints and spirits through different signs. Each sign is explained differently and is a signal that different things are occurring in an individual. Through the different signs, each individual can understand the saints and spirits. Nevertheless, what I can feel as signals from my spirits can combine with what another brother's spirit is sensing.

This can sometimes be seen in the agitation which spirits sense. One can feel this in the spiritual frame of the individual (*cuadro espiritual*). Certain spiritual frames are serene and not in agitation. One can see these spirits within each of the mediums. If serene spirits who are not in turmoil are seen, they can be identified as cheerful (*simpático*). Here the spirit is ready for a different evolutionary level.

I went looking for spiritual work, but I had to find a Godfather for everything. In many ways, it is like being a physician because they can dedicate themselves to different parts of the human body. Well, in spiritual work, there are different types of workers of the spirits. One then has different persons who dedicate themselves to one thing or another within Spiritism (Spiritualism).

The spirits are worked for different reasons. About half of those practicing Spiritism (Spiritualism) are interested in nothing else but the material: making money. But the material assistance which some Spiritists look for is based on self enrichment. Meeting the material needs of individuals is viewed as winning the lottery or playing the right number on the streets. If a believer doesn't hit the number, there is no belief in the spirits.

Other Spiritists are advanced and have acquired greater protection from the spirits. These Spiritists have respect for the spiritual world and take greater care. They look to help the spirits and attempt to secure the tranquility of spirits. The Spiritists whose primary concern in working the spirits is not for wealth, will receive material blessings because of their sacrifice. One can acquire wealth as a secondary aspect of working the spirits. But one whose motivation to work the spirits is material will not acquire riches.

Every person arrives with certain spiritual qualities. Many of these qualities are spiritual as well as material. As an example, a person can arrive with a high hierarchy in the material area; it could be a highly developed mind. Maybe it is a person who can invent things. But that person needs a well-developed set of spirits as well. For example, there are those individuals who have very little formal education. They have not felt compelled to receive a baccalaureate, but they can invent something or put something into practice. They do it because of the love they put into a particular object. That love is spiritual.

The spiritual is complicated, and there are variations on how that spiritual aspect is received. Each spiritual brother receives his currents (*fluidos*) differently. Because the mind is weak, it is often difficult for individuals to comprehend the spirit currents.

How is it that the mind is weak? The spiritual aspect of an individual can be quite powerful. Nevertheless, the material aspects of an individual's life could be problematic. An individual could be detained in his spiritual development because of his material concerns.

These material concerns evolve into trials which have to be worked as *causas*. Sometimes individuals have been victims of sorcery. These individuals who have *causas* needing work often turn to individual Spiritists (Spiritualists) who represent that half which is looking for material wealth. They have confided in a Spiritist (Spiritualist) only to be fooled.

This situation tends to confuse the public. We must understand these details about the public's experience. The public expects to arrive at the *centro* and be cured. It does not occur in that manner. A Spiritist is not a God.

The Spiritist must work as if he's a physician, a material doctor. One can expect the types of problems encountered by physicians. There are people who visit a physician for many years and are never cured. At one point, the individual will leave the physician and attempt to find another who will provide better results. It is common today for persons to seek second opinions on their illnesses. What individuals seek is certainty.

In work with the spirits, there are variations on the level of second opinion. When some members of the public arrive here for the first time, I request that they see a material doctor. I do this because the spirits told me that this or that particular individual needs a material cure. After I inform them that they need a material doctor, they may go to another Spiritist for a second opinion.

That person can go to another Spiritist and be told something different. The opinion could be the same as the one I gave or be more complicated than I thought. It could be that the seriousness of the material concerns was not properly communicated to me by the guides.

Sometimes, especially with members of the public, I decide to keep the seriousness of a situation to myself. I am concerned, when individuals are sick, that they are not made worse by information they cannot handle. Sometimes people once given information about their illness complicate their own existence. Each person has to be worked differently, and each person must be taken care of differently.

It is my understanding that if I go to a medical doctor and I do not like the manner in which he treats my material being, I will leave that doctor. This dislike for a material doctor can be made worse if he has not confided in me while my chronic ailment continued. This occurs among Spiritists, but material doctors communicate with one another about their opinions. Spiritists should be like material doctors. In this manner Spiritists, like material doctors, can request information about a *causa* from the first Spiritist's treatment. In this religion, Spiritists should be capable of communicating with one another.

The more important factor is, if Spiritists communicated, there would be greater faith in the work and less blocks (*cruces*) to treat. The level of cooperation would be better, especially since not everyone can do the work of the spirits, even though everyone can have *causas* worked.

There are those who work the spirits whom we call know-it-alls. For instance, I can tell an individual he needs some work for his benefit, his prosperity, or his health. He will go to another Spiritist. In order for that other Spiritist to gain this same individual's confidence, he will tell him that his new treatment will be more beneficial. All this does is create a block to the original treatment. In actuality, in the working of spirits, we are really all alike. The problem is that of securing confidence. If blocks are purposely created, a lack of confidence continues to grow which prevents the mediums from doing their work. Consequently, a lack of communication between Spiritist and public exists everywhere.

There are those among the public who can control their spirits. There are others unable to control their spirits due to economic or health problems. The health problem can be complicated when a physician is truthful, especially with cancer victims. It is correct to eventually tell a sick individual about his inevitability. But in telling someone he has cancer, the doctor runs a risk the individual will not build moral strength or maintain a sense of security. Should one tell an individual he is not going to die? Lying does not help. But a person's sense of self must be fortified before he is told he has cancer. In my work, we don't tell an individual anything until we've fortified their spirits because they have weak spirits. This will help prevent personal tragedies, such as committing suicide. Material doctors can often be in error.

Errors exist for everyone. Those of us who come to work the spiritual know there are trials caused by sickness. Often these trials which involve sickness are caused by distrust. But the manner in which a second opinion is handled is important; it can create the block which prevents the necessary confidence to ensure success in the working of a *causa* and the elimination of a trial.

There are beliefs within our Puerto Rican race within a certain group, who can be said to be zealots (*fanaticos*). This group practices *Santería*. Then there is another certain percentage who are enthusiasts in the area of herbal healing. Although there are many types of zealots, they all have their starting point in Spiritism. We have to understand that different people are attracted to different aspects of Spiritism (Spiritualism). As a consequence, the mediums come to work the spirits with a specialty in working the dead or in healing with herbs. This creates a disorganization within the Spiritist (Spiritualist) religion.

This disorganization can prejudice a Spiritist (Spiritualist) into incorrectly working the spirits. Each person is a world unto himself, and the mediums must each be viewed as a world. Each medium orients himself to those things which he feels enthusiastic about and understands. This brings many a good medium. But, because a medium must feel comfortable, it becomes the basis of underdevelopment for those mediums who fear doing the charitable work because they do not feel enthusiastic about it.

Let us take my development as medium as an example of the problems that can create underdevelopment in one's ability to do charitable work. It took two years of work to be seated next to the Spiritist who taught me how to work the table. As President of the table, there were two strong mediums, one to his right and another to his left. One of those Head Mediums was absent and he called on me to take her place. He asked me, "What do you see that woman dragging?" This woman was right in front of me. I told the Spiritist, "I see nothing." He insisted I see something and I insisted I saw nothing. This woman remained at the front and seemed to become annoyed at me because I told her the truth.

The following week, he sat me next to him for a second time. Everyone would purify himself and go into possession. I would feel nothing. But all of a sudden I felt these hot-cold sensations. I felt these strange sensations. I thought to myself, "What is this?" They placed me at the table even though I could not speak in tongues because they felt I had certain spiritual qualities. I did not give proofs of the evils which were causing certain *causas*.

As I developed, I couldn't work the dead but I had learned to give proof of the origin of a *causa* because of my developed spirit guides. At one point, a woman came up to the table and I told her what affected her. Everyone was amazed, even the President of the table. Although I feared working the spirits, I began to give proof that I was correctly working *causas*.

The first *causa* I worked was that of the godchild Doña Isabel. She was the first person I worked. She had been going to that *centro* for many years but had never had her *causa* worked. When I sat down that third time, the President of the table said, "You want to find some member of the congregation to work?" I went for a walk into the congregation and I saw Doña Isabel.

I informed her that it was presumptuous for me to attempt working her *causa* because I could not work the dead. I asked her to forgive me, but we should try anyway. What choice did I have? The Spiritist told me to "move on" since I did not do much at the *centro*. She had a rebellious spirit which made my attempt to see what was occurring difficult. To facilitate my sensing the spirit's troubles and search for light, I asked for Doña Isabel's hand. Asking for someone's hand was unusual at this *centro*, but when a person has a difficult spirit asking for the hand makes the reading easier.

When her hand touched mine, I felt the entire world go before me. I jumped back. The chair I was sitting on broke and I almost broke a shoulder bone. The congregation picked me up from the floor and I didn't remember what had happened.

According to the President of the table and Doña Isabel, they had to tie me to a chair. I broke everything within reach. These breakdowns in an individual's ability to control himself while treating a *causa* are caused by a lack of learning about the spirit world. This situation only served to break up the services. In any case, they said they struggled with me for about a half hour. I will never forget it because it occurred two days before Father's Day. Doña Isabel showed up on Father's Day at the *centro* and gave me my first payment of $25.00 for working her *causa*. I felt then that I could work the spirits. That was 20 years ago and those $25.00 are still on my altar. Doña Isabel is now a godchild at this *centro*. I worked at several Spiritist *centros*, often being asked to leave. The last place I was forced to leave from was that of my children's Roman Catholic godfather. I had to leave because he never wanted to help me develop. That conflict with my sons own Godfather was a trial. In the end, I became resigned and said, "Let whatever happens be God's will."

What happened was that he prohibited me from speaking to members of the public. He also prohibited me from arriving at the services early. I was looking for opportunities to work the spirits, so I would arrive a half hour early and wait outside until the services started.

I couldn't believe this manipulation from a man who said he respected me. He used to give me a lot of attention. He told me to sit among the public; he took me away from the mediums and placed me back in the public. I thought, "Well, I also need the charitable work of having my *causas* worked." For several weeks this placing me in the public continued. I had lost my place at his right side. In the end, he told me "you have to leave the *centro.*"

Once I left, I stayed home and remained undisturbed. I hadn't learned how to prepare an herbal bath. I was inexperienced with the world of the spirits. I thought of many things I should have attempted in trying to work the spirits, but I was unable to attempt them. I felt I didn't know how to do it. I couldn't spiritually clean my own home, and personal fears about this lack of understanding of the spirits grew.

Nevertheless, it must be remembered that this Spiritist was not very good; his ability to provide proofs from the dead was poor. I wanted him to let me stay at the table another month, but he wouldn't allow it because he knew he really wasn't teaching anything and he did not provide his mediums with herbal baths. I left that *centro,* but I was going to continue working the spirits. I felt as if I had wasted 10 years of my life. I also knew that his forcing me to leave would make it impossible to keep his congregation intact. It happened just as I thought. He closed his *centro* a short time after I left.

I spent three years going from place to place. Sometimes I would go to different *centros* hoping to find that experience I so badly needed. I would go to these *centros* and sit with the public. I would go as a know-it-all; I couldn't go to a *centro* and say I'm a medium. They would ask, "Who is that person?" The President of the table would ask me to come forward so that I could be recognized for my spiritual powers. They understood that my hierarchy of spirit communication was highly developed and would throw me out of the centros.

I have struggled to learn. The learning I have acquired is not much. I manifest the spirits because I have faith, but also because of my own interest in working the spirits. It comes from within me, what we call, from my own material (mental/body) interest. I practice this and make a great sacrifice. My purpose is to help those disoriented souls who are putting people through trials (*pruebas*). These trials help us learn and this spiritual work never ends.

One learns through years of spiritual work. By being baptized, the Godfather takes on the obligation to do the work of teaching his godchildren. The obligation must be kept until death. But what usually happens is that the material trials create a lack of confidence in the belief system. This lack of confidence brings about underdevelopment. This underdevelopment ignites forces in the individual which do not allow him to continue his work with the spirits. People fail to look for guidance from the Godfather because they distrust him or because a personal problem has transpired.

You can understand the problem of trusting a Godfather. Many Godfathers baptize individuals and those individuals develop a series of learnings which are incorrect. The problem is one of placing the godchild between development and underdevelopment. Consequently, the individual believes, which is a forward movement, but practices incorrectly, which is a backward movement. This creates underdevelopment. This situation has occurred to many. Then how can I create trust and confidence? They have to find their development elsewhere.

Some godchildren feel their first letdown when they start working the table. No Godfather can tell an individual what to say while working the table. It is a slow process of development.

For my own development, even at this very moment, I need certain sacraments. I need certain preparations called for by some of my spiritual guides. These spiritual guides want greater depth in my performance and ability to work *causas*. This a profoundly complicated task.

It is like learning to speak to my saints in tongues again. Especially, it is like learning the words all over again. I must learn the language necessary for spirits in the upper reaches of the hierarchy. I still have to learn about the complications involved in divining with cowrie shells.[1] Further, I must learn to read the coconuts when they are thrown. I must deepen my knowledge of the signs which saints use to communicate and interpret what they are asking for. Here is a list of the things I need to further develop spiritually, but these are acquired little by little and are products of good work at the table.

I do what the spirits demand. But the Godfather must develop a greater understanding because he also has to be a medium. The spirits not only order that one develop his mediumistic powers, but that the other mediums also develop theirs. It is only through a series of sacraments that I can improve.

The Godfather provides the sacrament of baptism in the Spiritist (Spiritualist) sense of it. The Godfather also has to develop some sense of how good a medium the individual he is baptizing will be. Therefore, the medium must be understood to be one who works the table or is a helper. There are those mediums who are unable to manifest the dead because only certain individuals arrive to work the dead. There are those mediums who work the dead (*muertera*) and there are mediums who cure (*curanderia*). Some mediums can do both working the dead and curing.

A medium has certain advantages because she can communicate with spirits of light. These spirits are demanding since they will only do for us if we give them something in return. But the spirits give us more than what we give them. Nevertheless, if we fall into a trial because they need it or because of our material lives, the spirits will attend to us and help us through the spiritual work.

Everyone brings with them a spiritual richness and it is represented like a rainbow in the everday personality. There are also the currents maifested in an indivdual. Each person brings with them currents which represent a spirit of the dead which that individual carries. These currents can be felt as cold or hot when a medium or someone with the potential for mediumship comes close to an individual. Sometimes the spirits can be sensed as a refreshing air that radiates from an individual.

Yet, the interesting thing is that there are individuals who bring an umderstanding of the spirits and yet have never worked the table. These individuals who have felt the spirits and have never worked them have been underdeveloped (*atrasados*). These untapped abilities are caused by dead relatives, such as someone's grandparent or mother.

Mediums can tell which individual will have spirits guiding their development from the higher reaches of the hierarchy. The medium's own principal protectors will inform her what type of spirits an individual brings with them.

The consultations are an important means of determining the type of spirits available to an individual because within the consultations, there is more time to determine these things. At the consultation we search for the things a given individual lacks and we attempt to give him this knowledge. More importantly, we can search out the spiritual chain of dead family members who had enlightened spirits. Often times spirits will withdraw from an individual as soon as they approach the *centro*. It is of utmost importance that one knows how to distinguish the spirits brought by an individual. The dead are an intelligent lot.

I keep two principal forces who are mediums at the corners of the table. This helps balance the table through their saints who are powerful. They are very important. I would rather leave their chairs empty if I couldn't find substitutes who were as powerfully developed. The rest of the mediums are still learning. But we are all learning here at this *centro*.

We are all participants, but some of us have developed more than others. The experience is based on the amount of time each one of us has spent working the table. One must also see experience as representing types of spirits worked, not just time spent at the table. Then there are those who can receive spirits of light better than others and can then learn faster how to work the spirits. Sometimes someone has no need to be taught because she knows how to do the things the saints request.

At this late date in my life, the spirits have been giving me trials. God only knows the type of trials I suffer. I can say these trials have tested my sense of dignity. Trials can manifest themselves in many areas, such as economic, personal, or material (bodily).

I learn in the manner every other individual learns, through trials. One must recognize trials and understand oneself while going through the trials. Further, one must understand how one acquires these trials and then understand how to put these trials into practice in spiritual work. These are the factors which help in an individual's development. This development takes faith and knowledge. Faith can only be gained through the help of the Guardian Angel and spirit protectors.

The saints sustain me and help me. They prevent me from falling to the wayside. These saints are my protectors because they make sure that I develop an understanding of unjust criticisms which evolve from out of the public. The saints prevent the tragedies that could engulf my very existence because I have faith. I do everything correctly, as they request it. I take the saints seriously, and they help me work my way through trials. There is no one at this *centro* who can prevent a trial. No one can take a trial away from an individual that has been placed by God. Who am I not to go through worse? Understanding this has provided me with sustenance. Consequently, I put more interest into my work and I strengthen my spirits. I have now arrived at the point where I can instruct others about the world of spirits.

The Godfather must orient his godchildren, and he ensures that they go through the spiritual sacraments. I have St. Francis of Assisi (*Orunla*), Santa Barbara (*Changó*), Our Lady of Regla (*Yemayá*), and I am also a full son of *Our Lady of La Caridad del Cobre*. I am a son of these saints who force me to keep them placed high on top of my altar. The Holy Guardian Angel (*Elegguá*) must be counted on most of all because without him you cannot petition the saints to help in serving people.

The President of the Table is the Godfather

Being a good medium is a precondition for the role of Godfather. Just as important is the ability to recognize the saints as they manifest themselves in different members of the public. An individual must continually grow in the Spiritualist belief system; otherwise the medium will be unable to work complicated *causas*. The Head Medium wanting to establish herself as a future Godmother struggles to prove herself competent and skillful. She can either displace the present Godfather, the Godfather can leave or the Head Medium leaves. Moreover, a medium gains the respect of the public because she has proven herself trustworthy and efficient in diagnosing *causas* and, as a result, has developed a repertoire of relieving *causas*.

It is understood that the Godfather is also the President of the table in the Spiritist tradition and, as a consequence, has worked his way up the hierarchy of mediums. It is hoped that through consultations with the Godfather, the Head Mediums will develop the skills needed for conducting consultations themselves. They will have to establish their own *centros* for this purpose. This is possible for the Head Mediums because they have participated in consultations as part of the public, godchildren, apprentice mediums and mediums.

The interview provided insight into the role of the Godfather (Stage V), a self-employed, full-time Spiritualist. In his role as Godfather, he mediates the ensemble of constituent parts represented at the *centro* through his involvement with the public, the associates, the godchildren, and the mediums. He focuses his attention on helping the mediums relieve *causas* during services. Later, he treats *causas* by himself in private consultations. He also engages in spiritual operations in private group sessions with the mediums and godchildren, and in public sessions. He becomes involved in recruiting individuals from the public for associate status.

Stage I: Relating to the Public

Those who arrive at the *centro* for the first time, as the public, and who are in the process of integrating themselves into the associates, use the term Spiritist (*Espiritista*) to refer to the Godfather. No one refers to him in Spanish as a Spiritist (*Espiritista*) after the first or second visit to the *centro*. They have learned to refer to him as Godfather (*Padrino*). The Godfather is never referred to in Spanish as a Spiritualist (*Espiritualista*).

Those in the public are individuals who arrive to "check things out" and remain near the rear of the *centro*. They come to the services in the hope that the Godfather will work their *causas*. The Godfather impresses the public with his spiritual powers and in this manner hopes to recruit dues-paying associates.

Stage II: Relating to the Transition from an Associate to Godchild

The Godfather usually recruits associates for the role of godchildren.

The godchild role is entered after a ritual baptism to which the individual must consent. During this transition period, new prohibitions appear. Lessons also begin about protectors, guides, and malicious spirits. This learning integrates the individual into the godchildren. Some succeed in this transition to godchild while others remain as associates or withdraw from the *centro*. Significantly, the language of *Santería* begins to make an appearance as home altars begin to incorporate *Orishas* out of *Cuban Santería*.

Stage III: Relating to the Godchildren

The godchildren make up that group which helps in spirit communication. They also secure spiritual protection through prayers for all present. The godchildren see themselves as a "family" and have established an in-group mechanism of control in which the Godfather and the mediums set the tone and are the role models. The male godchildren help the mediums during spirit communication by restraining the public, holding mediums during possession, and securing spiritually uncontaminated water for better communication with the dead. The role of the male godchild is highly sensualized, and physical. There is a dress code from *Santería* which makes its appearance, and the bead necklaces are enumerated on the bases of relatedness to both the Yorubaland Orishas and the Catholic Saints which the Godchild begins to manifest (*montar*). Greater efforts to incorporate the language of *Santería* is made as the dead manifest with prescriptions for the relief of *causas*.

Stage IV: Relating to the Mediums

The eight mediums represent the core working group within the *centro*. They work the *causas* and ensure spirit communication. In this manner the Godfather can analyze the *causa* causing an individual's affliction through the spirits. The Godfather helps the mediums understand the different types of spirits with whom they communicate. Rituals of *Santería* such as incorporating the spirits of nature involve the Godfather in outings to the mountains. The use of language now begins to point to an increase in the rituals of *Cuban Santería* as the Godfather refers to *asiento* and the divining system of Ifa.

The Godfather and the mediums have reached an understanding: The *centro* is to remain the Godfather's!   The saints decide who is to establish her own *centro*.   The medium who is required to start her own *Centro* must first withdraw from this *centro*.   The Godfather established this *centro* and the Head Mediums have not expressed a desire to divide the public by manipulating its loyalty.

Stage V The Godfather

The godfather must be on guard against the development of spiritual blocks while working a *causa*, as well as during the preparation of treatments.   Further, he must be conscious of betrayal, treason (*traición*), and attempts to have him ingest evil (object intrusion). These are methods used to combat the "good" he represents.

The Godfather feels burdened because he can only confide in the Head Mediums and possibly the auxiliaries. His greatest concern is treason, since the godchildren could betray him through their involvement in some evil sorcery which, unknown to him, might cause a block to his work at the *centro*.   He is frustrated by treason, which is manifested in a loss of godchildren who, instead of spreading light, become involved in darkness.   In the end, lost godchildren who continue working spirits on their own become involved in breaking marriages, theft of souls, and the use of malicious spirits; that is, low-level sorcery.

The Godfather is often invited out to eat. He must be careful for his spiritual development in the same way he is careful of the continued development of his godchildren. He does not like to eat out. He is concerned that someone would put an object of sorcery into his food, especially into his plantain meat pies (*pasteles*). The ingestion of evil would cause him to lose spiritual powers.   In this context, the concept of object intrusion out of *Santería* receives a new emphasis.   These worries are trials in themselves that must be judiciously dealt with if he is going to spiritually protect an entire *centro*.

The Godfather must be on guard at all times to prevent his good intentions from becoming a block to his work. Being on guard is in itself a spiritual trial or a trial of his belief. His wife, the Godmother, understands that a good Spiritist (Spiritualist) is tested every day, and she is on the alert so as not to allow herself to be provoked into jealous behavior, especially by what another woman at the *centro* might say her husband has done.

The Godmother refuses to participate in working *causas*. In this manner, she does not create blocks because of her relationship to her husband. She feels people do not trust husband and wife teams at a table because their personal family problems could be absorbed into the working of another individual's *causa*. Lack of trust and inability to work together are trials of one's character by the spirits.

There are several types of rumors caused by envy that the Godfather considers very negative spiritually and which create blocks at the *centro*. One such rumor is that he makes plaster images of saints to sell to the congregation. Another rumor contends he is a *Santero* and makes saints (*Asiento Ritual*) of people. He feels he is but a "lowly worm," without power to make saints out of anyone in the congregation as Cuban *Santeros* do.

The most distinctive rumor suggests that he uses his hands too freely when treating women. This rumor creates blocks in women who need treatment for a *causa*, but have closed themselves off spiritually because they distrust the Godfather. The treatment of women is a major problem and without trust in the Godfather there can be no relief from a *causa*. The Godfather asks permission of the spirits before ritual treatments, especially if they require close personal contact. Women who lack confidence in the treatment create blocks.

The Godfather speaks to husbands before treatments. He asks the husbands to pardon him if they should think his purpose is anything other than an honorable concern for the *causas* affecting their wives. The purpose of this is to prevent any individual member of a family from building blocks to the spiritual treatment. If individuals are properly forewarned and if they trust the Godfather, the spirits will ensure that the treatment works.

The herbal baths prepared by the Godfather, as well as the reading of spirit currents, must be done with care for people's sensibilities. The misreading of a *causa* because of a created block to spirit currents (*fluidos*) during consultations, would make the herbal baths useless. The Godfather also warns that thoughts of impending evil can serve to create blocks which are counterproductive to relieving a *causa*.

Two Types of Sorcery

Information is given about the two types of sorcery available in the world. Individuals must be informed during consultations that Spiritism (Spiritualism) works for "the good," while practices like *Santería* are used to do evil. The Godfather says that there are evil-looking rituals which can just as easily be called Spiritism (Spiritualism) but they are done for "the good" of an individual.

One type of sorcery is helping people get a "balance in their lives between evil and good." In certain cases of sorcery, there is a need to get people's spirits returned to them. Often sorcerers use spirits for evil purposes and use photographs to steal spirits from individuals. The medium must work the spirits in many ways to solve those types of *causas* which have their origin in the evil sorcery of *Santería*.

Preparations are made by the Godfather to secure that evil sorcery is driven from an individual with a *causa*. Herbs and plants are prepared for the purifying baths for individuals suffering the ill effects of a *Santero's* or sorcerer's work. The potions for curing individuals are secrets of the Godfather. He is an expert at mixing herbs and plants in a given order, which are then used to make sure that the spirits are relieved. The Principal Head Medium (*Mediaunidad de Mano Dere-cha*) often helps in the preparation of herbal baths.

Combating Sorcery With Herbal Baths

Baths are common preparations for spiritual cleansing and protection. They are provided in large gallon plastic jugs. The cost of the bath varies with the prescription needed. The liquid in the jugs becomes a pink milk-like substance. When it is intended as a spiritual cleansing for one's home, it is a light green. The baths are usually prepared before individuals arrive at the *centro*. If the baths cannot be prepared before an individual arrives, then they are mixed in front of those arriving for a consultation. Perfumes used in the herbal baths can cost up to $50.00 per four fluid ounces. The baths are made by combining the herbs, holy water, plants and fragrances.

Baths can be provided for an entire family. It is often the case that the house and the body have to be cleansed of evil spiritual influences.

Some individuals end up carrying three gallon jugs home in an effort to secure spiritual protection. The jugs filled with prepared herbal baths are kept under the pews near the altar where the godchildren sit.

The cost of a consultation does not cover the prescriptions for baths. Because of the rapidity with which the Godfather must work, he sometimes leaves the consultation room talking out loud about an individual's herbal bath prescriptions. They must pay for the baths, extra herbs required by the saints or spirits, and for the divining that occurs during the consultation. The Godfather does not like working on credit! The ingredients are costly and the *botánica* does not sell on credit. The Godfather feels that people take advantage of him because he cannot refuse a charitable case seeking spiritual work.

He has asked several individuals to pay for a bath and they responded by telling him that they can get the bath cheaper at the *botánica*. He feels insulted, but remains silent. The *botánica* (herbal magical-religious shop) sells the ingredients as well as factory-prepared baths. The Godfather also feels the commercial baths are cheaper, but factory-prepared baths are made without the individual's *causa* in mind. All too often, members of the public are unable to distinguish between commercial baths and those made by the Godfather.

The problems which individuals encounter with baths are many. Sometimes the issue is not one of commercially versus *centro* -prepared, but of expecting more from the baths than is reasonable. Even if an individual has the ability to pay for an expensive bath, if the expectation is unreasonable the bath will be blamed for the failure instead of evaluating the reasonableness of their expectations.

Unreasonable Expectations

The Godfather pointed to a young woman entering the *centro* as an example of unreasonable expectations. As she came down the aisle, one could not help but notice that she was well-dressed and her hair was finely styled. The door to the *centro* was left open behind her, providing a view of her four-door luxury sedan blocking the corner crosswalk in front of the *centro*. In a hurry, she explained she had arrived to pick up her mother's baths. She took the baths from the Godfather and went out the door carrying two gallon jugs of herbal baths. The Godfather said the young woman and her mother own an expensive beauty salon in the North Bronx. The young woman's mother will leave soon on a business trip to Puerto Rico and wants to ensure its success with an herbal bath. If the business trip doesn't go well, they will blame the baths intended as spiritual protection.

He turned to those who waited for a consultation in the *centro* and said, "If I asked that young woman for $50.00 per bath, I would get more respect from her." He was annoyed by her middle class elitism and brashness, but more importantly, he was concerned about their unreasonable expectations. As she left, the Godfather shook his head and held his hands up high in helplessness.

The Godfather as Teacher

The Godfather increases the intensity of his involvement with each successive Stage of socialization into the *centro*. In stages II through IV, unlike Stage I, individuals clearly enter roles that require greater participation at the *centro*. The Godfather involves himself with the public and associates of Stage I, yet his involvement is less active since it is primarily aimed at either curing *causas* during services or gaining contributors to the *centro*. In the other stages he initiates a process of teaching which involves individuals in occupying the more significant roles at the *centro*.

The Godfather begins informing individuals in private consultations about the belief system. In these private consultations with the mediums, he begins to distinguish the type of spiritual work a perspective godchild is suited to undertake. He must also help the mediums identify the type of specialty they bring with them to the table such as *curanderia* (spiritual curing) or *muertera* (worker of the dead). One type works the dead (*muertera*), while the other works as a healer (*curandera*). A medium can be trained to both heal and work the dead. Most mediums feel they are better at either one or the other. The *curandera* at this *centro* sits to the left of the Godfather, signalling a privileged position among the mediums.[2]

The Godfather helps the inexperienced godchildren to distinguish multiple types of spirits. He facilitates the godchildren's ability to distinguish between the spirits out to betray the medium and those intent on confusing the medium as she communicates with the spirit world. A medium's ability to learn from the Godfather how to distinguish the different spirits enables her to properly work a *causa.*

The method by which *causas* develop must also be considered; they must be analyzed by divining (diagnosing) the types of sorcery responsible. The Godfather details the different types of sorcery, their composition, their purpose, and the manner in which they were prepared.

Group Sessions

The Godfather conducts group sessions in which the godchildren and the mediums participate. The sessions are aimed at reviewing the manner in which the godchildren and mediums prepare spiritually to arrive at the *centro.* Often the sessions are aimed at helping them distinguish between the material (physical-economic-familial) and the spiritual. Other times the Godfather is more interested in pinpointing and counteracting the negative material problems which the godchildren may unconsciously bring with them to the *centro.* He makes a special effort to provide baths to the godchildren and to help them maintain themselves spiritually pure.

The godchildren are told they can progress to mediumship by following the Godfather's instructions only. The public and associates, as well as the godchildren and mediums, continue private consultations with the Godfather. In these private consultations the godchildren measure their progress and secure information on ritual protection.

Private Consultations

During private consultation sessions, the Godfather helps the godchildren counter their material fears of spirits and helps them work against their doubts in the spirit world. The Godfather intervenes to secure his godchildren's confidence in the spirits by helping them with problems which might serve to undermine either growth or trust in the spirits. Confidence in the Godfather's intervention is reflected in an individual's understanding that the spirits are real.

The Godfather is distinguished as an exemplary model of spiritual patience, unbiased understanding, and knowledge of the dead. This

view of the Godfather is especially held by those in need of an understanding of how to communicate with the dead. He helps the godchildren in their quest for higher spiritual development. He informs the
godchildren that they are special, that they must primarily distinguish
themselves from the rest of mankind as individuals with patience.

The Belief System of the Godfather

Spiritism (Spiritualism) calls for a lifelong commitment and trials
occur more frequently as one becomes more involved as a believer. The
trials (*pruebas*) gather strength and can spiritually consume (*envolver*)
those not properly trained. These trials have been known to gather
sufficient strength to drive individuals crazy (*loco*). One member of the
congregation went crazy because he did not take his involvement in
Spiritualism seriously. Consequently, the Godfather feels one must
initially be taught spiritual self-control. Understanding the problems of
communicating with the dead can lead to trials (*pruebas*) which are
beyond the individual's abilities to comprehend.

It is useless to view the spirits as a panacea in a world filled with dark
forces and lack of faith in enlightenment. Spirits themselves are searching for enlightenment. These spirits' search creates the trials which individuals experience as *causas*. The Spiritualist, in working *causas*, re-
lieves trials and increases his own understanding of the spirit world. He
helps the spirits evolve up the hierarchy from their place of darkness
(lack of knowledge) to their place of light (knowledgeable). If the
Godfather incorrectly works the spirits, he himself remains in the dark
while alive and insures that his spirits remain in the dark once he is dead,
instead of becoming enlightened (knowledgeable).

In general, some spiritualists work in half light because they fail at
working some of the darker spirits. At first, their own darker sides
remain hidden. All the *causas* with darker sides that they later encounter remain in darkness. It is in other's spirits that you see your own dark
spirits. There is no place in Spiritualism for hypocrisy. If there is a lack
of truth, then there is a lack of faith. This combination of lack of truth
and faith contributes to the general public's distrust in Spiritualists. This
distrust can be said to be an uneasy feeling, a lack of confidence and a
distrust in the Spiritualist, especially by women. This distrust is trans-

formed into a lack of faith in the spirit world and later into blocks which reinforce a lifelong commitment to darkness and its forces. These forces undermine one's faith. If the combined lack of faith and resultant blocks are not eliminated, a *causa* can develop into a trial as spirits search for light. If a sufficient number of trials go untreated, or most dangerously, poorly treated, they can consume an individual. It can lead to forms of insanity which the family can't explain, and are unexpected. Unrelieved trials end with a dark spirit's search for light in its after life.

The Godfather himself faces trials and, if he cannot heal himself because of spiritual underdevelopment, he cannot help the members of his *centro* with their *causas*. In other words, the doctor must heal himself because he might be sicker (darker) than the patient, causing more damage to an already sick individual.

The Godfather and I have spoken for hours. He is tired. His evening is about to begin. He is a heavy set man, but not sluggish. No one would ever recognize him as a Spiritualist upon seeing him walking down the street. He uses a formal Spanish. A Spanish which seems out of place in the South Bronx, a Spanish that is respected as if it were a museum piece. That is, a very consciously constructed Spanish intended to get points across without being pointed, brash, or intimidating. It is only after you've walked away, while recalling the conversation, that you understand how cleverly constructed his point was.

It is late afternoon and the faithful have begun to arrive at the *centro*. I feel relieved that the Godfather must tend to his flock. He doesn't want to walk away. I can feel it. The Godfather does walk away, but half way down the *centro* he returns to the rear where I am standing. He looks at me while walking toward me with his hand outstretched, then shakes my hand. I sense, after all these years, that today I may have to run away. He begins to walk away again and turns to me. He smiles. I look down at the floor in respect. He asks me, "how is your stomach this week Andrés?" I say "I am okay" and of course I lied. At the same time I wonder to myself, how did he know? I am filled with apprehension. I feel a darker spirit and acknowledge a distrust racing inside me. The Godfather knowingly smiles a big welcoming smile. I smile back, all the while feeling a sense of misfortune caused by a new nakedness simultaneously occurring with a cascading hot and cold feeling down my arms that made my hairs stand on end. I experienced a hot and cold sweat; an anxiety unlike anything I had ever felt before; a darkness seeping from deep inside. I rationalized the feeling. "It's hot in here; it must be a material thing, I'm sure."

The Godfather as Specialist

The Godfather does not understand what makes him a better Spiritualist than most. On the other hand, he admits he is one of few Spiritualists in the South Bronx who teaches his godchildren about the spirit world.

The Godfather talks of the trials he suffered when he first arrived in the United States and the difficulties of finding employment as an electrician or as a film projectionist. He sympathizes with the problems of new arrivals from Puerto Rico who have skills, but cannot work in the United States because of the language barrier or because their licenses are only valid in Puerto Rico.

Nevertheless, the Godfather feels he has a job he must do and it requires working with spirits. He works especially well with malicious spirits which have arrived from one's prior existence. These malicious spirits may be out to do harm and must be worked as *causas* needing enlightenment. It is more than employment says the Godfather: it is a "specialty."

The Spiritist (Spiritualist) must know how to relieve a *causa* and the type of ritual-ceremonial paraphernalia required. What often takes precedence is the thinking between the Spiritualist and the individuals involved in a *causa*. The thinking of the Godfather must be considered along with that of the person with the *causa*. The Godfather says one must be conscious of the thinking of women with *causas*. One must be consistently conscious of those things which could cause a block.

Women, Blocks, and *Causas*

Many problems can be complicated and require precautions to prevent blocks, but the working of *causas* has to be carefully developed, especially for women, in the privacy of the consultation room. Intimate cures, says the Godfather, are sometimes required for women. Material misunderstandings can occur which evolve into criticisms of the manner in which the Godfather has treated a woman. These misunderstandings can be especially damaging during intimate body readings. One of the worst things that can happen is that rumors are spread about what occurred between an individual under treatment and the Godfather.

If these rumors are spread in a conscious effort to undermine or betray the Godfather, it creates blocks which might be unknown to the Spiritualist as he works on a believer. In an effort to avoid such rumors, he informs women about what is going to take place in the privacy of his consultation room. He will also bring the husband into the consultation room or explain to him the intimate details of what the ritual requires. In this manner he hopes to avoid rumors or unpleasant situations, especially with jealous husbands.

The Godfather himself does not belong to a grouping of godchildren. He is not a member of a house with a *Babaláo* to help him learn. He laments that he is not fully developed as a Spiritist (Spiritualist) because he has not found a Godfather (*Babaláo*) for his spiritual development.

Many feel the *centro* has no involvement with *Santería*. What is practiced at the *centro* is viewed as cleaner and purer than Cuban *Santería*. Contrary to what members of the congregation say, the Godfather says he does not fear *Santeros*. He works the saints to secure guidance and keeps the Seven African Powers as the preeminent saints at the altar. The saints possess (*montar*) individual godchildren during services and a list of godchildren and their corresponding saints is kept near the consultation room.

The Godfather chastises the congregation because, all too often, a godchild expects to be possessed by one particular saint, but learns he is mistaken about which saint has possessed him. The Godfather feels that no one should predetermine which saint is going to possess him. This is true even if the individual has had a lifelong commitment to a given saint prior to arriving at the *centro*. Whatever saint was given to that individual by providence will possess him. Each individual brings a given saint with him. It has nothing to do with what saint an individual wants as a possessor.

One member of the public had been attending the *centro* for over three years and was devoted to *Santa Barbara* (Saint Barbara), often the revered Saint of homosexuals. He always left offerings to her on his altar. During one of the ceremonies in which the purifications through fire occurred, he lost his balance and fell. The Godfather informed him that he should reevaluate what saint he was to manifest during spirit possession. He now feels Saint Lazarus is more likely to manifest himself in him during possession because Saint Lazarus walks on crutches to ensure his balance.

The Godfather has rejected the whole concept in *Santería* of making saints out of individuals through the *asiento* ceremony.[3] He informs the congregation they should not allow anyone to ceremonially pour chicken blood over their heads. He makes a point of telling those who come to the *centro* for the first time that he does not make saints. He is a Spiritist (Spiritualist). He uses ritually sacrificed animals for spiritual cleansing (*despojo*), usually a dove.

Unlike the *Santeros*, he never uses the blood of ritually sacrificed animals to attract ancestor spirits to the *centro*. He neither pours blood over the rocks that attract the Congo spirits (spirits of the Bantu) to the *centro*, nor uses blood to acknowledge the saints which manifest (*montar*) themselves in his godchildren. He keeps near the altar a cross-listing of the names of Godchildren and the saint which manifests itself in each godchild. This is done even though the *centro* does not perform the *asiento* ceremony of *Santería*.

The Problem of *Santería* and Puerto Ricans

A problem identified within the *centro* is the immense amount of exploitation of Puerto Rican Spiritist believers by Cuban *Santeros*. They make saints of individuals in the ceremony of *asiento* which the Puerto Rican Spiritualist must then undo. The Godfather informs the congregation that they are not to allow anyone to pour chicken blood on their heads. He considers it a complicated ritual requiring rigorous training by a *Santero* of the neophyte, and is prohibitively expensive. Without such training, the neophyte's spirits can go into darkness.

Puerto Ricans needing the services of a Spiritist will often confuse the Spiritist with the *Santero*. The Spiritist and the *Santero* work the spirits differently and do not use the same methods for working *causas*. Cuban *Santeros* are much more expensive and considered less trustworthy than the Puerto Rican Spiritist because it is said that *Santeros* work for the highest bidder. The Godfather belittles the *Santero* as a worker of evil. He often says this "*Santerismo* stuff" is very dangerous.[4]

A Reference Library for Working *Causas*

Since *causas* are complicated to resolve, the Godfather keeps a library in the consultation room, hidden above eye level, which he does not allow anyone to touch. He regularly adds books which he buys from the *botánica* (herbal magico-religious shop). He also keeps books given to him by members of the congregation. He recently added, for the second time, *El Monte* by Lydia Cabrera because his first copy was stolen. He was surprised that what he considers the "*Bible of Santeros*" now costs $15.00. He recently added the Gonzales-Wippler book, *Santería*. He evaluated both books and decided they were dangerous since they contained appendixes of prescriptions for sorcery. He felt this knowledge of sorcery and how to work evil spirits could get into the hands of individuals with malicious intentions on the streets.

There are many people who can use the prescriptions for sorcery to injure others whom they envy. The end result, he fears, is the spread of those prescriptions (*recetas*) for sorcery from *Santería* beyond their present isolation in the Hispanic community. The spread of sorcery even begins to harm the sorcerers themselves as they attempt greater evils in envious rivalry.

All the godchildren are told to keep The Book of Mediums by Kardec at home. It details the different methods for spirit communications and explains the sensations which accompany the arrival of possessing spirits.

The Godfather feels obligated not to follow Kardec's rules for Spiritist meetings explicitly because he cannot turn away a person who lacks membership at the *centro*. He has advised the associates that if they do not financially support the *centro* through contributions, he will be forced to close the *centro* to the public. He would then only treat the *causas* of dues-paying members. The associates feel it is their charitable duty to ensure that *causas* are worked from the public. The associates nevertheless want the public to contribute during the passing of the collection box. This will ensure the material well-being of the *centro*.

To the Mountains (*Al Monte*)

The saints demand the Godfather go into seclusion with the godchildren once a year.   In the mountains, he speaks to his saints and protector spirits.   These saints provide the Godfather with advice on handling complicated spiritual/material *causas*.

The saints manifest themselves in the Godfather and are ritually fed. In this manner the Head Mediums learn to satisfy the demands from their saints.   The ritual feeding of the saints will ensure the enlightenment of the spirit protectors and guides.   Some food offerings are left in the woods of the state parks.

The Godfather Works a *Causa*

The story of Negrita, her mother Carmen and her son René, gives us an account of the Godfather's methods in solving one family's *causa*.

René is eight years old.   His skin is a dark brown, he has a wide smile, and is interested in everything out of the ordinary.   He is curious and intelligent.   He has a heavy build but is not fat.   His wide body, especially at the soldiers, makes him stand out all the more because Negrita, his mother, is very thin.   René stands on his toes and can almost reach Negrita's height.   He does this and looks her in the eye with a severe intensity, mimicking the manner in which she looks at him when she orders him to do something.   He is always well-clothed, clean, neat, and respectful of adults.

Both René's mother and grandmother are associates.   They are preparing to become godchildren.   René lives in his grandmother's low income housing project apartment along with his mother and uncle.

Negrita and Carmen both regularly go for consultations with the Godfather.   They are concerned with how wide spread evil is in the South Bronx.   They feel René must be spiritually protected to secure his continued safe progress through life. The bead necklaces help, but often individuals need the Godfather to cleanse their hair (*despojo*) of accumulated malicious spiritual influences.   René has been getting his hair spiritually cleansed (*despojo*) once a week. This is done after a consultation with either the mother or grandmother.   René enjoys getting his hair washed with the coconut soap and is disappointed if the ritual does not occur. The *despojo* spiritually protects René for the week. The Godfather has had to postpone the hair washing because of a lack of hot water at the building where the *centro* is located.

A *Causa* Gains Momentum

Negrita, with René tagging along behind her, arrived one day for an emergency consultation. She said, "I usually go in by myself, but this time he's going in because he did something that surprised the hell out of me! So I am going to tell the Spiritualist."

René stole money from his uncle's room. His mother adds that he did it to buy a comic book after she told him she could not afford it. She pulled out of her pocketbook one of the comic books René bought. She added that he did this by stealing one dollar and getting another dollar from a friend. She repeats, the other dollar belongs to his friend and René asks, "It does?" She reminds René he said that he had gotten the other dollar from his friend. René's mother had gone to the friend and asked about the money. He said he didn't know anything about the money. In frustration, Negrita admits she can't trust anything said by René's friend either, because he would say anything to "save his own skin." She turns to René, who looks at her with a blank expression, and says to him, "you not only stole, you lied."

Negrita begins to discuss the reasons why she is at the *centro* by requesting a special consultation with the Spiritist (Spiritualist). She says René is lucky she is not the violent type.

> I would have gotten him and punched him out at the house. Maybe I would have hit him on the head with a stick. The Godfather has informed me I should be careful because in one of these blind rages I could knock him out. So, I hope that the Godfather punishes him and gives him a talking to.

She feels that the problem with René's behavior has gone beyond the talking stage. She does not know what the Spiritist (Spiritualist) is going to do. Nevertheless, she is determined not to feel guilty no matter what he decides.

Negrita feels that the only reason René has any respect for her is that she takes things he enjoys away from him. That is why he has no choice but to respect her.   Negrita recently took a Special Education course on behavior modification techniques, at the City University of New York. This has worked out very well for her in her job as a teacher's aide. René breaks in and says, "but that's what I've been telling you to do; do one on me."   He believes behavior modification is something similar to sorcery.   Negrita says in anger, "but can't you see, I gave up on you!"

René was given the white beads and a chain with the Seven African Powers.   All these beads and charms are to protect him and keep him out of trouble.   As Negrita reaches over to see René's beads she says, "Oh, my God, they're gone."   René breathes deeply and repeats, "Oh, my God, they're gone!"   René accuses his mother of having taken the beads and charms off the night before and forgetting to fasten them on to him again in the morning.   Negrita quickly says she does not remember.

The Godfather walks out of the consultation room, walks over to René and, without looking at him, asks him to enter the consultation room.   A sure sign that he is to be disciplined.   He spends about three minutes with René, and then he walks back out and tells René's mother to join them.   Three minutes later all three walk to the altar area; René with his head hanging to his chest and the Godfather with an angry expression on his face.

The Godfather took René by the shoulder and asked him to stand at the front of the altar.   He then asked that a towel be found and placed on the floor.   René was asked to kneel on the towel and hold on to the edge of the altar with both hands.   The Godfather told René he was not to stand for half an hour.   René looked at the Godfather and then looked behind him at the pews where 10 people were waiting for a consultation and staring at him.   René turned red in the face, looked forward and up at the altar.   You could hear a deep sigh escape from his chest.   He remained there until the Godfather informed him that his half hour of punishment was over.

The Material, Spiritual, and the Consultation

Negrita complained about the Godfather's intervention in the past because she felt René's problems were not spiritual but material.   She feels René is like his father who had an "attitude problem."   In other words, a "heredity thing" that brings this problem outside the spiritual realm and makes the problem material in origin. Negrita sees it as material, while René's grandmother Carmen sees it as spiritual. The material/spiritual debate has created arguments between Negrita and her mother when dealing with René. Recently the argument between the two about René's behavior took a new turn. Negrita has questioned Carmen's right to discipline René. Negrita says, "my mother is taking my authority away!"

The Godfather intervened in the situation as the grandmother's advocate, seeing the situation as potentially spiritual. His feeling is that, even if the problem with René is material, a spiritual problem between mother and daughter has developed.

Malicious spirits have intervened to create a poor relationship between them. The Godfather became concerned when the grandmother informed him she was having problems communicating with her daughter. Negrita felt the lack of communication with her mother was the end result of a "little rift" caused by René's behavior, especially after the Godfather took her mother's side.

René upsets Negrita with his tantrums. She says when he goes into tantrums he "takes off on tangents of all types, [and] as they say, 'he's really troublesome'. I ignore the tantrums most of the time. I would rather not have ulcers. I'm telling you, I can't take it! Then when he gets home he fights with my mother."

Negrita sometimes wishes the Godfather would not get involved in her personal material problems. But she admits that his advice in the past has helped her with René. After working 6 to 10 hours a day at school with 10 children in need of disciplining, she feels too exhausted to start all over again when she gets home.

Toward the end of the summer of 1980, while Negrita and Carmen were at the beach arguing about René's behavior in the water, the Godfather was in his consultation room speaking to the saints. At the next consultation with Negrita, he informed her that the saints had told him her summer job had provided the necessary material (money) resources for her to move out of her mother's home. Now Carmen is reluctantly helping her daughter to satisfy the demands of the saints. This move is a trial that the saints require to prevent material concerns from interfering in the spiritual development of these two associates

who want to become Godchildren.   Women are more spiritually oriented and will make the necessary sacrifices on the road to mediumship.

ENDNOTES

¹ The desire by the Godfather for training in the use of cowrie shells for divining (diagnostic) purposes is a significant element in furthering syncretism and it propels Puerto Rican Spiritualism further into the realm of Cuban *Santería*. This is distinquished from the Brazilian system which is used as a part of *Cantumblé*. Brazilians use divining chains with cowrie shells at the ends while Cubans, in general, use either the circular or rectangular divining tray. It can be said that Puerto Rican Spiritualism is going to inherit the divining system out of Cuban *Santería*. For a discussion of the differences between the use of cowrie shells for divining purposes used in *Santería* and the divining chains used in Brazil, see William Bascom's discussion of the different systems of Yoruba divination in West Africa (1969).

² In *Santería*, the traditional role of the *curandero* is healer through the preparation of spells (*hechizos*). As a result, the role of the *curandero* is regarded as one of the most vital. See Fernando Ortiz, 1973. Within Puerto Rican Spiritualism, the differentiation of *curanderia* and *muertera*, with a privileged position being given to the *curanderia*, reflects a similar occurrence to that found in *Santería*.

³ For a discussion of the ceremony of *asiento* see the most recent contribution to the literature by Migene Gonzalez-Wippler (1989). She describes the traditional *Santería* rite of *asiento* in exacting detail.

⁴ *Santerismo* among Cubans usually refers to a syncretism of Cuban *Santería* and Kardecian Spiritism. Puerto Rican Spiritualists will often times refer to *Santería* as *Santerismo*.

CHAPTER VIII

Conclusions

Afro-Latin cultural beliefs are going through dynamic changes here in the United Sates as Hispanics begin to exchange customs. Nationally based cultural customs, that were far flung from one another geographically, have been compressed into survival in the metropolis. This provides a unique opportunity to observe syncretism and to define it in a more dynamic manner. Role enactment with participants at the *centro* becomes the best way of determining intensity of involvement in Spiritualism. The *centro* provides avenues of expression for the traditional as well as for the unexpected. Pressures on women to conform to traditional roles has created unusual role behaviors where their position is seemingly powerful but where, in fact, real power remains with men. There are new opportunities for research providing comparative possibilities.

M ost of the literature on syncretism views it in a static, non-historical manner and, most damaging, without consideration of the social forces which ignite the syncretism. The cultural forces contributing to the process of religious amalgamation are present independently and prior to the onset of religious syncretism. The process of syncretism arises out of tensions within the society. Puerto Ricans in the United States were active participants in the struggles of the 1960's, often for equal access to education, civil rights and the movement against the Vietnam War.

Syncretism has not received much attention in the last fifteen years. The positive reappraisal of African "retentions" in the English speaking

African-American Community spilled over into the Puerto Rican Community and a search for African retentions began among Puerto Ricans. The Puerto Rican minority in the United States is reaffirming its ancestor worship and at the same time distancing themselves from religious practices of English-speaking African Americans with whom they cohabit many Northeastern urban areas. Religious distancing is strongly directed against present-day North American Roman Catholicism.

While less distancing from African-American cultural expressions is exhibited, Puerto Ricans are conspicuously absent from English Speaking African-American congregations. What has evolved in the Puerto Rican Community is a search for relatedness which has manifested itself in a syncretism of Cuban *Santería* and French Spiritism from the Island. This is a reflection of an initial political distancing by the leaders of the Puerto Rican Community in the U.S. from the larger culture during the 1960's. The Puerto Rican Community turned inward resulting in a distancing from the Roman Catholic Church and from the religious expressions found in the African American Community. Today the Spiritualist beliefs of the Puerto Rican Community have at their core the paraphernalia of Cuban *Santería*. It is a declaration of independence and a return to ancestor worship.

Belief in spirits was found among the *Taíno* native American population of Puerto Rico during the Spanish conquest. This historical trajectory was later replenished by the belief in ancestor worship practiced by Puerto Rico's population of African descent. The later element of ancestor worship was a politically motivated movement based on Kardec's Spiritist formulations. French Kardecian Spiritism generally displaced African practices by the late 1880's. Spiritism underwent a dynamic change among Puerto Ricans in the United States during the 1960's through the manifestation of African cultural practices which were dormant in Puerto Rico. This belief in spirits cannot be viewed as an anomaly because it has remained a constant factor in the historical trajectory of the Puerto Rican people.

An insufficient historical background of the configuration of the Puerto Rican nation has flawed much of the research in the area of Afro-Latin beliefs. This lack of understanding has caused confusion which can most clearly be seen in the research literature discussing Spiritism (*espiritismo*), which often goes undifferentiated from Spiritualism (*es-*

piritualismo). Similarly, all forms of sorcery are equated with *Santería*, thereby overlooking the fact that certain forms of sorcery are independent of *Santería*.

The distinguishing characteristics among these three belief systems are all important. For example, French Spiritism has none of the paraphernalia of Roman Catholicism and does not involve sorcery. *Santería* can be distinguished from Spiritism because it has elements of Roman Catholicism and aspects of African sorcery. Puerto Rican Spiritualism, which is often unwittingly identified by Puerto Ricans as a form of French Spiritism, combines all three: that is, aspects of French Spiritism, traditional Roman Catholicism, and an extensive use of the paraphernalia and ritual sorcery of Afro-Cuban *Santería*. As a result, research on sorcery that evolves from either Puerto Rican Spiritualism or Afro-Cuban *Santería* has not been distinguished from French Spiritism by most researchers in the United States. Further, the combined, and intertwined religious practices of Cuban *Santería*, *brujería*, Spiritism, Spiritualism and other multifaceted forms of ancestor worship have not been differentiated.

It is important for the researcher to avoid confusing these distinct religious forms within the Hispanic community. This lack of discrimination tends toward making for a simplistic view of the religious background of Hispanics. In addition to, and independent of belief in Spiritualism, there is also at the *centro* a tendency to view Haitian *Vodun* sorcery as most powerful.

Significantly, aspects of Cuban *Palomayombe* approximate forms of *Vodum*, and there are many aspects of *Palo* which are commonly used in Cuban *Santería*. *Palomayombe* sorcery out of *Santería* is now making inroads into Puerto Rican Spiritualism. This serves to create new challenges for researchers, especially those working on new forms of religious syncretism among Hispanics in the United States.

There is a substantial body of research on Afro-Brazilian religions relevant to an understanding of Puerto Rican Spiritualism. Puerto Rican Spiritualism has its historical equivalent in Brazilian *Umbanda*. The newly evolved ancestor worship among Puerto Ricans can be called either Puerto Rican Spiritualism or Puerto Rican *Umbanda*. Puerto Rican Spiritualism as a social phenomenon is a manifestation of Afro-Latin cultures in the Americas. By linking this Spiritualism to its historical equivalent in Brazilian *Umbanda,* we get a whole new dimension in theoretical and comparative possibilities.

The Particularism of Spiritualism Among Puerto Ricans

The belief system, as practiced at the *centro espiritista,* requires that individuals not "doubt" the world of the spirits or the motives of the Godfather. This requirement is combined with a rejection of *Santería* or *Santerismo,* which believers at the *centro* equate as one and the same. The rejection of *Santería* is consciously engaged in even though the *centro* has incorporated many of the ritual paraphernalia and behaviors associated with Cuban *Santería.* This renunciation of *Santería* and incorporation of the ritual is not an antagonistic contradiction and can be viewed as a rational development.

The ritual and paraphernalia of *Santería* has brought with it a relatively new means of justifying payment for services to Puerto Rican Spiritualist-Godfathers. Payment for services among Puerto Rican Kardecian Spiritists is unjustifiable in the belief system. For the *Santero,* however, payment for services is a prerequisite. The basis for justifying payment in *Santería* has traditionally been that "the saints only work for those who pay," a concept now incorporated into Puerto Rican Spiritualism along with the paraphernalia of *Santería.* The incorporation of this concept can be viewed as a professionalization of Kardecian Spiritist practitioners and a desire to build an ethnic socioeconomic organization through the recruitment of godchildren. This organization can then compete with the Cuban houses (*casas*) of worship in *Santería.* Further, in the struggle for clients, it brings the Spiritualist-Godfather to a level where he can legitimize a national demarcation between himself and the Cuban *Santero.* This demarcation represents on the one hand an increase in the trappings and paraphernalia of *Santería,* while on the other hand the continued use of the nomenclature which operates out of Kardec's Spiritism. These are then employed to discourage individuals from going to a Cuban *Santero.*

Research has not determined levels of participation in Spiritism or Spiritualism within geographic and economic cross sections of the Puerto Rican population. Consequently, research should go beyond those using mental health services or participating in a *centro* to determine prevalence in the general Puerto Rican population. There is, therefore, no means of generalizing about the impact of this syncretized belief in spirits among Puerto Ricans until this survey of prevalence is undertaken. The survey must go beyond the question of consultations to that of role enactment within the belief system. A consultation with a medium cannot be construed as anything other than the workings of an Afro-Latin Caribbean culture. This book's data suggests that an encounter with a spiritualist at a *centro* is sought as a part of the individual's life style. A prior condition needing spiritual work becomes the justification for the *consulta*.

The belief in the spirit world necessitates the existence of *centros*, and of significant others who act in roles primarily aimed at eliminating either conditions or problems which are viewed as *causas*. As a result, "envy" has evolved from Spiritism as the main etiological motivation providing for the development of *causas* within Puerto Rican Spiritualism. The implications of "envy" continuing as the etiological category from Spiritism to Spiritualism leads one to assume that it is the end result of severe insecurity affecting an ethnic community.

The belief in the spirits as worshipped at the *centro* also has built into it a collective paranoid structure because one must always guard oneself from falling a victim of a *causa*, and "envy" is due to financial success, familial relations, congeniality, or sexual appeal. Any of these factors causing "envy" can either unconsciously create a *causa* by the envious or can be consciously conjured into a force through the use of a sorcerer (*brujo*). Defeat, doubt, and personal problems become agents to negatively reinforce the belief system. Further, any of these problems are viewed as spiritual trials (*pruebas*) or tests of one's belief; therefore, concrete worldly situations are spiritually reified. No matter what the reported condition at the *centro*, the spirits are held responsible, and the individual's energies are forced away from concrete issues encountered and projected beyond the control of significant others. Never are the agencies or institutions representative of the society held responsible for detrimental actions against a believer in spiritualism. Interestingly, it is the individuals within institutions who are held responsible, not the larger society.

Socialization of Men and Women Into Roles at the *Centro*

There is a continuum among those who believe and participate in a *centro espiritista* that ranges from minimal participation in the periphery to intense involvement in the core. Further, men tend to be less involved than are women believers and also seem less likely to adhere to long term Spiritualist solutions. The outcome of the socialization process into the Spiritualist belief system involves role differentiation between men and women. Involvement in Spiritualism is unconsciously viewed for women as sex-appropriate behavior. Parental "warmth" through affectionate gestures between mothers and their daughters before the age of five were recalled by the mothers as greater than affection between mothers and their sons. Further, Maccoby & Jacklin, 1974, point to this as a significant contributor to the differentiation in the socialization of male and female children (p. 313). This difference in affection between mothers and their under-five-years-of-age female children is reflected inside the *centro*. Motherly warmth toward female children during services reinforces socialization into participation in the *centro*. Male children receive less warmth and consequently receive less positive reinforcement for participating in the services. Male children are usually placed between the wall and the last adult in a pew during services, unlike female children, who sit with their mothers and are affectionately reinforced.

There is also a tendency for the Godfather to become an agent of punishment for delinquent male behavior, especially for single mothers who request that the Godfather discipline their male children. It can be said, therefore, that the socialization process from childhood through belonging to the *centro's* hierarchy is a mirror image of society. What is built into the *centro* is the use of women at a "symbolic" level, because "girls do tend to conform more readily than boys to directives from parents and teachers" (Maccoby & Jacklin, 1974, p. 272) and "although it has not been demonstrated, it appears likely that in adulthood as well they (women) will 'take orders' from authority figures with less coercion" (Maccoby & Jacklin, 1974, p. 371).

If this is the case, the belief system is reflecting the male at the top of the hierarchy of power in a "more highly valued place in the material process of life" (Godelier, 1981, p. 12).

To this end, males are featured as materially motivated while women are viewed as primarily spiritually motivated. Consequently, it is no surprise to find that the male godchildren became actively involved in the *centro* when they were unemployed, suspending their involvement once employed on a full time job.

Therefore, for men it can be assumed that full time employment is equated with minimal participation in the belief system because they are materially interested. Once men are viewed as more materially oriented the tendency is to recruit them into the associates, who have a primary duty to financially contribute to the upkeep of the *centro*. They need spiritual protection to fulfill their materially based role.

There are usually 15 godchildren, 3 of whom are male. During a three-year period, only one of the three male godchildren has sat at the table as an apprentice medium. There are more women involved in the congregation (public and associates), as godchildren, and especially as mediums. This greater participation of women can be quantitatively located in the findings. In the first place, it can be located in the tallies of participants in the *centro* where women represented a maximum difference of three females to every male. Secondly, this difference of male-female participation can also be seen in that two-thirds of the *causas* worked by the mediums in a three-week period belonged to women. Thirdly, women predominate in consultations with the Godfather, which indicates a tendency for women to attempt to work out their problems through the belief system.

Impact on roles

Damon (1983) suggests that in the use of Mead's role taking theory that the individual is adjusting to the "social group as a whole to which he belongs" (p. 117). Language becomes the means to socialize an individual as they accommodate the speaker to the listener through symbols that insure adjustment to the social group. Puerto Rican Spiritualism is fluid, slowly incorporating language from Cuban *Santería*, while retaining some of the language of the world of the spirits as represented by French Spiritism. Yet, few participants understand this on-going development.

It is at the level of "perspective discrepancies" where the major obstacles to role taking can be found. I have detailed where it is that individuals fail to fulfill their role and the reasons for this failure. The effort here is to jettison a view of sameness or "individual homogeneity" all too often found in symbolic interactionalism (Damon, 1983, p. 118). In addressing this shortcoming, this book enumerates the errors to role attainment by explicitly dealing with failure to achieve a given role. This is similarly done with those factors which contribute to successful role achievement. Importantly, transitional stages between roles are never addressed as a part of symbolic interactionalist literature and an effort is made here to address this weakness.

Reasons for Role Achievement Failure

In Stage I, the simplest level of involvement occurs. It is here that *causas* are relieved or cured for members of the public. Those who do not intensify their involvement beyond the initial consultation remain at the level of the public and are considered to have failed in their quest for enlightenment. In general, it is mostly men who become associates, and remain a part of the public, contributing to the upkeep of the *centro*. Women are expected to intensify their participation.

In Stage II we find a transitional role to the godchild. The failure to arrive at role fulfillment is caused by doubting the existence of the spirit world, while at the same time not having trust in the intentions of the Godfather, especially by women. Failing to maintain a home altar, not following assigned rituals and dressing inappropriately for services become the basis for failure. This usually results in a cancellation of baptism, thus preventing one from becoming a member of the godchildren.

In Stage III, the godchildren are apprentice mediums and are taught about the sensations of spirits as they manifest themselves in the mediums' bodies. If a godchild is either afraid to speak to the dead or unable to reveal through divination the forms which sorcery takes, they remain as apprentices and are often not allowed to sit at the table with the mediums. Some godchildren not perceiving an improvement in their mediumistic powers withdraw from the activities of the *centro*.

Stage IV is represented by the mediums. They are hierarchically arranged on the basis of ability and experience. The process of going from godchild to sitting at the table as an apprentice medium, can be described as one where the medium senses the spirits, is willing to divine and recognizes what ails the person with the *causa*. Failure occurs when material concerns such as marital problems begin to interfere with the work of the *centro*. Material concerns create blocks which undermine one's potential as a medium. It also prevents one having spirits enlightened for the purpose of relieving *causas*.

In Stage V it is understood that the Principal Head Medium who sits to his right is closest to the Godfather. She is expected to leave the *centro* rather than divide the loyalties of the members of the *centro*. The Godfather openly acknowledges he was forced to leave several centros in his search for "learnings" about Spiritualism. All godchildren are instructed that their loyalty is to the Godfather. A Head Medium who undermines (blocks) or works against the Godfather initiates a process of spiritual conflicts (*envolvimientos*) which frustrates the primary purpose of the *centro* : the relief of *causas* and the enlightenment of the spirit world.

A tool to further dissect role performance at the *centro* is provided by Robert K. Merton. He codifies functions which are "manifest" and those which are "latent." Manifest functions are defined as the intended consequences of group behavior while latent functions are defined as unintended consequences. As a manifest function or intended consequences, the *centro espiritista* exhibits levels of participation which are reflected not only in role performance but in a tendency for women to predominate in significant roles. The *centro* can also be seen as providing a sense of community, a manifestation of "retention" of African cultural practices, and an atmosphere where individual "accumulated frustrations" can be expressed. These beneficial aspects are all the more important for primarily Spanish-speaking women barred from the greater institutions of the society.

The latent function or unintended consequences of the *centro espiritista* tends toward reproducing male dominance. This male dominance is immediately noticeable in three ways. The first is through male exceptionalism discerned in the baptism of men into the godchildren who maintain "doubts" about their belief in the world of spirits. Two of the three male godchildren refused to alter familial antagonisms which undermined their belief in the spirit world and created blocks (*cruces*);

243

an aspect of their role performance which is unlike that of any of the women, who act out the expectations required of their role.

The third aspect reinforcing male domination is the role of the Godfather. On the symbolic level, the Godfather maintains his domination by being the only male medium at the table. In the Godfather, moreover, one finds the only person making a full-time living from the *centro*, thereby providing an economic element to his domination. Consequently, what seems as "symbolic" dominance also characterizes itself in the economic realm as well. Furthermore, on a political level he exerts control over the ensemble of individuals at the *centro* by politically mediating the distinctions between French Spiritism and the paraphernalia of Cuban *Santería*. He also exerts control by confirming the divining of *causas* and as a result the training of mediums. The Godfather fulfills all three levels needed to secure male domination: symbolic, economic, and political (Godelier, 1981, p. 5), while women remain at the symbolic level.

The latent function unconsciously reproduces and imposes a mechanism of dominance over women. Women's energies are expended in a reified fringe of the Puerto Rican community, unlike the men who are primarily interested in self-fulfillment in the material world. This dichotomy between a latent function which gears women to the spiritually reified while gearing men to the material is operating at this *centro espiritista*.

Toward reinforcing this latent aspect for women, the Godfather surrounds himself with a core group of women with the most competent women required to leave the *centro* without challenging the Godfather's leadership because the saints demand it. The women at the *centro espiritista* do not report challenging the Spiritualist's authority. The objective measure of capabilities is suppressed to ensure the domination of the male at the top of the power hierarchy.

In this *centro espiritista* the belief system sanctions divorce or separation if the marriage becomes a block (*cruz*) to one's personal Spiritualist development. Divorce or separation cannot be justified by concurrent issues, but instead by its unfavorable impact on a woman's development in the reified world of spirits. As a consequence, women are unconsciously being instructed not to challenge male authority through concrete issues. Once a godchild becomes a medium she is instructed that treating *causas* that have to do with extramarital affairs is wasteful, conditioning women mediums to accept on the one hand that extramarital affairs have no spiritual etiology thereby undermining the meaning and importance of the affair, while on the other hand, preconditioning women to view the affair as activated by sorcery (*brujería*). Never are interpersonal problems of everyday married life considered as contributors to breakdowns in relationships; therefore, the only means of countering sorcery is through either a cleansing ritual (*despojo*) or through a more powerful use of sorcery.

Some women report that their husbands object to their continued participation at the *centro*. They stopped their husband's objections by jokingly threatening them with sorcery. This is no joke to the men. Men openly distrust women and are especially fearful of women who can engage in revengeful sorcery.

Broadly speaking, it seems that even in the fringes of society male dominance is reflected in a hierarchy of power although, by recruiting primarily women, the mechanism for maintaining male dominance takes on a unexpected form. Whereas one would think that an institution would be less likely to reinforce androcentrism by the number of women involved in an organization, the implication here is that male dominance is not a matter of the proportion of women to men in a power hierarchy.

These findings suggest that research in the past has been androcentric and has failed to see Spiritualism as a mechanism that provides a false sense of power in Puerto Rican women, further alienating them from consciousness of their real powerlessness. These findings also suggest that spiritualism tends toward keeping some women away from the formal hierarchies of the larger society while mirroring societal mechanisms of male domination. Nevertheless, at no point do the women mediums consciously think of themselves as perpetuating male dominance and they demonstrate deep concern about the lack of males in the core grouping.

It is incorrect to stereotype Puerto Ricans as uniformly motivated by the Spiritualist belief system, even if they attend consultations with mediums. The implications for mental health workers is that adherence to the belief system must be measured against the role that the individual plays in the behavioral-ritual nexus of the *centro*. Similarly, with the physician, the level of resistance to treatment by a believer in Spiritualism must be viewed in relation to the role a believer occupies at a *centro*.

The case study approach is self-limiting because of its exploratory nature. The findings, nevertheless, become a vehicle by which to consider future research. Consequently, this research shows what's going on in one *centro espiritista*. The primary purpose of this book is to understand the various roles available at this *centro*. The research findings do not lend themselves to generalizing about adherence to the belief system by the Puerto Rican populace of New York City. Whereas the findings provide a point of departure for research into role enactment, they do not automatically mean that a similar situation will be reflected at other *centros*. As a result, the manner in which roles are articulated at other *centros* may be different.

Religious syncretism between Puerto Rican Spiritism and Cuban *Santería* is an on-going process in the United States, but is being transported to Puerto Rico as part of return migration to the Island. It leads us to assume that there will be greater African retentions of Spiritualist beliefs among Puerto Ricans who have resided in the United States than among those who have remained on the Island. More and more, this Puerto Rican Spiritualism is rapidly becoming an Afro-Cuban inundated Spiritualism, alive with the iconography, paraphernalia, music and chants of Cuban *Santería*. It is strongest among the great mass of Puerto Rican people who do not totally accept Eurocentric conceptions of religious beliefs.

This book brings into focus a series of issues that affect the manner in which Afro-Latin beliefs among Puerto Ricans is viewed. The syncretic development of Puerto Rican Spiritualism in the United States and its historical base in Puerto Rico have never been delineated in the research literature. The idiosyncratic dictionary provides new dimensions to the meaning of Puerto Rican Spiritualism, giving future researchers a better means of understanding what believers are articulating. The men and women who practice this Spiritualism have never before explained the intimate sensations of allowing long dead ancestors from West Africa, who today are represented by the Saints of the Roman Church, to penetrate their bodies. The spirits arrive with their own identifying sensations. These intimate feelings which mediums experience as spirit manifestation are revealed for the first time.

Men and women who believe in Spiritualism are very different in their practice. This difference, we can now say, without doubt, is a manifestation of the role each individual plays within the *centro espiritista*. An in-depth look at these roles at different stages of development has never been documented in the existing research literature. We have now made it available.

The Hispanic population of the United States is a growing population whose culture is little understood. It is usually viewed as religiously monolithic and its Afro-Latin religious practices are not considered. Such cultural misconceptions with regard to this Spanish-speaking population can no longer be entertained. Research into the Afro-Latin religious practices within the Latino Community reveal constant evolution and sociological complexity. As the Hispanic population in the United States continues to grow and their religious beliefs continue to flourish, it is inevitable that we will be confronted with these complex religious expressions. An informed understanding of the specifics of this process is essential for scholars as well as for the wider community.

GLOSSARY

Perspective of Observer

These definitions are not from the participant's perspective, but are terms judged appropriate by the researcher for inclusion in this glossary. Many of these terms can be found in either historical accounts, ethnographical descriptions, or have been gleaned from informants on ancestor worship in the Americas.

Ataque
Fit. Clinically a hyperkinetic seizure. Mostly viewed as occurring among Puerto Rican women and identified as caused by unexpressed evil intentions, envy, and malicious thoughts directed towards an innocent or spiritually unprotected individual. These repressed sentiments attach themselves to that unprotected individual.

Ahijados
See Godchildren

Babalao (Babalawo)
Santería high priest who maintains a house of worship. His followers are referred to as the Godchildren in a ritual kinship system. There are women babalaos and most were trained in Cuba. Both male and female babalaos can be found in the United States. Most often babalaos belong to the Cuban cult house of Orunmila and are master diviners. The babalao practices divination through spiritual intercession and geomancy using the cowrie shells. Unlike the followers of the cult house of Ifa, where cowrie

shells attached to necklaces are used for divination, the cult house of Orunmila uses loose cowrie shells. The most powerful babalao is a Santero who works Palo, and is keeper of a cult house of Orunmila. Puerto Rican Spiritualists are not initiated into the cult house of Orunmila. Puerto Rican Spiritualist divination relies solely on spirit intercession. See Godfather, Padrino, Santería, Puerto Rican Spiritualism, Palo, Palomayombe.

Babalú-Ayé
The Santería god of earth, of epidemics, and infectious diseases; syncretized in Cuba with Saint Lazarus, the great healer, the medieval leper.

Botánica
An herbal magico-religious shop selling remedies, and religious objects which are primarily used by believers in ancestor worship.

Brujería
The term "sorcery" (brujería) is often translated as witchcraft. Those practicing this belief system are considered to have powers used to affect others. The sorcery of a Santero falls under the category of brujería, but the belief is rarely referred to as brujería unless disparagingly referring to the belief system. See: Brujo.

Brujo
Someone who engages in brujería (sorcery) exclusively. A "brujo/a barato/a", a derogatory term, used to describe a practitioner of low level malicious sorcery who is inexpensive. Although many Paleros are exclusively sorcerers they are rarely referred to as brujos. See: Palo; also, Palomayombe.

Cadena espiritual
Literally a "chain" from the past due to an ancestor who worked the spirits. This ancestor secures one's ability to communicate with the dead or to be a sorcerer. Also, among Puerto Rican Spiritualists, a means of closing the ceremonies at centros by holding

hands as done in the Roman Catholic mass as a result of Vatican Council II.

Candomblé
A syncretic religion in Brazil which uses aspects of Yorubaland practices and Roman Catholicism. It is similar to Cuban Santería in practice and in ideological content. In the English speaking West Indies as well as in some geographical areas of Brazil the practice is called Changó.

Causa
A spiritually caused discomfort, ailment, or disease, sometimes identified as the result of sorcery.

Changó
The Santería god of fire and thunder, syncretized in the Afro-Latin Caribbean with Santa Barbara.

Collares
Necklaces made of colored beads representing the different Yoruba deities and saints with which one has been protected. A practice out of Santería now found in Puerto Rican Spiritualism.

Comprobado
A public affirmation by the congregation of a medium's correct divining of a causa during spirit possession.

Consulta
Individual spiritual consultation session with a godfather, god-mother, babalao, palero, or high level medium.

Corriente
Vibes viewed as an electrical current, and representing the spiritual world.

Cuadros
A frame. A series of spirits, guides, and protectors which represent the believer in Puerto Rican Spiritualism and protects her or him.

Daño, un
A harm. Seduction of a virgin or rape. Also a magical harm believed to be caused by a sorcerer.

Darle luz
Giving the spirits enlightenment.

Despojo
A spiritually cleansing bath. A process of spiritual cleansing whereby a person becomes separated and protected from evil spirits and influences. These baths may contain herbs, flowers, essences, fragrances, and can be combined with other rituals.

Eleggúa
The Santería God of opportunity and keeper of the doors. Often syncretized with the Holy Guardian Angel or more recently in the South Bronx with Saint Martin of Porres.

Envidia
Repressed envy which harms the envied. A major etiology in Puerto Rican Spiritualism, and a concept culturally shared by other members from the Afro-Latin Caribbean.

Espiritismo
See Spiritism.

Evidencias
Evidence divined during spirit possession revealing the types of sorcery used against the believer and the malicious intent involved. If the person with the causa confirms that evidence of sorcery was found by the believer and that the malicious intent was reified in their lives, then the congregation says "compro-

bado". See Comprobado.

Facultades
Talents or abilities to communicate with the spirit world which manifest themselves during preadolescent trails or "pruebas".

Fluido
A spirit's ability to communicate its existence to a medium. Presently the rationale for the use of goblets of water to attract the spirits.

Godchildren (ahijados)
Individuals who have been initiated into a Puerto Rican Spiritualist Center. Traditionally used in reference to individuals initiated into a house of Cuban Santería. All godchildren become related in a fictive kinship system, unlike the natural kinship system based on marriage or descent from a common ancestor. Fictive kinship can also be referred to as ritual kinship.

Godfather or Godmother
The head of a Puerto Rican Spiritualist Center. Although referred to as godfather or godmother they have not been initiated into the cult house of Orunmila. The godfather/godmother of a Puerto Rican Spiritualist Center initiates individuals; however, they are never referred to as a babalao. Traditionally, the title godfather/godmother is used in reference to the head of a Cuban house (casa) of worshipers of Santería. See Babaláo, Padrino.

Guía Principal
Principal guide is usually identified as the guardian angel; but when Spiritism becomes syncretized with Santería it can be identified with either the Guardian Angel or an orisha (deity) from the Yorubaland Pantheon or both.

Hot and Cold

A system for treating disease from ancient Greece, where "cold" diseases were treated with "hot" medications and foods, and "hot" diseases treated with "cold" foods or medications. In Spiritism the system of "hot" and "cold" has evolved to include disease categories, foods, medications, and spirits which penetrate the body of the medium.

Kardec, Allan

Pseudonym of Leon Denizarth Hippolyte Rivall, 1803-1869. Founder of French Spiritism, also known as Scientific Spiritism, as a means of communicating with the dead. See Spiritism.

Kardician Spiritism

See Spiritism, Kardec.

Macumba

A Brazilian syncretism of ancestor worship that also uses Yorubaland practices. The ideological impact of Allan Kardec's Spiritism is not readably noticeable. It is the root belief system of Umbanda where there is a clear manifestation of Kardec's spiritism. See Umbanda.

Madrina, La

Godmother. Female spiritual leader in Santería, and in spiritualism. Also, the wife of a Santero, or the President of a Centro. See Godfather.

Materia

Non spiritual aspects of a person or the tangible aspects of an individual. Commonly used by believers in the Kardec's Spiritist tradition. The concept has made some inroads into Santería.

Medium

An individual who can be possessed by spirits and who the spirits speak through. Terms differentiating the roles available for the mediums (mediaunidad) facilitate an understanding of their hierarchy, e.g. head, apprentice, and auxiliary. These terms are not used in the belief system. See spiritism.

Mediaunidad
Medium.

Mesa blanca
The "white table" ancestor worship identifies followers of Kardec's French Spiritist tradition in Puerto Rico. It is my opinion that it is called "white table" spiritism because other forms of ancestor worship emanate from the Black population where sorcery - black magic is used. Nevertheless, some sorcery from Santería is now operative in Puerto Rican Spiritualism while at the same time they are followers of white table French Spiritism.

Montar
The process in Santería of having an orisha manifest itself in a babalao/a or Santero/a. Presently, in Puerto Rican Spiritualism the mediums are manifesting the orishas and the spirits during possession. Never are the orishas and the spirits manifested simultaneously during services. There is a clear demarcation between possession aspects which are out of Santería and those out of are French Spiritism.

Obatalá
The Santería creation divinity seen as male, female, father, mother, and syncretized in Cuba with the Virgin of Mercy (Nuestra Señora de las Mercedes).

Ochún
The Santería goddess of the river and the owner of money, love, honey, and everything sweet; rules over the genitals and the lower abdomen. Syncretized with the Virgin of Charity (Nuestra Señora de la Caridad del Cobre), patron saint of Cuba.

Oggún
The Santería god of metal and war, syncretized with St. Peter.

Orishas
Spanish spelling for the deities in the Yoruba Pantheon used in Santería. Luso Brazilian spelling for the Yorubaland deities is Orixás.

Orúnla
The Santería god of wisdom; syncretized in Cuba with St. Francis of Assisi.

Padrino, El
Godfather, head of church, master medium, minister. The high priest who is the leader of the ritual kinship in Santería. The individual may or may not be a babalao. This term is now being used by believers in Puerto Rican Spiritualism. See babalao.

Palo
Sticks. The materials from the woods (el monte) used in Palomayombe magic. A form of sorcery which usually disavows the use of Roman Catholicism although some Santeros are also Paleros. Often Santería becomes the cover for the practice of Palo. Paleros are distinguished by their unflinching sentiment with sorcery and their commitment to clients. They use an extensive repertory of sorcery; Occidental conceptions of good and evil do not operate in this belief system, as they often do in Santería. See Palomayombe; also Santería.

Palomayombe
A Palomayombero is a perpetrator of Congo-Bantu sorcery in Cuba; they are now present in the United States. A highly complicated and secretive sect with high priests often prepared prior to birth through sexual rituals to become a Palero sorcerer. The power is inherited through descent from a blood line that traces itself to a powerful Palero/a, and there is a prohibition against

initiating individuals who have no blood line to a sorcerer. There are no non-Cubans within the belief system, except as clients or followers (godchildren) of a powerful Palero/a. This decent aspect does not operate in Santería. Palo sorcery is the source of much of the magic in Santería, but Palo is complicated in practice due to Cuban regional differentiation possibly caused by African national, linguistic and ethnic settlements during the slave era. Paleros have rites involving the use of nature e.g. woods, rivers, rocks, soils, herbs, plants, human body parts from the deceased, body fluids especially blood, semen, and urine. They are particularly adept at working the spirits of the dead. Palo also includes blood letting rituals - most often the sacrificial use of animals. They are expensive sorcerers who will often guarantee their work. The true Palero/a rejects any Homeric, or Christian conception of the duality of good and evil. Paleros, like many a Santero, speak and sing in Yoruba especially during spirit possession, divination, ceremonies, rituals, and rites.

Pases
Symbolic gestures used to read the aura performed for curative purposes by mediums.

Presidente
In French Spiritism the officiating medium.

Protectores
Protectors, guides, or spirits which are assigned to accompany an individual through life. They help the believer by protecting him or her from evil influences, and contagious malicious spirits. Everyone has these guides to some degree, but they must be ritually reinforced to make them more powerful. When Santería is involved the protectors are worn as necklaces (collares) which represent the deities of the Yoruba Pantheon spiritually assigned to the individual.

Prueba

These are predestined trials by spirits, testing a person's forbearance while in the process of developing faculties as a medium. Preadolescent trials are viewed as a sign that the child was born to work the spirits of the dead as a medium. Later, in adulthood "pruebas" are identified as tests of one's faith in the world of spirits.

Puerto Rican Spiritualism

A system of belief among Puerto Ricans in the United States which uses the three component parts of the civilizations which make up the roots of Puerto Rican culture: African, European, and Taíno - native indians. In this syncretic belief system one can find paraphernalia of Cuban Santería which include Roman Catholicism, Kardician Spiritism, and the use of either North American or West Indian spirits. Puerto Rican Spiritualism is closer to Umbanda from Brazil. There are two forces propelling this belief system onto the Puerto Rican mainland. The first is return migration by Puerto Ricans from the United States and the second is the resettlement of Cubans in Puerto Rico since the Cuban Revolution. See Umbanda, Macumba.

Puerto Rican Umbanda

See Umbanda; Puerto Rican Spiritualism.

Santería

An Afro-Cuban religion which is a contentious combination (syncretism) of the worship of Roman Catholic saints and Yorubaland mythology. The high priest is of great importance and is called a Babalao. He initiates individuals into a house of worship, called a "casa de Santería". Sometimes there is a strong belief in the rituals of The Roman Catholic Church, especially in Baptism and Holy Communion. It is an orally transmitted belief system which uses spirit communication, black and white forms of magic, sorcery, and the use of shells for divining. The Babalao also uses herbs and plants in the process of healing or doing sorcery. Much of the blood letting sacrifices and sorcery in Santería have their origin in Palomayombe. There is some confusion about the conception of the quality of good and evil in this belief system. Most Santeros believe in the duality of good and evil while most Paleros do not. Some Santeros, like most Paleros, feel that to attain good, evil must be done, or vice versa. The Santero who has a line of decent in Palo remembers his childhood ritual of initiation which will forever tie him/her to one of the deities of the Yoruba Pantheon. It can be a dangerous initiation ritual within Santería conducted secretly by a significant member of the family and done outdoors. It is intended to prove an individual is the continuation of a line of descent in Palo. See Palo, Palomayombe, Babalao.

Santiguador(a)
An individual who engages in a spiritual curing process where oils are rubbed on the affected part of the body.

Seres
Lower ranking souls in the spiritual hierarchy.

Siete Potencias Africanas, Las
The Seven African Powers are major ancestor spirits from African Yorubaland mythology used by Santeros in the United States and in Brazil. There are several combinations available. The deities reflect the national or ethnic group practicing a form of African ancestor worship. The more predominant Yorubaland deities used in the Afro-Latin Caribbean are Changó, Elegguá, Obatalá, Ochún, Oggún, Orúnla, and Yemayá. Caution must be taken since there is no all inclusive list. There is no mention made of the Seven African Powers in the anthropological literature on Santería from Cuba.

Spiritism (Espiritismo)
A belief system founded in France by Allan Kardec which made an impact on Latin America in the 1890s. The belief system did away with all vestiges of Roman Catholicism. Services were not con-

ducted in front of a congregation. Communication with spirits was made either by an individual or a small group of persons in a home. Associations of Spiritist groups developed in Europe during the late 1800s. The belief system was pro-republican and liberal during the nineteenth century and includes a formal organizational structure with titles, such as President of the table (Presidente de la mesa), Secretary, Treasurer and other officers.

Syncretism

Coalescing. A contentious combination. The reconciling of elements that are seemingly contradictory. A synthesis of beliefs. The end result of civilizations clashing bringing with it the imposition of religious ideological hegemony by the more powerful. As a consequence a syncretic belief system develops as a means of resistance. The content of the belief system is altered as pitched battles occur on an ideological plane. This affects the belief of those wielding ideological hegemony as well as those who counter the hegemony. An example is Cuban Santería where Roman Catholicism imposed by the conquering Spanish becomes identified with Yorubaland beliefs in the orishas. See Santería, Umbanda, Puerto Rican Spiritualism.

Spiritualism

Spiritualism was originally used to refer to the Anglo-North American Spiritualist phenomenon of the Fox sisters, during the Anglo-American religious revival of the 1840's. Spiritualism was condemned by Allan Kardec, founder of French Spiritism. Today, however, among Puerto Ricans it is a mistranslation of the term Spiritism from the Spanish into the English. Consequently, when a believer speaks in Spanish the term will be heard as Spiritism (Espiritismo), while if the same person is speaking in English he/she uses the term Spiritualism. The Spanish term for Spiritualism (Espiritualismo) is rarely used by Puerto Rican believers, especially those who are combining French Kardecian Spiritism and Santería.

Transmición espiritual
Spiritual divination. Used in Puerto Rican Spiritualism solely.

Umbanda
A combination (syncretism) of the religious orientations of the three major racial groups which make up the Brazilian people. These three components can be identified as African through the worship of orishas in Candomblé. Secondly, European through the use of Allan Kardec's Spiritism as well as the Roman Catholic Saints, and lastly the worship of native indian spirits. This belief system's true counterpart can now be found in Puerto Rican Spiritualism in the United States which contains the three component parts and syncretized elements of Brazilian Umbanda.

Yemayá
The Roman Catholic Saint - Virgin of Regla, patron of the harbor of Havana and syncretized in Santería with Yemayá, one of the deities of the Yoruba Pantheon. In Santería she rules the intestines.

Yoruba
West African people living chiefly in southwestern Nigeria.

BIBLIOGRAPHY

Abad, V., Boyce, E. "Issues in Psychiatric Evaluation of Puerto Ricans: A Socio-Cultural Perspective." Journal of Operational Psychiatry, 10, 1979: 28-39.

Aron, R. Main Currents in Sociological Thought I. Harmondsworth, England. Penguin, 1965.

Asociación Escuela Cientifica Basilio. Curso para Auxiliares, Libro Primero. Buenos Aires, Argentina: Asociación Escuela Cientifica Basilio Culto Espiritista, 1975.

Asociación Escuela Cientifica Basilio. Curso para Auxiliares, Libro Segundo. Buenos Aires, Argentina: Asociación Escuela Cientifica Basilio Culto Espiritista, 1976.

Bascom, W. R. "The Focus of Cuban Santería." In M. Horowitz (Ed.), Peoples and Cultures in the Caribbean. Garden City, N.Y.: Natural History Press, 1971: 522-527.

Bascom, W. Ifa Divination. Bloomington: Indiana University Press, 1969.

Bastide, R. African Civilizations in the New World (P. Green, Trans.). New York: Harper Torchbooks, 1971.

Bastide, R. African Religions of Brazil (Helen Sebba, Trans.). Baltimore: Johns Hopkins University Press, 1978.

Becker, H.S., Geer, B., Hughes, E. C., & Strauss, A. L. Boys in White. Chicago: University of Chicago Press, 1961.

Boggs, C. Gramsci's Marxism. London: Pluto Press, 1976.

Borrello, M.A., & Mathias, E. "Botanicas: Puerto Rican Folk Pharmacies." Natural History, 86(7), 1977: 65-72.

Bram, J. "Spirits, Mediums, and Believers in Contemporary Puerto Rico." In E. Fernandez Mendez (Ed.), Portrait of a Society. Rio Priedras: University of Puerto Rico Press, 1972: 371-377.

Brameld, T. The Remaking of a Culture. New York: Harper & Row, 1959.

Cabrera, L. El Monte. Miami: Ediciones Universal, 1975.

Cadwallader, M. E. Hydesville in History. Chicago: The Progressive Thinker Publishing House, 1917.

Capetillo, L. Memories of the Free Federation. In A. Quintero Rivera (Ed.), Workers Struggle in Puerto Rico: A Documentary History. New York: Monthly Review Press, 1976: 40-50.

Carr, E. H. Saint-Simon: The Precursor (1950). Studies in Revolution. New York: Universal Library, Grosset & Dunlap, 1964.

Compact Edition of the Oxford English Dictionary, (Vol. 1). S. V. "Calixtin." Oxford: Oxford University Press, 1971.

Cook, S. "The Prophets: A Revivalistic Folk Religious Movement in Puerto Rico." In M. Horowitz (Ed.), Peoples and Cultures in the Caribbean. Garden City, N.Y.: Natural History Press, 1971: 560-579.

Coser, L. A. Masters of Sociological Thought (2nd Ed.). New York: Harcourt Brace Jovanovich, 1977.

Damon, W. Social and Personality Development. New York: W. W. Norton & Comapany, 1983.

Diaz Soler, L. M. Resendo Matienzo Cintron, Orientador Y Guardian de una Cultura (Tomo 1). Puerto Rico: Ediciones del Instituto de Literatura Puertoriqueña, Universidad de Puerto Rico, 1960.

Engels, F. Socialism--Utopian and Scientific. Chicago: Charles H. Kerr & Company, 1908.

Engels, F. Natural Science and the Spirit World. Dialectics of Nature. New York: International Publishers, 1940.

Erickson, M. H. "Further Clinical Techniques of Hypnosis: Utilization of Techniques." American Journal of Clinical Hypnosis, 2, 1959: 3-21.

Falcon, Nieves, L. Personal Communication, 1980.

Federal Party of Puerto Rico. Platform found at the Department of Puerto Rican Studies, City College, City University of New York, 1898.

Fenton, J. Understanding the Religious Background of the Puerto Rican. In CIDOC--Centro Intercultural de Documentacion--SONDEOS (No. 52, Apdo. 479). Cuernavaca, Mexico, 1969: 0.1-6.2.

Fernandez Mendez, E. Historia Cultural de Puerto Rico. San Juan, P.R.: Ediciones "El Cemi," 1969.

Fitzpatrick, J. P. Puerto Rican Americans. Englewood Cliffs, N.J.: Prentice-Hall, Inc., 1971.

Garcia, E. P. "La Iglesia Protestante y La Americanizacion de Puerto Rico 1898-1971." Revista de Ciencias Sociales, 18, (1-2), 1974: 99-122.

Garrison, V. Espiritismo: Implications for Provision of Mental Health Services to Puerto Rican Populations. Paper delivered at the 8th Annual Meeting of the Southern Anthropology Society, February, 1972.

Garrison, V. "Doctor, Espiritista or Psychiatrist? Health-Seeking Behavior in a Puerto Rican Neighborhood of New York City." Medical Anthropology, 1(2), 1977, (a): 65-180.

Garrison, V. "The 'Puerto Rican Syndrome' in Psychiatry and Espiritismo." In V. Crapanzano & V. Garrison (Eds.), Case Studies in Spirit Possession. New York: John Wiley & Sons, Inc., 1977, (b): 383-449.

Garrison, V. "Support Systems of Schizophrenic and Nonschizophrenic Puerto Rican Migrant Women in New York City." Schizophrenic Bulletin, 4(4), 1978: 561-596.

Gaviria, M., & Wintrob, R. "Supernatural Influence in Psychopathology--Puerto Rican Folk Beliefs about Mental Illness." Canadian Psychiatric Association Journal, 21, 1976: 361-369.

Gaviria, M., & Wintrob, R. "Spiritist or Psychiatrist: Treatment of Mental Illness Among Puerto Ricans in Two Connecticut Towns." Journal of Operational Psychiatry, 10, 1979: 40-46.

Glazer, N., & Moynihan, D. P. Beyond the Melting Pot. Cambridge, Mass.; The MIT Press, 1963.

Godelier, M. "The Origins of Male Domination." New Left Review, 127, 1981: 3-17.

Gonzalez-Wippler, M. Santería. New York: Doubleday, 1975.

Gonzalez-Wippler, M. Personal Communication, 1980.

Gonzalez-Wippler, M. The Santería Experience. New York: Original Publications, 1982.

Gonzalez-Wippler, M. Santería the Religion. New York: Harmony Books, 1989.

Griffith, E. E. H., & Ruiz, P. "Cultural Factors in the Training of Psychiatric Residents in a Hispanic Urban Community." Psychiatric Quarterly, 49, 1977: 29-37.

Halifax, J., & Weidman, H. H. "Religion as a Mediating Institution in Acculturation: The Case of Santería in Greater Miami." In R. H. Cox (Ed.), Religious Systems and Psychotherapy. Springfield, Ill.: Charles C. Thomas, 1973.

Haring, C. H. The Spanish Empire in America. New York: Harcourt, Brace, & World, 1963.

Harwood, A. "Puerto Rican Spiritism: Description and Analysis of An Alternative Psychotherapeutic Approach." In Culture, Medicine and Psychiatry, I. Dordrecht, Holland: D. Reidel Publishing Company, (a), 1977: 69-95.

Harwood, A. "Puerto Rican Spiritism: An Institution With Preventive and Therapeutic Functions in Community Psychiatry." In Culture, Medicine and Psychiatry, I. Dordrecht, Holland: D. Reidel Publishing Company, (b), 1977: 135-153.

Harwood, A. Rx: Spiritist As Needed: A Study of Puerto Rican Community Mental Health Resource. New York: John Wiley & Sons, 1977, (c) .

Heilbroner, R. L. The Worldly Philosophers. New York: Simon & Schuster, 1972.

Herring, H. A History of Latin America. New York: Alfred A. Knopf, 1968.

Herskovits, M. J. "African Gods and Catholic Saints in New World Negro Belief." Originally appeared in American Anthropologist New Series XXXIX, No. 4, (1937) and was reprinted in F. S. Herskovits (Ed.), The New World Negro. Bloomington: Indiana University Press, 1966: 321-329.

Hillway, T. Handbook of Educational Research. Boston: Houghton Mifflin Comlpany, 1969.

Jahn, J. Muntu An Outline of a New African Culture (M. Green, Trans.). New York: Grove Press, Inc., 1961.

Jones, R. A., & Day, R. A. "Social Psychology as Symbolic Interaction." In C. Hendrick (Ed.), Perspectives in Social Psychology. New York: John Wiley & Sons, Inc., 1977: 75-112.

Jung, C. G. The Psychology of Transference. Princeton, N.J.: Princeton University Press, 1954.

Kardec, A. El Evangelio Segun El Espiritismo (Anonymous trans. into Spanish). New York: Stadium Corporation, 1969.

Kardec, A. Book of Mediums (E. A. Wood, Trans.). New York: Samuel Weiser, 1970.

Kardec, A. El Libro de Los Espiritus. Barcelona: M. Pareja-Montana, 1975.

Koss, J. D. "Therapeutic Aspects of Puerto Rican Cult Practices." Psychiatry, 38, 1975: 160-171.

Koss, J. D. "Social Process, Healing, and Self-Defeat Among Puerto Rican Spiritists." American Ethnologist, 4, 1977, (a): 453-469.

Koss, J. D. "Spirits as Socializing Agents: A Case Study of a Puerto Rican Girl Reared in a Matricentric Family." In V. Crapanzano & V. Garrison (Eds.), Case Studies in Spirit Possession. New York: John Wiley & Sons, 1977, (b): 365-381.

Langness, L. L. The Life History in Anthropological Science. New York: Holt, Rinehart, & Winston, 1965.

Leutz, W. N. "The Informal Community Caregiver: A Link Between the Health Care System and Local Residents." American Journal of Orthopsychiatry, **46, 1976: 678-688.**

Lewis, G. K. Puerto Rico Freedom and Power in the Caribbean. New York: Harper Torchbooks, Harper & Row Publishers, **1963.**

Lewis, O. La Vida. New York: Vintage Books, Alfred A. Knopf, Inc., & Random House, **1965.**

Lubchansky, I., Egri, G., & Stokes, J. "Puerto Rican Spiritualists View Mental Illness: The Faith Healer as Paraprofessional." American Journal of Psychiatry, **127, 1970: 312-321.**

Maccoby, E. E., & Jacklin, C. N. The Psychology of Sex Differences. Stanford, CA.: Stanford University Press, **1974.**

Marques, R. The Docile Puerto Rican (B. B. Aponte, Trans.). Philadelphia: Temple University Press, **1976.**

Mead, G. H. Mind, Self and Society (C. W. Morris, Ed.). Chicago: University of Chicago Press, **1962.**

Merton, R. K. Social Theory and Social Struture. New York: The Free Press, **1968.**

Mintz, S. W. Worker in the Cane. New York: W. W. Norton & Company, Inc., **1960.**

Morales Carrion, A. Albores Historicos del Capitalismo en Puerto Rico. Rio Priedras: Editorial Universitaria, Universidad de Puerto Rico, **1972.**

Morales Carrion, A. Puerto Rico and the Non-Hispanic Caribbean. Rio Piedras: University of Puerto Rico, **1974.**

Morton-Williams, P. "The Influence of Habitat and Trade on the Politices of Oyo and Ashanti." In **M. Douglas & P. M. Kaberry** (Eds.), Man in Africa. Garden City, N.Y.: Anchor Books, **1971**: 80-99.

Mumford, E. Puerto Rican Perspectives on Mental Illness. New York: Department of Psychiatry, Mount Sinai School of Medicine of the City University of New York, **1972**.

Nash, June. We Eat the Mines and The Mines Eat Us. New York: Columbia University Press, **1979**.

Nisbet, R. History of the Idea of Progress. New York: Basic Books, **1980**.

Ortiz, F. Los Negros Brujos. Miami: New House Publishers, **1973**.

Padilla, E. Up From Puerto Rico. New York: Columbia University, **1958**.

Pane, R. "Relacion de Fray Ramon Pane Acera de Las Antiquedades de Los Indios, Las Cuales, Con Diligencia, Como Hombre que Sabe Su Idioma, Recogio Por Mandata del Almirante." **Ano 1505**. In **E. Fernandez Mendez** (Ed.), Cronicas de Puerto Rico Desde La Conquista Hasta Nuestros Dias (1493-1955). Rio Priedras: Editorial Universitaria, Universidad de Puerto Rico, **1969**.

Pérez y Mena, A. I. "Spiritualism As An Adaptive Mechanism Among Puerto Ricans in the United States." Cornell Journal of Social Relations, **12, 1977**: 125-136.

Pérez y Mena, A. I. "A Synthesis of Puerto Rican Spiritualism and Modern Psychology." Paper read at the American Psychological Association, Division of Humanistic Psychology, Toronto, Canada, **1978**.

Ramos, A. O Folklore Negro No Brazil. Rio de Janeiro: Civilizaçao Brasileira, 1935.

Ramos, A. O Negro Brasileiro. Rio de Janeiro: Civilizaçao Brasileira, 1940.

Ramos, A. Introduçao a Anthropologia Brasiliera. Rio de Janeiro: n.pub., 1943.

Ramos, A. Las Poblaciones del Brazil. Mexico City: n.pub., 1944.

Ramos, G. A. "The Development of an Annexationist Politics in Twentieth Century Puerto Rico." In A. Lopez (Ed.), The Puerto Ricans. Cambridge, Mass.: Schenkman Publishing Company, Inc., 1980: 257-272.

Read, M. Culture, Health, and Disease. Philadelphia: Tavistock Publications, J. B. Lippincott Company, 1966.

Republican Party of Puerto Rico. Platform found at the Department of Puerto Rican Studies, City College, City University of New York, 1898.

Rogler, L. H., & Hollingshead, A. B. "Puerto Rican Spiritualist as Psychiatrist." In F. Cordasco & E. Bucchioni (Eds.), The Puerto Rican Community and Its Children. Metuchen, N.J.: The Scarecrow Press, Inc., 1972: 49-55.

Rosario, J. C. The Development of the Puerto Rican Jibaro and His Present Attitudes Towards Society. New York: Arno Press, 1975.

Rude, G. Ideology and Popular Protest. New York: Pantheon Books, 1980.

Ruiz, P. "Spiritism, Mental Health, and the Puerto Ricans: An Overview." Transcultural Psychiatric Research Review, 16. 1979: 28-43.

Ruiz, P., & Langrod, J.   The Role of Folk Healers in Community Mental Health Services. Mental Health Journal, 12, 1976: 392-398.

Salgado, R. M.   The Role of the Puerto Rican Spiritist in Helping Puerto Ricans With Problems of Family Relations.   Unpublished doctoral dissertation, Teachers College, Columbia University, 1974.

Sandoval, M. "Santería: Afrocuban Concepts of Disease and Its Treatment in Miami." Journal of Operational Psychiatry, 8(2), 1977: 52-63.

Sandoval, M.   Santería in Miami.   Paper read at the Annual Meeting of African Studies Association, Baltimore, MD., 1978.

Sariola, S.   The Puerto Rican Dilemma.   Port Washington, N.Y.: Kinnikat Press Corp, 1979.

Sebo, E. A.   Systematization of Selected Concepts of George Herbert Mead: Toward a Research Application of Social Behaviorist Theory.   Unpublished doctoral dissertation, Teachers College, Columbia University, 1976.

Seda Bonilla, E.   Interaccion Social y Personalidad en una Communidad en Puerto Rico (2nd ed.).   San Juan: Ediciones Juan Ponce de Leon, 1969.

Selltiz, C. Jahoda, M., Deutsch, M., & Cook, S. W.   Research Methods in Social Relations.   New York: Holt, Rinehart, & Winston, 1959.

Showerman, G. Syncretism.   Encyclopedia Britanica (11th ed.), 26, 1910-1911: 292-293.

Sidgwick, E. M. Spiritualism. The Encyclopedia Britanica (11th ed.), 25, 1910-1911: 705-708.

Steiner, S. The Islands. New York: Harper & Row, 1974.

Stevens-Arroyo, Antonio M. Cave of the Jugua. University of New Mexico Press, Albuquerque, 1988.

Tallant, R. Voodoo in New Orleans. New York: The Macmillan Company, 1971.

The Puerto Rican New Yorkers: A Recent History of Their Distribution and Population and Household Characterstics. New York City Department of City Planning - December 1982.

Thomas, N. W. Divination. The Encyclopedia Britanica (11th ed.), 8, 1910-1911: 332-333.

Turner, J. H. Interaction Theory. The Structure of Sociological Theory. Homewood, Ill.: The Dorsey Press, 1974.

Valle, N. Luisa Capetillo. San Juan de Puerto Rico: n.pub., 1975.

Wagenheim, K. Puerto Rico: A Profile. New York: Praeger Publishers, 1970.

Wakefield, D. The World of the Spirits. Island in the City. Boston: Houghton Mifflin Company, 1960.

Whyte, W. F. Street Corner Society. Chicago: The University of Chicago Press, 1970.

Wolf, K. L. "Growing Up and Its Price in Three Puerto Rican Subcultures." In E. F. Mendez (Ed.), Portrait of a Society. Rio Piedras: University of Puerto Rico Press, 1972: 233-275.

INDEX

34. Wesley R. Hurt. *Manzano: A Study of Community Disorganization.*
35. Chava Weissler. *Making Judaism Meaningful: Ambivalence and Tradition in a Havurah Community.*
36. Carolyn Stickney Beck. *Our Own Vine and Fig Tree: The Persistence of the Mother Bethel Family.*
37. Charles C. Muzny. *The Vietnamese in Oklahoma City: A Study of Ethnic Change.*
38. Sathi Dasgupta. *On the Trail of an Uncertain Dream: Indian Immigrant Experience in America.*
39. Deborah Padgett. *Settlers and Sojourners: A Study of Serbian Adaptation in Milwaukee, Wisconsin.*
40. Margaret S. Boone. *Capital Cubans: Refugee Adaptation in Washington, D.C.*
41. George James Patterson, Jr. *The Unassimilated Greeks of Denver.*
42. Mark M. Stolarik. *Immigration and Urbanization: The Slovak Experience.*
43. Dorita Sewell. *Knowing People: A Mexican-American Community's Concept of a Person.*
44. M. Ann Walko. *Rejecting the Second Generation Hypothesis: Maintaining Estonian Ethnicity in Lakewood, New Jersey.*
45. Peter D. Goldsmith. *When I Rise Cryin' Holy: African-American Denominationalism on the Georgia Coast.*
46. Emily Bradley Massara. *¡Qué Gordita!: A Study of Weight Among Women in a Puerto Rican Community.*
47. Stephen L. Cabral. *Tradition and Transformation: Portuguese Feasting in New Bedford.*
48. Usha R. Jain. *The Gujaratis of San Francisco.*
49. Aleksandras Gedemintas. *An Interesting Bit of Identity: The Dynamics of Ethnic Identity in a Lithuanian-American Community.*
50. Suzanne J. Terrel. *This Other Kind of Doctors: Traditional Medical Systems in Black Neighborhoods in Austin, Texas.*
51. Annamma Joy. *Ethnicity in Canada: Social Accomodation and Cultural Persistence Among the Sikhs and the Portuguese.*
52. Maria Andrea Miralles. *A Matter of Life and Death: Health-seeking Behavior of Guatemalan Refugees in South Florida.*
53. Greta E. Swenson. *Festivals of Sharing: Family Reunions in America.*
54. Tekle Mariam Woldemikael. *Becoming Black American: Haitians and American Institutions in Evanston, Illinois*
55. Louis James Cononelos. *In Search of Gold Paved Streets: Greek Immigrant Labor in the Far West, 1900–1920.*
56. Terry J. Prewitt. *German-American Settlement in an Oklahoma Town: Ecologic, Ethnic and Cultural Change.*
57. Myrna Silverman. *Strategies for Social Mobility: Family, Kinship and Ethnicity within Jewish Families in Pittsburgh.*
58. Peter Vasiliadis. *Whose Are You?: Identity and Ethnicity Among the Toronto Macedonians.*
59. Iftikhar Haider Malik. *Pakistanis in Michigan: A Study of Third Culture and Acculturation.*
60. Koozma J. Tarasoff. *Spells, Splits, and Survival in a Russian Canadian Community: A Study of Russian Organizations in the Greater Vancouver Area.*
61. Alice H. Reich. *The Cultural Construction of Ethnicity: Chicanos in the University.*
62. Greta Kwik. *The Indos in Southern California.*
63. Laurence Marshall Carucci, et al. *Shared Spaces: Contexts of Interaction in Chicago's Ethnic Communities.*
64. Frances White Chapin. *Tides of Migration: A Study of Migration Decision-Making and Social Progress in São Miguel, Azores.*
65. Robert B. Klymasz. *The Ukrainian Folk Ballad in Canada.* With Musical Transcriptions by Kenneth Peacock.
66. Elaine H. Maas. *The Jews of Houston: An Ethnographic Study.*
67. James W. Kiriazis. *Children of the Colossus: The Rhodian Greek Immigrants in the United States.*
68. Donna Misner Collins. *Ethnic Identification: The Greek Americans of Houston, Texas.*
69. Keum Young Pang. *Korean Elderly Women in America: Everyday Life, Health and Illness.*
70. Rose-Marie Cassagnol Chierici. *Demele: "Making It." Migration and Adaptation Among Haitian Boat People in the United States.*
71. Dana Shenk. *Aging and Retirement in a Lebanese-American Community.*
72. Robert W. Franco. *Samoan Perceptions of Work: Moving Up and Moving Around.*

DATE DUE

NOV 7 '98			